365 days of stories

Published in the UK by Byeway Books,
Chichester, West Sussex. www.autumnpublishing.co.uk
Published in the US by Byeway Books Inc,
Lenexa KS 66219 Tel 866.4BYEWAY www.byewaybooks.com

Printed in China

ISBN 1 85997 953 X

365 days of stories

Stories by:
Annie Murant
Didier Baravd
Christian Demilly

BYEWAY
BOOKS

The threadbare teddy bear

Peter and his sister Sally were spending the day at their grandparents' house.

'Let's go up into the attic!' said Peter, who loved searching through the dusty chests for hidden treasures. Sometimes, the children dressed up in the old clothes they found. But this time, instead of searching through the chests, Peter and Sally ran over to an old wardrobe they had never noticed.

'I wonder what's inside?' asked Sally.

'I can't open the doors!' said Peter, tugging hard.

'If only we could open the doors,' Sally said, wistfully.

Peter wasn't going to give up. He searched everywhere for the key, but the attic was such a mess it was impossible to find anything.

'Oh, I give up!' sighed Peter, leaning against the wardrobe. Then, as if by magic, the door gave a little creak and opened!

'The door wasn't locked, after all!' giggled Sally.

Inside the wardrobe, the children found a pile of baby clothes and sitting in a dusty box, a threadbare teddy bear with a foot missing.

'Grandma,' called Peter, running downstairs holding the teddy bear. "Look what we found in the attic!"

'Ah, you've found Scruffy!' said his grandma. 'He belonged to your dad. When he was a little boy, he couldn't sleep without Scruffy beside him in bed.'

Peter and Sally laughed as they tried to imagine their dad with a teddy bear.

Busy buzzy bee

We buzz and we sting! Well, that's what they say, but you shouldn't believe everything you hear about bees.

Take me for example, I've got just about everything needed to make you dislike me. Think about it! I've got a nasty sting, plenty of venom, a pair of wings that will carry me miles from my hive, and I make a very shrill noise when I'm angry. But just because I'm buzzing, it doesn't mean I'm coming to annoy you.

My sisters and I work hard. During the day we search for nectar to make honey, then in the evenings we look after the queen bee and the baby bees.

We don't like visitors very much, and if an animal or a human comes too near to the hive, we let them know that it would be better if they left us alone.

First, we go *bzzzz* quietly. But if the intruder doesn't move on, we put on the turbo *BZZZZZZZ!*

Remember, if you approach a hive, don't stand in front of the entrance because you might get in our way. It is very difficult to do tricky flying moves when carrying a ball of pollen on each leg and a crop of nectar on your back!

At some point, one of us busy bees will notice that you are being a nuisance or getting too close, and then watch out for a sharp sting! *Ooh! Ouch!*

The moral of my story is: don't come too close as we busy bees don't like to be disturbed. But when I'm gathering pollen from the flowers, come and watch me from a distance and I won't mind a bit. Promise!

Jimmy the duckling

No matter how hard he tries, Jimmy the little yellow duckling always ends up arguing with the other ducks! It's not his fault that he doesn't like waddling into the pond water. Instead, he prefers perching on low branches and then jumping down. *Wheeeee!* It almost feels like he's flying!

Jimmy's mother has said to him a thousand times, 'My sweet little son, we are farm ducks. We don't fly! Be wary of these silly bird thoughts in your head.'

'But Ma, what about those birds up there? They're flying!'

'Yes, but they're different. Those are wild ducks, and wild ducks fly, you don't! Aren't you happy down here on the ground? It's much safer. There are no eagles hunting you or hunters trying to shoot you.'

Jimmy knows his mother is right, but she is keeping something from him. She wouldn't explain why Uncle Duckford suddenly disappeared last year. And, thought Jimmy, what about all the missing eggs? Who takes them each morning?

Jimmy says as soon as he grows up he is going to climb to the roof of the barn and fly away. Then he will find answers to all his questions.

Jimmy wants to be like those birds he saw settling onto the pond, their wings slowing as their feet touched the water. But when Jimmy went down to see the birds, but they had already flown. Up there in the clear blue sky, their outstretched wings looked like the wings of a plane. Jimmy tried to copy them. He beat his wings up and down, and up and down. No matter how hard he tried, he remained on the ground. Perhaps his ma had been right all the time!

No sole mates

ere we go again! Another quarrel and, as usual, it is about the same, old thing!

'Phew, you really smell!' said one shoe.

'And I suppose you think you smell of sweet roses, do you?' said the other.

that's the problem. It is what James's sister Emily describes as a 'very nasty whiff'. His trainers are truly very smelly!

The red shoe would do almost anything to get away from the smell, but a shoe cannot travel alone. So, it will have to put up with the pong until morning.

'Me, sir? I'm a lady's shoe, not a stinky, mud-filled boot like you!'

All the family's shoes are kept in the hall cupboard under the stairs. Each evening, the shoes are thrown into the cupboard, and pairs of shoes that have been together for always are separated. Each shoe has no idea who will be next to it.

One evening, one of Jane's pretty red court shoes finished up next to one of James's mud-covered trainers. But it's not just the mud

Next morning, James looks for his trainers in the cupboard, but he isn't particularly careful. As far as he is concerned, Jane's Sunday-best red shoes are just shoes like any others. When a red shoe tumbles out, he can't even be bothered to pick it up. He kicks it into the back of cupboard and shuts the door.

Now, the poor red shoe finds itself lying next to something even worse than stinky trainers. It is Dad's really, truly, stinky, smelly fishing boots!

Clippety-clop!

lippety-clop, clippety-clop, all along the roads and lanes. In all weathers, Clippety, the little white donkey, loves to trot along in front of her cart. When it's cold, her breath makes a fluffy cloud in front of her nostrils.

Clippety stops whenever she wants. Her kind master, Mr Foster, the old farrier, never argues or makes her walk-on. They have criss-crossed the country together for so long that Clippety knows the way home like she knows the back of her hoof. When she reaches home, she neighs to wake her dozing master. But even Clippety's very noisy neigh is sometimes not enough to wake Mr Foster.

One snowy day, Clippety had been neighing at the top of her voice, stamping her feet, and banging the cart against the wall, but Mr Foster didn't stir. If it were possible, Clippety would have taken off her harness and carried the old man's bed to the cart so that Mr Foster could sleep and travel in comfort! But she was a cold little donkey, a couple of paces from her cosy, warm stable, and her hay. So all Clippety could do was neigh.

All night Clippety waited for Mr Foster to wake up, but he didn't. At dawn, Clippety knew that her master must have gone to heaven.

Sad and lonely, Clippety slipped out of her harness and wandered down the road. I found her a little later, in front of my house, and that is how we met.

Clippety and I have since become good friends. She lives in my garden and every morning I give her a bowl of oats. Clippety misses Mr Foster, but she knows that wherever he is, he is smiling down at her.

What if?

he universe seems like an endless space full of huge planets and sparkling stars. We can use telescopes to look deep into the sky and see the things that our eyes cannot see. You know that and so do I, but...

What if the stars were just hung on the sky like pretty pictures on a wall?

What if the black blanket of the night started to run and dribble like very wet paint on a sheet of paper?

What if the moon lost its balance and fell down?

What if the planets decided they wanted to be somewhere else?

What if somewhere far away, there were little children looking at our planet saying, 'What if that planet over there had people on it?'

'And what if on that planet there are children like us, looking up at the stars?'

What if questions are wonderful, but where are the answers?

Maybe you will discover the answers to all these questions in your dreams. Anything can happen in dreams. You might, in your dreams, meet the little children who live on other planets, even though you don't know if they exist. Sometimes, you just have to believe in something to make it happen.

Try it tonight and you'll see.

The janitor's bird

aw, the janitor's bird, is very funny. Sitting inside his cage that hangs on the balcony, Caw whistles, tweets, and talks all day long. He can mimic human and animal voices after hearing them once!

Caroline loves Caw, but she thinks it's sad that he's kept in a cage all day. She's tried to persuade his master to set him free, but was told that Caw isn't unhappy in his cage because he can see everything that's going on.

'Well I'd like to see *you* in a cage,' Caroline thought. 'I bet you would soon want to get out!'

A week later, Caroline had an idea. When she walked by Caw's cage, she said loudly, 'Open the bird cage! Set me free!'

Every day, Caroline would say the same thing, in the hope that Caw would repeat the words to his owner. But so far, Caw had not reacted.

Caroline wasn't the only person to have tried to make the bird repeat words. Tommy, a horrid boy from the third floor had uttered all sorts of naughty words, but Caw had never mimicked any of them. Then, this morning, as soon as the janitor went into his room, Caw said over and over again all the new words he had learned!

'Oooooopen the bird cage! Set me free! Idiotic old man! I'm going to get you!'

At first, the janitor thought it funny and laughed. By late afternoon, though, Caw's insults were beginning to get very annoying. 'Perhaps I should set you free,' said the janitor as he opened the door of the cage.

Caroline smiled as the bird flew away, free at last!

Sam's sums

Sam was a very lively black dog with pointed ears and a wagging tail. He was so gentle he would never hurt anything, not even Polo the naughty goat, who was always up to tricks that would annoy Sam.

Believe it or not, Sam could count. Not by saying 'one, two, three' as you or I would do. No, Sam counted in a way that no one, at least no-one human, could understand. Somehow, he always knew exactly how many goats there were in the pen. When new goats were born on the farm, Sam would simply add that number to the total.

One day, Annie the shepherdess took the herd along a new path which was crossed by a fence. The goats jumped the fence easily, but something was not right and Sam knew it. One of the goats was missing!

Sam ran back towards the goats' pen where he expected to see Bonny, a lazy old thing, sound asleep. But the pen was empty, so Sam sped back to the herd and counted the goats again.

This time, the goat count was exactly right. No one, not even Bonny, was missing. Poor Sam couldn't understand what had happened. He knew that his counting was never wrong!

What Sam didn't know was that Bonny had taken a different path because she didn't want to jump over the fence. And, while Sam was away, lazy Bonny had joined the herd as if nothing had happened.

Who says animals are less intelligent that humans!

The hungry wolf!

For as long as they could remember the woolly sheep of Fern Valley had had to put up with a big, bad wolf chasing them around and eating them for dinner. Well, enough was enough. The sheep called a meeting.

Now, it was the first time there had ever been a meeting of any kind among the sheep, for it was in the sheep's nature to follow each other in everything. However, the wolf had become a serious problem, and so sheep came from all over to discuss it.

The meeting went on until late in the evening because the sheep couldn't decide what to do.

Eventually, they asked the wise owl. He told the sheep about a powerful goblin that he knew who could help them. The owl went to talk to the goblin.

'The goblin said that he will help you, but he wants payment in gold'.

'Where can we get gold?' bleated the sheep

'If you all sold your wool, you could get the gold to pay the goblin,' said the owl.

And so, the sheep sold their wool and the goblin said a magic spell. The sheep slept soundly that night, but the next day they were terrified when they saw the wolf running toward them, licking his lips. Suddenly, the wolf stopped and picked up a lettuce. The goblin had made the wolf a vegetarian!'

The magician

erald was a happy magician, but one day something happened that bothered him indeed.

It was a Sunday, and Gerald was doing housework. He would glide around the house tapping each untidy object with his wand, and magically each object would put itself back in its proper place.

Casper, his magical cat, would sit on the side of the sink watching Gerald's magical robes scrubbing themselves clean.

This particular Sunday, however, was not like others. No washing was being done and Gerald's magical books scattered themselves untidily all over the floor. Gerald sat sadly in his armchair in the corner.

'Whatever is the matter?' Casper asked, leaping onto Gerald's lap.

Gerald put his hand into the pocket of his velvet robe and pulled out his wand. It was broken!

'This is a serious problem,' thought Casper. How can a magician do magic without his wand? And who could fix his wand on a Sunday? All magical shops were shut.

'Why don't you repair your magic wand with magic!' said Casper, excitedly.

'What a fantastic idea!' came the reply. 'But if I can use magic to repair the wand, do I really need my magic wand at all?'

The wolf and the horse

No one can gallop as fast as Lightning. When he races the other wild horses, he always wins. Lightning is a very beautiful horse. He has a long mane, a gleaming white coat, and big, black eyes!

Lightning spends his days grazing in a valley where lush green grass grows as far as the eye can see.

One day, as Lightning was gazing at the horizon, he saw a tiny black spot in the distance. He continued watching as this strange black spot came closer and closer, getting larger every second. Lightning pricked up his ears and sniffed the air, trying to work out what was approaching.

Lightning was a wild horse and very suspicious, but he wasn't too bothered about anything creeping up to attack him. After all, he knew of no animal or human who was fast enough to catch him.

By late evening, Lightning was able to see the 'black spot' more clearly. It was a skinny old wolf from the other end of the valley. Now as Lightning knew well, a lone wolf in this poor condition was not much of a threat to him, so he ignored it.

All day, every time Lightning walked a few steps, so did the wolf, staying as close as he dared to the beautiful white horse. By the end of the week, Lightning was used to seeing the old wolf. Then one day, the wolf disappeared and this saddened Lightning very much. Lightning felt as though he had lost a friend.

One hump or two?

In the beginning, Carrie the camel had a single hump, just like her cousin Cleo. Carrie lived in a desert, where the sand was so hot it burned her feet. She really wanted to find a tree to stand under, but trees were very hard to find in the desert.

One day, Carrie came across a hole in the rocks. Unfortunately, the black hole wasn't quite big enough for her to squeeze through. As she stood by the hole, a cooling breeze blew from inside the cave. How lovely it would be, she thought, to be in the cave and out of the hot sun!

Carrie decided to try to get into the cave. Now, have you ever tried to get a camel into a tiny hole? It's just about impossible! But Carrie wasn't going to give easily. She pushed and pushed, and wriggled and jiggled until a hump and a rump were firmly wedged in the hole.

The poor camel couldn't go forward or backward. Her nose was enjoying the cool breeze, but her rear was still in the sun! All day she struggled to free herself, but it was no use. The skin on Carrie's back was grazed and sore, and the sun only made her feel worse!

Carrie decided it was now or never. She made one last big push… and pushed herself out of the hole.

All the pushing and squeezing had given Carrie a second hump, just behind the first hump. It really hurt, but Carrie didn't complain. She was happy to have wriggled out of the hole.

'Well,' said Carrie's cousin, trying not to laugh, 'you've got an extra hump now!'

Tall as the treetops!

emma the giraffe is very shy and doesn't think she's pretty at all.

'Not very pretty?!' shouted her friend, Prickly the porcupine. 'But you have such beautiful eyes with long, dark lashes and your nose is the prettiest thing I have ever seen! Oh, and I think your neck is so graceful and elegant! I assure you, you are very beautiful. Not like me, with my nasty prickly prickles!'

'Thank you, Prickly,' shouted Gemma, blushing. 'I don't think your prickles are nasty at all. In fact, I think they are really very impressive.'

You might have worked out by now that Prickly the porcupine and Gemma the giraffe are good friends. Their only problem is hearing what each other says.

Gemma's head is higher than the treetops, while Prickly can just touch Gemma's knees if she stands on tippy-toes and stretches. Gemma can bend her long neck, but she can't stay like it for very long because it gives her a terrible headache.

So, what can they do? It was Stripey, the anteater, who finally thought of a solution.

'At the end of the savannah there is an enormous rock. If you scramble onto it, Prickly, then Gemma won't have to lower her head,' said Stripey, who was famous for his clever ideas.

Now, Prickly sits on the enormous rock and Gemma happily listens to him chatter away. Gemma still has to lower her head a little, but the pair of chatting friends does make a funny sight!

Little blue cloud

It was such a small cloud, that no one ever noticed it moving across the sky. It was born this morning after the rain fell, when the sun began to warm the sea. The tiny, brand-new cloud drifted all alone in the big sky. He wasn't very confident because there were no other clouds in sight. There was only the little blue cloud, who was almost invisible.

But Julie had seen the little cloud. She was sitting in the garden with her Aunt Jane when the fluffy cloud drifted past.

'Jane, can you see that little cloud?' said Julie. 'It looks really odd.'

'Mmm,' mumbled Aunt Jane.

'Jane, please look!' said Julie.

'Can you let me finish this book, please?' said Jane, impatiently.

'But it's really strange cloud. It's really pale has a silver lining,' Julie went on.

'Oh, that's nice,' said Jane, not even looking up from her book.

Strange things like this need an explanation, so Julie called to the cloud, 'Little blue cloud, where are you going?'

A voice, soft like cotton wool whispered in her ear, 'You don't need to shout, I can hear you. Where am I going? Wherever the wind takes me. But I'm very sad because I'm all alone!'

Then the little cloud began to cry, and raindrops fell from the sky. Jane was annoyed that it had begun to rain and went inside. But how can you explain to grown-ups that clouds feel sad when they are on their own?

Hands can speak, too!

This year there is a new student in the class. Josh is just like any other little boy, except for one thing–he cannot hear anything. Josh has made a big impression on Lisa because she has never met anyone who cannot hear before. Lisa never stops talking, and she wondered what she could do to make Josh understand her.

'Josh cannot hear, but he can lip read,' the teacher explained. 'So, you must face him when you are talking and speak clearly.'

Lisa tried this and it worked. Josh could understand everything she said!

On Wednesday afternoon, Lisa met Josh in the street. He was with another girl and boy who Lisa didn't know. They were making strange gestures with their hands and laughing, but they weren't saying a word. Lisa wanted to know what they were doing.

The next day, Lisa asked Josh, 'Can you speak using your hands, Josh?'

Josh answered by writing on a sheet of paper, 'Yes, it's called sign language.'

Lisa asked her teacher if she knew how to do sign language. 'No,' said her teacher. 'But perhaps we could all learn it together. Josh, what do you think? Could you teach us?'

Josh was happy to teach his new friends, and every break-time, the other children stood around him and learned how to speak with their hands.

Smudge in a pickle!

Smudge, the little kitten, stayed in the house just like his father had asked him. The children were at school, and their parents were at work, so Smudge was all alone. Smudge's Dad was sleeping in the garden.

Now, Smudge had everything he could possibly want. He had a big bowl of milk, a lovely cushion on the sofa, and his friend, Bubbles the goldfish, to keep him company. But fish aren't very chatty and Smudge soon became bored. So, what do kittens usually do when they're bored? That's right, they get into mischief!

Smudge began by knocking over her bowl of milk (an accident, of course). Then, he jumped onto the kitchen table to chase after a buzzing fly. In the process, he sent a large jug of water crashing to the floor where it smashed into a zillion pieces!

Smudge left the kitchen and jumped back onto the sofa. The sofa was a very safe place where he could not cause any trouble. Well, that is what Smudge thought. But as he settled into the cushions, he knocked some knitting with his paw and a ball of yarn rolled across the sofa and tumbled onto the carpet.

Smudge's coat bristled. What was that furry round thing with the thin tail that went on and on and on? Was it a mouse with a really long tail?

Smudge had never seen a mouse before so he wasn't sure. He leaped upon the furry thing and stuck his razor-sharp claws into it. He wrestled with it and rolled about on the floor, first this way and then that way. Soon the yarn was wrapped around him and Smudge was trapped and unable to move at all.

Oh dear, Smudge is going to feel very silly when his Dad returns and sees him like that. His Dad will also not be pleased when he sees the mess in the kitchen!

Splish, splash!

Ben loves walking through puddles. They go splish, splash! It's such fun. But Ben's parents don't think it's very amusing and try to stop him doing it. Ben is sure that when they were young, they must have liked splish, splashing in puddles. His parents, though, would never admit it, of course.

It had rained all night and on the way to school Ben just couldn't resist the temptation.

'*Splish! Splash!*' His clothes were soaking wet! Ben hung back a bit in the school yard to dry off before the school bell rang for morning lessons.

Ben's shoes were full of cold, squelchy water and his trousers were dripping wet. His teacher spotted the state of his clothes straight away.

'Ben, come here, please. What happened to you? You're soaked through !' said Mrs Morris.

'Nothing. It was…' began Ben who was going to say that a passing car had splashed him. But Ben couldn't do it. He may have been naughty for getting himself wet, but he wasn't going to tell a lie.

'Come on, take off your shoes and put them on the window sill in the sun,' said his teacher.

Ben was beginning to feel a bit cold. He would have to spend the morning in his wet socks with his wet trousers sticking to his legs.

At break, all the other children rushed outside. 'Ben, you'll have to stay in the class,' his teacher said, 'I don't want you catching a cold.'

And so Ben sat by the window, watching his friends playing ball. From then on, Ben always thought twice before jumping splish-splash in puddles!

Something fishy

Yesterday John's class went on a special trip to the aquarium where they saw lots of fish of all different shapes and sizes. There was even a special see-through, underwater tunnel that you could walk through and where sharks swam above, around and below you!

John noticed a low aquarium where something was pressed against the glass. He bent down to take a look and saw an octopus, sticking to a glass wall of the tank with the suckers on its long tentacles.

The octopus was looking straight at John! Even though this gave John a shock, it did not frighten him. This wasn't because John was extra brave or because he knew the octopus could not escape from its tank. What John felt was sorry for the octopus, whose big, sad eyes seemed to want to tell him something.

John smiled, and without knowing why, he placed his hand against the glass. The octopus moved a tentacle so that it was pressed against the glass near John's hand. John could not believe what he saw, but he knew he was experiencing something very special. At that moment, the teacher said it was time to leave the aquarium.

How could John explain this to his teacher? 'Sorry, can you wait just one more minute, I'm trying to talk to an octopus.'

That evening, John told his parents what had happened. 'I know the octopus wanted to tell me something! Oh, why can't octopus live with us and not in tanks?' he asked.

John's parents found it difficult to answer his questions. The only thing she said was that octopus are very clever, maybe as intelligent as us, but John had already worked that out.

Silly seals

oday, a big blizzard is blowing across the glaciers. But that doesn't stop three little seal cubs from having fun. They play at trying to hide from each other in the dense, swirling snow.

'Can you see me?' calls Neil, sliding away from his brothers.

'Yes, we can still see your nose and your eyes!' yells Steven.

Neil moves further away. 'Can you see me now?' he calls, but there was no answer. 'You can't see me! You can't see me! Ha ha, I win!' triumphs Neil.

After a while Neil wants to rejoin his brothers, but he can't see them in the fog.

'Where are you?' Neil calls again. 'Come on, that's enough! Stop playing around, you two!' But there was no reply.

Neil begins to walk in the direction he thought his brothers'

voices had come from, but all he can see in every direction is white snow. Everything is white! Neil decides he ought to stop calling his brothers because there might be a hungry polar bear listening.

Neil starts to feel scared. A polar bear? Oh, no! That would be awful. Poor Neil curls up in the snow and begins to cry.

Suddenly, he hears a deep voice, 'I'm going to eat you!'

Neil jumps up and discovers it's his brothers. 'You idiots! I thought it was a polar bear,' he scolds as their laughing comes to a sudden stop.

'A polar bear!' they gasp. 'Quick, let's get home and make it quick!'

One unhappy bunny

Farmer Johnson sat in his barn and played the violin every morning. Why did he play in the barn when he lived in a big house? Well, it was because he did not want to wake his children. But Farmer Johnson wasn't alone when he played. He had a very loyal audience of two: Chaffie, the chaffinch, and Poppy, a black cat. Perched on the farmer's shoulders, they listened to his wonderful music.

Someone else listened to Farmer Johnson's morning concerts. It was a little blue toy rabbit. You see, when the farmer's children grew up, they no longer wanted their stuffed toys. They either put them in the attic or threw them away! Luckily Eric, the little blue rabbit escaped this sad fate. He was was rescued by Farmer Johnson, who sat him on a bale of hay in the barn.

Now, once upon a time, Eric must have been a handsome toy. He did have a cute, rather mischievous look, but then one of his ears was torn and started to droop rather oddly. In his present state, Eric seemed a little sad to be honest.

Farmer Johnson had tried everything to make Eric smile. He had even sung special songs for him, but it had made no difference. The little blue rabbit still looked at him with sad eyes.

Then one day, the farmer secretly bought another toy rabbit. Farmer Johnson didn't want to tell anyone because he thought they would laugh at him. This little girl rabbit had big black eyes and a pretty blue ribbon tied around her neck. And from that day on, Eric the rabbit smiled all the time.

Spooky gets spooked!

pooky is a ghost, but instead of scaring others, he is the one who is scared. This is because he is convinced that someone is following him. But whenever he turns round, there is nobody there, and so he reckons this mysterious someone is invisible just like him.

Each time Spooky goes into the street, he can feel a presence. One day, he even felt something hold his hand as he crossed a busy road.

Spooky is a pretty scatty kind of ghost, and he doesn't pay much attention to what he's doing or where he's going!

Today, Spooky has decided to find out exactly who is following him! He hides behind a wall to wait for his mysterious 'something' to pass. But why hide when you are invisible?

'Why are you following me?' Spooky asks to no one. But there was no answer because, as you probably know, a ghost's voice can't be heard!

Getting angrier and angrier, and more scared by the minute,

Spooky says, 'If you continue following me, you will make me very cross!'

'Calm yourself,' says a whispered voice into Spooky's ear. 'There is no reason for you to be cross or afraid when I'm here.'

'Ah,' says Spooky, feeling pleased with himself. 'I was right! It is another ghost! So, are you going to tell me who you are? I know that you are always behind me. Show yourself now!'

'I'm here, little one, right next to you,' said the soft and gentle voice. 'I'm your mother and I stay with you to make sure you are always safe.'

Bet you didn't know that ghosts have mothers too?!

Poppy loses her cool

oppy is the greediest, most pampered kitten in the world. She is also very sweet and playful, and children adore her. She chases balls of yarn that she pretends are mice.

With the family gone to work and school, Poppy has a whole day in front of her. She can eat and sleep and eat and sleep. Then, perhaps do more some eating and a little more sleeping.

But first Poppy goes on a little tour of the kitchen to see if anyone has left a special treat on the table or on the worktop! Yes! There is a half-eaten plate of food on the table, and it looks absolutely delicious!

The first mouthful tastes as good as it looks, and so does the second. What a treat: cheese, meat, tomatoes, and something else that tastes a little strange. Chili! First, the spicy sauce burns her mouth and tongue, and then it slowly works its hot

way down her throat and into her tummy! It's burning!

Poppy looks around the kitchen for something to put out the fire that seems to be raging inside her. 'Perhaps, I'll explode!' thinks Poppy. But there's nothing she can see or do that will help.

Poppy drinks water from her bowl as quickly as she can, but it doesn't stop the burning pain. Oh, if only she hadn't been so greedy and stolen that food.

From now on, she'll only eat the biscuits and food that are put out for her. At least, there are no surprises with biscuits. They are always delicious and ever-so cool!

Chestnut's journey of discovery

 hestnut was a wild horse who lived in a lush valley. He had plenty of grass to eat and nobody bothered him, and that was the problem. No one bothered him, but no one spoke to him either! He was all alone in his sea of green grass.

One day, Chestnut decided to go and find himself some company. Even if that company annoyed him, it had to be better than talking to himself!

But which way should Chestnut go? Everywhere looked the same whichever way he turned. He decided to follow the setting sun all the way to the horizon. So Chestnut headed west, galloping across the pastures and fields.

Some time later, he saw two strange things with smoke pouring from holes at the top. They were the homes of two families, but Chestnut didn't know that. He had never seen humans before.

Opening his large nostrils, Chestnut sniffed the air and inhaled the familiar and pungent smell of fire. Sometimes when there is a storm, the valley goes up in flames and then the grass grows again, greener and sweeter than ever.

'Fire is a good sign,' thought Chestnut. 'I'll go and take a closer look.'

He went up to the houses and saw strange animals walking on two feet. He also saw lots of horses! One of them came toward him, gently shaking its head from side to side. It was a pretty black filly.

Chestnut had discovered humans and where they live, as well as more friends that he could ever have imagined!

Monkey trouble!

 arney, the little monkey told his mother he was going to see his grandpa, who lived in a tree nearby.

'Take care,' said Barney's ma. 'Remember, the forest can be a dangerous place, especially for little ones. If your Grandpa Pip isn't there, come home right away.'

To get to grandpa's home, Barney had to follow the river. Sometimes, he would sit for hours by the river watching the water flow by. Barney didn't know how to swim, but he had always wanted to learn.

'Wow, what's that?' said Barney to himself. 'It looks like a log with eyes!'

This log, though, looked odd and the eyes were a bit scary. Then, the log the started to speak to him in a very low voice.

'Hello, little monkey. Do you want to swim with me?'

For a moment, Barney was quite tempted. 'I would love to, but I don't know how to swim,' he replied, politely.

'Don't worry,' crooned the log. 'I'm a swimming teacher. You are completely safe with me. Come over here and I'll show you what to do.'

'But I'll sink!' said Barney, looking into the deep water.

'I'll hold you up,' said the log.

'My grandpa is waiting for me, and I'm very late. I think I should be on my way,' Barney decided.

'Good idea, Barney,' replied Grandpa, who had been listening and watching. 'Mr Crocodile, you can go and find something other than my grandson for your lunch!'

Barney was happy to see Grandpa, but even happier to see the crocodile swim away!

Are there monsters about?

lison isn't afraid of anything...well, almost anything. She isn't afraid of the dark. She isn't afraid of spiders. She isn't afraid of dogs. She isn't afraid of airplanes flying overhead and making a deafening noise as they pass. She isn't afraid of her teacher, even though she is really strict. She's not afraid of snakes, or mice, or lions, or aliens. But...

In Alison's bedroom there is a wardrobe, and Alison is certain that it contains monsters that are hiding and waiting to leap out at her! *Argh!*

Every night before Alison goes to bed, she makes sure the wardrobe doors are firmly shut. Sometimes, she even has to get out of bed to check them again. She thinks the monsters might come out while she is asleep, you see. Alison is not sure what they look like, but she knows that they are really scary.

During the night, Alison hears little scuttling noises followed by something much worse–a long, creepy silence. She is sure it is the monsters shifting about in the wardrobe. Sometimes they even steal the cookies that Alison hides on the top shelf. All that is left of the cookies are a few crumbs. The monsters also love chocolate! There were actually tooth marks in the last bar she left out. That time, Alison told her parents about the monsters in the wardrobe.

Together, Alison and her parents opened the wardrobe to spot the monsters. Instead of monsters, they saw a tiny grey shadow disappear through a tiny hole. It was a mouse! Alison isn't afraid of anything now that she has discovered that her monsters are only greedy little mice!

Maria's question quest

There are lots of things that Maria would like to know, but when she asks her parents questions they don't always give an answer. Sometimes she feels that they are not quite telling her the whole truth. One time, for example, when she asked, 'Dad, why am I a girl, not a boy?' Her father simply smiled and said 'That is the way you were made.'

Call that an answer?! If she said something like that at school when teacher asked a question she would be in big trouble! So she still doesn't know why she was born a girl not a boy.

The moon and the stars seemed to be similar problems. Poor dad tried his best. He began to explain that stars are like the sun and goodness knows what else, and that the moon...well... at this point, dad got a bit confused and couldn't remember what else he was going to say. Then it was time for dinner, so the question and its answer were totally forgotten.

How could Maria find out how children are made? It seemed her parents thought she was too young to know all the details. Did they think she was still a dumb baby? Why make such a mystery of everything! *Huh!* Who'd have parents?!

Another question that didn't seem to have an answer was how was the Earth made?

Uncle David gave her a story about a 'big bang', but Maria doubted that could be true. Big bang! It sounded ridiculous. No, thought Maria, grown-ups don't know much at all, and they don't want to admit it. Instead of making up crazy stories, why don't they just say they don't know!

A mouse in the house

 oor Kitty was worn out. She had spent a week chasing an invisible mouse. As she hunted for it day and night, Kitty began to wonder if the mouse really was invisible or whether it just didn't exist. Perhaps the invisible mouse was all in her imagination? There was no smell, trace, or sound of a mouse in the house, and yet...

It all began last Saturday when the family returned home from shopping. Kitty had stayed at home like the good guard-cat she is. The children were really excited when they got home and started unpacking everything.

'Careful,' said Dad. 'Let me do it. Where's the mouse, James?'

'In the box, Dad,' said James.

'Right,' said Kitty to herself, 'there's a mouse in a box somewhere around here, and I'm gonna get it!' Kitty jumped on the first box, clawed it open but didn't find a mouse.

'Kitty, get out of that box!' shouted Amber. 'Dad, Kitty's ruining everything!'

Kitty climbed onto the sofa to wait for things to calm down. As she waited, Kitty kept careful watch just in case the mouse suddenly appeared.

At last, she heard dad say, 'James, click on the mouse. No, not like that! Slide it across there!'

'They must have all gone mad,' thought Kitty, looking around. 'There's no mouse here, I'm sure of it!'

That was a week ago, and poor Kitty is still on guard duty looking out for a mouse in the house. She hasn't realised that the only mouse in this house is connected to a computer!

Owl sense

artin and his mother were driving home from school when Martin noticed a little brown ball in the road. It looked like a stuffed toy, or could it be a small animal?

'Stop! There's something in the road!' Martin shouted.

His mother stopped the car just in time. Martin got out and on the road was a little ball of soft, feathery down, struggling for its life.

'What is it?' asked Martin.

'It's a baby owl. It must have fallen out of its nest,' said Martin's mother.

'Can we take it home with us?' asked Martin. 'It's going to be run over if we leave it here.'

'No, Martin. We'll have to leave him here, but we'll take him off the road and put him under the trees,' said mother.

'Please can we take him home?' begged Martin. 'I promise I'll look after him, and when he's grown up I'll set him free.'

'We can't do that,' his mother explained. 'Baby owls often fall out of their nests. His parents will find him and pick him up. If we took him home, we wouldn't be able to look after him properly and he would die.'

Martin bent down to stroke the owl, but his mother stopped him.

'Don't touch him. His parents won't know his smell and they will abandon him,' she said. 'Go and get the box from the boot of the car and we'll use it to carry him to the trees.'

Martin went to get the box. He was sad, but at the same time glad that the baby owl would be fine. Now, whenever he hears the hoot of an owl, he thinks of the baby owl and his family.

The lonely snowman

It was very cold that evening. All the children had gone home to get warm. Even the birds had gone to their cosy nests, and the poor snowman was all alone in the middle of the park. It is always much colder if you're alone, even if you're a snowman.

There he was with his frozen feet, holding a broom in his hand, an old coat on his back and an icicle hanging on the end of his carrot nose.

'Oh, how miserable I feel,' he said sadly. 'And I'm afraid of the dark!'

Suddenly the snowman heard a beautiful voice, as sweet as vanilla ice cream saying, 'Have they left you all alone too? Is there a cold wind blowing around you over there? I'm starting to get cold. Can you see me?'

The young children had built a snow statue not far from the snowman. She wasn't wearing tatty clothes like the snowman. She looked like a real person and the last golden-red rays of sun shining on her made her look almost alive.

The snowman had forgotten all about her because he never thought she would look at him twice. After all, he was an ugly, old snowman with a fat tummy, a carrot nose, and grubby eyes made of coal. And yet, here she was talking to him!

Some sort of magic must have gone on that evening, because the following day the two figures in the park were standing side by side, and wrapped around their shoulders was the snowman's tatty coat.

The forgotten violin

There once was a very lonely violin that whiled away its hours locked up in a dusty attic. It sat among faded boxes, and played melancholy sad tunes while dreaming of days long gone.

You see this violin was not any old violin. It once belonged to a famous musician. He played the violin so beautifully that people flocked from miles away to hear his delightful music. The violin loved his master and put its heart and soul into making the music sound wonderful. But the musician grew old and his hands became too tired to play any more. So the violin was put in the attic many years ago.

Then one day, a muffled sound at the far end of the attic awoke the violin from his lonely daydreaming. It was the sound of the attic door being opened.

No one had opened the door for years! The violin held its breath excitedly as it saw rays of light flooded attic.

With shuffling steps, a wizened elderly man climbed the ladder, softly muttering to himself, 'It must be up here. I haven't seen it in years. Now, where are you, my pretty?'

It was the musician! And peeking from behind him was a little girl. The musician saw the violin and tears came to his eyes, 'Here he is, Daisy. Here's your extra special present. I used to play this violin in concerts many years ago. You must take good care of him, as he is a dear old friend of mine.'

The little girl nodded solemnly as her grandpa passed the precious instrument to her. The violin was never lonely again.

When wishes come true

There once was a giant who was so tall his head touched the clouds. There was also a little old man who was so small his belly touched his shoes. Each of them wished they were different.

The giant sighed, 'How I wish I was small!'

The little man sighed, 'How I wish I was tall!'

One day, the giant was really tired and wanted to find a bed that was big enough for him to sleep in. But there were no beds long enough for him. His feet always stuck out at the end.

'How I wish I was small!' the giant groaned. 'It would be so nice to be able to stretch out when I go to sleep!'

Just then a voice from below him called, 'And I wish I was tall! We could swap if you like. I know a magician who could help us get what we want.'

'Okay,' answered the giant without thinking. 'But can he do it quickly? I am feeling really tired and need to rest.'

Instantly the giant saw the mountains become enormous, then the trees and the flowers. He stretched out and went to sleep on an ever-so-comfy bed.

When the giant awoke a little later, it was very hot and he thought he could do with a cool cloud bath. Cloud baths were so refreshing. Forgetting how small he now was, he could not reach the clouds. Just then a huge, dark shadow fell over him. Far up in the sky, a voice moaned, 'Help! I am too tall and I want to be small again.'

Maybe next time the giant and the small man should think about what they wish for!

The day the cockerel didn't crow

William and Rachel didn't need an alarm clock because they had Colin, the cockerel. At day break, Colin would puff himself up and loudly announce the news to the world. 'Cockle-doodle-doo! It's morning!'

The problem was that cockerels never take a holiday or enjoy a lazy lie-in. Through all the seasons it's the same. Colin laughs when the radio announces that the clocks are going back back one hour. It isn't humans who decide the time, it is the sun!

One day, William and Rachel's pop said, 'Tomorrow I'm going to the market in town and I'm going to sell that noisy, old cockerel!'

But the next day, everyone awoke late because Colin the cockerel hadn't crowed. They went to look for Colin in the hen house, but he wasn't there!

The cockerel and the chickens had all vanished!

William and Rachel looked everywhere for Colin and the chickens. They even accused the foxes of eating them.

To make sure they didn't oversleep again, pop had to buy an alarm clock. The family soon noticed the difference.

What a horrible, clanging, nasty, tinny din that wind-up alarm clock made!

Colin used to crow quietly so as not to wake the babies, and then he would crow louder until everyone was awake. The alarm clock didn't know how to do that.

Only when everyone agreed that Colin the cockerel was better than any alarm clock did Colin bring the chickens back to the coop and return to his duty of crowing at day break.

The naughty imp

Tyke, the little imp, lived in Massif, the giant's house. Now Tyke couldn't help playing practical jokes. His bestest trick of all was tying the giant's shoelaces together when he was sleeping.

One day, when Massif went out in search of wood, Spike had a new idea. He knew the giant would want a mug of hot chocolate when he came home, so he decided to tip an entire packet of salt into the giant's milk pitcher. But before he had done it, Tyke slipped and fell into the pitcher!

'Help, I'm drowning!' he cried.

Massif arrived just in time to grab the little imp by the scruff of his neck.

'What's this?' boomed the giant. 'You're the naughty imp that messes with my shoelaces, aren't you? Were you about to play another trick on me? Speak up.'

'Yes, I wanted to play a joke on you,' gasped Tyke.

'And exactly what joke was that going to be?' asked the giant.

'I was going to pour salt into your milk. Please forgive me,' the imp spluttered.

'No, no,' said the giant, 'what a wonderful idea. I'll make you a delicious mug of hot chocolate with a big pinch of salt. Then, you can tell me what it's like. If you don't drink it, I'll throw you into the pitcher. Okay?'

Poor Tyke had to drink every last drop of the salty hot chocolate. It really was disgusting! The giant laughed so hard the house shook. Ever since the giant has slept peacefully, knowing that Tyke won't play silly tricks.

The land of the tamarisk pips

Do you know where the land of the tamarisk pips can be found? I didn't know even know there was such a place, until one day not very long ago.

I live in a big house near the forest and every day I go for a walk on the way home from school. Depending on the season, I pick strawberries and mushrooms to take home for supper.

On this particular day, I had taken a tangerine with me as a snack. I sat on the grass, I thought how delicious the tangerine smelled. Tangerines aren't very big, but they smell delicious, look beautiful, and taste just wonderful.

Just as I pierced the skin of the fruit with my fingernail, I heard a voice above my head say, 'If you eat that tangerine, you will never go to the land of the tamarisk pips.'

I looked up, but could see no one. I thought I must have been imagining things, so I carried on peeling the tangerine.

A moment later and the voice spoke again, and this time the voice was very, very close!

'Have you really thought about this?' boomed the voice.

I was sure there was no one there, and feeling more than a little foolish I asked, 'Where is the land of the tamarisk pips?'

I waited and waited, but there was no reply. 'I must be going mad,' I thought to myself.

But ever since that day, I have never been able to eat another tangerine, just in case it means I can never go to the land of the tamarisk pips, wherever that may be! I don't suppose you know, do you?

What a cheeky monkey!

Mikey was a baby monkey and although he still depended on his mother, he was eager to be independent.

Once, when he was playing in the bush, he came across Guffaw the hyena. Now, Mikey wasn't frightened at all. He copied what his dad did and puffed himself up, opening his mouth so that Guffaw could see his big teeth. He stamped his feet and hit his chest with his paws. *Boom, boom, boom!*

'Hiiii-hiiii!' laughed the hyena. 'Are you trying to scare me little monkey? How dangerous you are–like a warrior! But I'm the one who is going to eat you!'

Unafraid, Mikey bared his teeth even more. The hyena started to back off then ran away. Mikey felt very proud of himself.

'Yes! I'm the best! I scared that stupid hyena away!' he laughed.

'Hurrumph!' boomed a loud voice behind him. Terrified, Mikey spun round to see the most enormous animal he had ever seen. It had four big fat feet, and was as tall as a tree, with a big branch dangling off the end of its nose. Mikey was scooped up into the air with the branch. He closed his eyes in fear and cried, 'Please don't eat me!'

'Be quiet and stop wriggling!' said a big husky voice that sounded like Mikey's grandpa.

It was an elephant, and luckily, they don't eat monkeys. Not even cheeky ones like Mikey!

'Come on, I'll take you home, you little warrior!' said the kind elephant.

It's the swallows calling

This morning, all the swallows in the town were perching next to each other on the telephone wires, silently looking at the empty sky. What was going on? Were they waiting for a telephone call?

'Yes,' Gemma thought. 'That must be it. Why else would they be wasting their time sitting there when they love flying so much?'

When Gemma left school that afternoon there were no swallows on the telephone wire, nor in the sky above the town. She would have to ask her dad about it.

'Dad, can swallows make telephone calls?' asked Gemma.

'I don't think so,' smiled dad. 'They communicate with each other in a different way.'

'So why were the swallows lined up on the telephone wire this morning?' she said. 'Do you think they were going to have a race?'

'I suppose it's a sort of a race,' said dad. 'It's that time of the year when the swallows leave us. They don't like the cold, so they all fly off to find somewhere warm in the sun. They'll be back in the spring.'

'But will the birds remember where they live?' asked Gemma

'Don't worry, Gemma, they always come back to the same place,' said dad.

'I think it's sad to see the sky without birds in it!' said Gemma.

'But there are lots of other birds around. There's robins and there's sparrows, and other small birds. We can make a bird table for them on the patio this winter,' said dad. 'Then, they will be sure to visit us, and you won't even have to phone them!'

Seven little monsters

A little green monster. A little spiky monster. A little big-eared monster. A little grumpy monster. A little skinny monster. A little yellow monster.

That makes seven, doesn't it? Count them again, please. I think we're missing one. Oh, yes! That's right, the little invisible monster.

The seven monsters were always messing around. They were also terrible little liars.

When the little green monster stole candy from the store cupboard, he said it was the little big-eared monster, not him. When the little big-eared monster was punished for stealing the candy, he said the little spiky monster had taken the candy.

The spiky monster cried, 'It wasn't me! It was the little skinny monster! He stole them, the little grumpy monster hid them, and the little yellow monster ate them!'

The little invisible monster got up to invisible mischief, so you could never tell what he was doing. But one day, the seven monsters got what they deserved.

As usual, they had been into mischief. They poured the milk onto the sofa, deleted everything on the computer, and lots of other naughty things. They were just about to fall asleep in the monster den when they heard something terrible! It was a child's voice saying, 'Monsters don't exist!'

Zap! the monsters vanished! You see, if children don't believe in monsters, they disappear forever!

A narrow escape

 nowy, Spotty, and Silky the three little seals, liked to spend their days rolling around in the snow. They never got cold because they were covered in dense, thick fur.

One day, the seals heard a loud noise in the sky. A huge bird without wings was hovering overhead. It made all the snow around the seals fly up into the air. Like all little creatures, Snowy, Spotty, and Silky were very curious.

'Let's go and have a closer look,' said Snowy.

'No,' said Spotty. 'Mum told us never to talk to strangers.'

'But it's only a bird,' said Snowy, 'and if it has come from far away, it might have seen lots of really interesting things. I want to know what it has seen.'

'Look!' said Silky, pointing at the 'bird'.

Suddenly, some strange, two-legged creatures jumped out onto the ice and began running toward the three confused little seals.

Then, another strange big bird landed next to the first one, and for the first time in their lives, the seals heard a human voice.

'We are the police! Get back into your helicopter and leave now! Hunting seal cubs is banned.'

The creatures got back into the first bird, and then the two strange birds quickly flew off.

The young seals ran off to play in the snow, completely unaware how close they had just come to being trapped by hunters!

A letter from the dormouse family

We are the dormouse family and we live in the country. Like lots of other animals, we have a nice long sleep in the winter. As soon as the snow falls, we go back into our warm little hole and go to sleep. We snuggle up together through the winter until spring arrives. But before we can go to sleep, we have to prepare ourselves, and that can be very hard work!

First, we have to collect lots of hay to make a lovely soft bed, then we have to eat and eat and eat some more, so that we can store extra fat. We have to rush to get all this done before the snow comes.

But the problem is, we are always being interrupted by foxes, eagles, and humans. You humans have no idea of the trouble you cause. We know you don't mean to be thoughtless, but kicking stones when you trample around can be quite frightening for us.

To help us prepare in peace each day, one dormouse sits on a rock and keeps watch. At any sign of danger, he whistles loudly, and we all disappear as fast as we can. So, little human, if you ever hear whistling when you're walking in the country you must tread carefully less you trample us.

If you want to see us, you must keep very quiet. If you do that, then you might get to see our babies playing in the long grass. Now remember, we're counting on you to help us by explaining this to the grown-ups.

Maya and Rama

Maya lives in a village in the jungle and she loves watching the wild animals. Maya was really worried yesterday because she thought Rama, the rhinoceros, was going to die.

Two days ago, poachers had injured Rama while trying to capture her. She had charged at the poachers and they ran away. But then the rhino had been too ill to eat or drink. Maya wanted to help her, but she didn't dare go too close as Maya knew she might be dangerous if she was in a grumpy mood.

Suddenly, Maya heard an engine. A truck appeared with a man standing on the back. He was pointing a gun at Rama.

Maya shouted, 'No! Don't shoot!' But it was too late! The rhino collapsed to the ground and three men jumped from the truck. They ran up to the rhino and Maya ran after them. One of the men caught her.

'What are you doing here? I'd stand back if I were you. Once the vet has treated the rhino. she'll wake up in a bad temper,' said one of the men.

Maya was surprised. A vet? But they'd just shot the rhino! 'You are bad hunters, not vets. I saw that man fire his gun!' said Maya.

'I know,' said the vet, smiling. 'The gun was only loaded with something to make the rhino sleep so that I can treat her safely.'

Once the vet had done his work, the men got back into the truck. From a safe distance, Maya watched Rama awake and start plodding about. Maya decided she would like to be a vet and help animals in the jungle, too.

The talking stone

This morning, Farmer Fred took Flora the cow into a field full of lush, green grass. She was just about to take a huge mouthful of grass, when she came nose to nose with a strange-looking stone. The stone not only had a head, but it could talk as well!

'Can you be a little more careful. You almost swallowed me!' said the stone, crossly.

Now, Flora is a gentle cow but even she doesn't like to be spoken to like that. This large stone was very rude.

'I do beg your pardon, but we polite creatures usually start a sentence by saying 'hello'! And anyway, I *am* careful, and I *don't* eat stones!' said Flora.

'Well I don't think you are very careful,' said the 'stone'. 'It's unbelievable that you think I am a stone. Look at me. Have you ever seen a walking, talking stone? Well have you?'

And with that the 'stone' started ambling very slowly away. Flora couldn't believe her eyes. Was this possible? She had seen many strange things in her life, but never a walking, talking, breathing stone!

'And now I'm going to do something else you won't believe,' said the 'stone'.

'And what might that be?' said Flora, looking puzzled.

'I am going to go swimming! With that the 'stone' wandered to the edge of the pond and flopped into the water. Flora could see the 'stone' floating and actually swimming!

Before disappearing under the water. the stone called, 'See you later, cow! Tara the turtle wishes you well!'

Tulip and the orphan

Tulip was a pretty cow with big eyes and long, long eyelashes. She was feeling very unhappy because her calf had grown up and left her. From now on, she would only see him in the evenings when she got back to the barn. All day she stood beside the fence and sighed quietly to herself.

Growing nearby, was a fir tree forest and Tulip could smell the wild boar who lived there. Some mornings she would see that the grass in the pasture had been dug up by the wild boars the night before. *Eeeurgh!* It would smell like stinky pigs.

But one day, Tulip thought she could hear a baby animal crying. Maybe her calf had got lost, she frantically thought. She dashed to the forest and pricked up her ears. There was someone nearby, sobbing loudly. Tulip glanced back to the field and saw her calf playing with the other calves.

As Tulip started to walk away she heard a tiny voice cry, 'Help me! I'm all alone. I want my Ma!'

Tulip the cow turned back and said, 'Come here little one. Don't be frightened.'

A little brown hairy thing came timidly out from under the drooping branches of a tree.

'Come here. Are you lost? Are you hungry?' asked Tulip.

'Y-yes,' stuttered the baby wild boar. 'There were hunters in the woods yesterday, and I haven't seen my mother since!'

Tulip, the gentle cow, lay down next to the orphaned wild boar and nuzzled it until it felt safe again. Now that she had someone to care for, Tulip was no longer lonely or sad.

No more soup!

It's always the same. As soon as winter comes, Amy's mother says, 'It's getting cold. Tonight, I'm going to make some soup to warm us up.'

On hearing this, Amy would always say, 'Oh, no! You know I don't like soup!'

'We can't always eat what we like,' said Amy's mother one particularly chilly day.

'Why not?' asked Amy.

Well, it's a good question, isn't it? Why can't we just eat things that we like? Amy knew what her mother's answer would be...

'If I let you eat anything, you would only eat chocolate, and that's not good for your teeth!'

'That's not true. I also like crisps and ice cream and ketchup!' said Amy.

'Exactly,' said her mother. 'What about vegetables and fruit? If you just ate what you liked, you would put on lots of weight, have terrible teeth, and would not be very healthy, at all!'

After much thought, Amy smiled and said, 'I wouldn't mind. When we met Mrs Jones, she said, 'My how big you've grown, Amy' and you answered, 'Yes, she is big for her age'. I don't care whether I'm big or small, but I don't like soup!'

Just then, Amy's grandma arrived. She asked what was going on and then thought for a while before saying, 'Why don't you cook lots of different vegetables, and Amy can choose three that she likes and eat them with ketchup poured over. What do you think of that idea, Amy?'

Amy thought for a second then said, 'I think that's a great idea!'

Time for bed, Stuart!

ven if his Dad has promised to tell him a bedtime story, Stuart always tries to avoid going to bed. He always tries to stay up as late as he possibly can.

Then every morning, because he's so tired, Stuart eats his breakfast like a zombie, pulls on his coat, and stumbles into the car to go to school. If he remembers, he gives his mother a quick kiss on the cheek, and mumbles, 'See you later.'

It's no better in the evenings. There's barely time for dinner with all the homework he has to do. Stuart would love to have a bit of time to sit on the sofa with his parents, and watch the television or chat for a while. But instead, he's on his own in his room because his mother's cooking dinner and sorting things for the next day, and dad's working on office stuff.

What happens every night goes like this: the three of them eat dinner, then Stuart has a quick bath, and then it's time for bed because tomorrow is a school or work day. Before you know it, the routine starts all over again!

So, Stuart always takes as long as possible to eat his meal, and pretends not to hear when his mothers tells him it is time for a bath. Sometimes, Stuart can stretch a tiny job like cleaning his teeth to take an hour. Mind you, his teeth shine!

When Stuart is finally ready for bed, he runs downstairs and sits on his dad's lap. But dad always says, 'You can only sit here for a minute. Remember, you've got a busy day at school tomorrow.'

'School, school, school! It's always school. What about having a few little cuddles?' Stuart grumbles giving dad a huge bear hug.

Meg's lovely locks

My friend Meg has lovely red hair. It's not bright red like a traffic light, it's a soft, warm copper-red like my grandma's saucepans. I haven't told Meg that her hair reminds me of my grandma's saucepans yet! I don't know if she'd take it as a compliment, or think I was just being rude. Girls are complicated and I'm shy, so I admire her hair in secret.

Meg doesn't like people talking about her hair because there are lots of boys who tease her about it in our class at school.

Our teacher has red hair, but you can see that she isn't really a natural redhead. I think it must be dyed.

One day, a naughty boy called Jim asked this question to our teacher, 'Do your parents have red hair, Miss?'

'That's a strange question to ask me, Jim,' said the teacher.

Jim sniggered, then asked another question. 'Are your children redheads?' he persisted.

I think the teacher understood what Jim was getting at when she saw Meg blushing.

'I regret to say that no one in my family has hair as red or as beautiful as Meg's,' smiled the teacher. 'I'm afraid I have to dye mine so it looks a little bit like Meg's.'

'Really?' smiled Meg, suddenly very proud of her red locks. 'Perhaps my hair isn't so bad, after all.'

From then on, the other children in the class stopped teasing Meg about her red hair. In fact, some of the girls said they wished they had red hair, too!

The horrible new car

ittle Pete's father decided to buy a new car. The old one still worked, but it didn't have a fast engine, lights all over the dashboard, or gleaming metallic finish. Pete used to like sitting in the back of the old car with his dog. Now everything was more complicated. For one thing, dad was always shouting, 'Be careful! Don't slam the door! Stop making the seats dirty!'

Pete wasn't allowed to wind down the windows in the new car or eat biscuits on a long journey. His dog wasn't even allowed in the car! Going anywhere by car was no fun at all. In fact, it was really, really boring!

There was no radio in their old car, so Pete and his family always used to sing or play a guessing game when they went on holiday. But now they don't even talk to each other. All his parents want to do is listen to horrible music blasting out of the new radio. It's not even possible for Pete to singalong because he doesn't know any of the words.

The worst of the new car thing was that Pete didn't get a new bike. His parents said his old bike was still fine to ride.

Pete said, 'The old car was fine too, but you swapped it for a newer model.'

'That was different,' said dad.

Of course, that was the sort of dad-answer Pete expected! 'When I'm grown-up, I'm going to drive an old car!' said Pete. 'Old cars are fun!'

Big, bad dog or not?

There has been a kennel in next door's yard for a few days now. Inside the kennel sits a huge dog with big fangs and a squashed nose.

Minky and Fluffball, our two kittens, don't think he looks at all friendly. The big fierce dog isn't tied up, so they can't go and make faces at him like they do to the little yappy dog across the road.

The big dog seems to sleep all day, so the kittens have decided that they'll have to find a new way to their friend Blanche's house. In fact, the kitten have just spotted Blanche walking across the lawn just a couple of feet away from the kennel!

Oh, no! The nasty big dog might pounce on her! He could swallow her whole! Quick! Scurry up that tree, Blanche.

Minky and Fluffball shook with fright. What would become of their friend? She's acting completely mad!

Blanche is now actually walking toward the vicious dog! The two kittens long to warn her before it's too late. But without a care in the world, Blanche saunters up to the kennel and sniffs the dog's food. The dog lifts his large head, gives a huge yawn that shows all of his gigantic teeth and...oh, no!...he smiles at Blanche. It's unbelievable!

Today, Minky and Fluffball have learned a very important lesson: you should never judge anyone by how he or she looks.

The greedy shark

azor is an enormous shark. He is called Razor because of his incredibly sharp teeth. He is the kind of shark that eats everything yet is always hungry.

The other day he saw something moving behind the coral. Food! Perfect timing for a hungry shark! Razor darted over, with his mouth wide open, ready to swallow and bite. Instead of finding a tasty fish lurking in the coral, there was only a rusty anchor sinking to the seabed.

But Razor saw the anchor too late! His huge jaws snapped shut around the large chunk of metal. *Ow! Ow! Ow!* His teeth hurt so much that for once he didn't feel the slightest bit hungry.

Even though he isn't exactly loveable, Razor has one loyal friend. It is Piccolo, a tiny fish who follows him everywhere. Piccolo is too small for Razor to bother eating, so they have become friends.

Razor could not understand why his mouth was hurting, so Piccolo offered to help.

'Open wide and say *'ahhhh'!'* said Piccolo. 'Oh, come on! You can open wider than that!'

The enormous shark opened his mouth and the tiny little fish swam in to inspect his teeth.

'Oh dear, dear me! You've broken a tooth, you poor, old thing. Don't worry another one will grow to replace it in no time,' said Piccolo, swimming quickly out of Razor's mouth. After all, would you trust a shark in a bad mood?

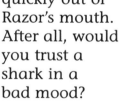

The snail race

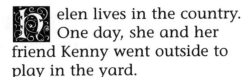elen lives in the country. One day, she and her friend Kenny went outside to play in the yard.

'I know what we can do!' said Helen. 'Let's have a snail race!'

Kenny didn't look too impressed. 'Snails can race? Well that's news to me!' he scoffed.

'It's brilliant,' said Helen. 'You put them all on a start line and the first one to reach the end is the winner.'

The friends went to look for some contestants. Helen chose a purple snail with a yellow shell. Kenny found a fat brown snail. Kenny thought that large snail would be stronger and therefore faster. Helen drew a line across the path with a crayon, and placed the snails behind it.

'Ready, steady, GO!' said Helen.

The grey snail took the lead. But the purple one set off in the wrong direction, then stopped and eyed his opponent and turned to follow him. This lost the snail time and it became clear he was going to lose.

But Helen was determined to win. She took a piece of lettuce out of her pocket and waved it in front of her snail. The purple snail suddenly perked up! He slid past the big snail and was first across the finish line.

'I won!' shouted Helen.

'Oh, really? What's that in your hand?' asked Kenny.

'Nothing,' said Helen, trying to hide the lettuce in her pocket.

'I'm not gonna play with you any more,' said Kenny. As Helen and Kenny argued, the snails slowly slithered home.

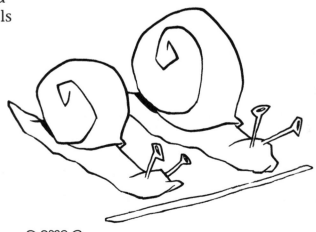

A meal on wheels?

Floating in the river with just his nose and eyes poking up above the water, little Croc was having a nap.

It was very hot. The birds were quiet because the heat would dry their throats. The gazelles were resting in the shade of the trees, but still watchful of an approaching lion.

But who would run in heat like this? Everyone was waiting for nightfall when they could go and drink from the river. At times like this there is a water 'truce'. The animals don't bother each other because they are all too thirsty.

But Croc was a crocodile and although it looked like he was sleeping, he was always ready to catch anything that passed by his big, gaping mouth.

Now, Croc didn't mean to be bad, it was just that nature had made all crocodiles greedy. And because of this, nobody wanted to be his friend. Anyone who saw him would quickly run or swim away.

Suddenly, Croc saw something approaching. He had never seen anything like it before. What could it be? It was a square beast with four round feet and it was making a loud, roaring noise! It splashed into the water and almost landed on Croc's nose! Thinking fast, Croc dived under the water and swam home to complain about this new beast to his mother.

'Well, it's lucky you didn't try to eat it!' said Mrs Crocodile, knowing only too well that her young son had a huge appetite. 'You know I'm always telling you to watch what you eat. The thing you saw was a truck. Trucks are very, very hard to swallow and they're not even very tasty!'

Miss Moonflower

There was once a puppet called Miss Moonflower. She lived in a big box with other puppets. When the puppeteer opened the box to take out the puppets for a show, he always started with Miss Moonflower because she was extra special!

Miss Moonflower was very pretty, but she was very also mischievous, especially when it came to Prince Carlo, her boyfriend. She pulled his hair, pinched him, and once she even ruined his beautiful blue silk costume. Poor Prince Carlo! During the show, she would always try to tangle his strings.

The other puppets were fed up with Miss Moonflower's naughty tricks, so they called upon a special fairy. The puppets asked the fairy to 'magic' Miss Moonflower into a real person. Then, she could live in the real world and leave the puppets to live together in peace.

Prince Carlo begged the fairy not to cast any sort of spell that would change Miss Moonflower.

'Why so kind when she is so awful to you?" asked the fairy.

'I don't mind because I love her,' replied Prince Carlo.

'As you wish,' said the fairy. So with one wave of her magic wand, the fairy transformed both the puppets. Prince Carlo became a handsome young man, and Miss Moonflower became part of the moon. Ever since then, the other puppets in the box have been able to sleep peacefully. Prince Carlo married a real princess, and every once in a while he looks at the moon and smiles, remembering the naughty Miss Moonflower.

The baby silver birch

n Rosewood Forest there was a little silver birch tree. Unfortunately, the poor little birch was squashed between two huge fir trees.

The big fir trees stretched out their branches, and the poor little silver birch never got any sunlight. A silver birch needs lots of sun and warmth if it is to grow properly. Every day, the silver birch wished it could be growing in a different part of the forest.

'If you're not happy here, then go somewhere else,' snapped one of the fir trees.

'But how could I do that?' answered the silver birch. 'My roots are stuck into the ground.'

'You haven't even tried,' said the fir tree. '*Pull!* Come on, *pull!* I can move whenever I like, look!'

The fir tree pulled at its roots as hard as it could, but he didn't move even the tiniest bit. So, the north wind said, 'Do you want me to help you?'

'Yes, that's a good idea,' said the stupid fir tree. 'Blow as hard as you can!'

'No!' he said to the wind. 'Please don't do that! If he falls, he'll die.'

But the fir tree said, 'Be quiet, titch! You'll see!'

The wind blew and the fir tree fell to the ground with a crash. The little birch felt sad for his foolish companion, but it was nice to feel the sunshine at last!

Ghostly goings-on!

eorge the little ghost, was very cross. He had told his friend the owl, who lived in the bell tower, exactly why he was so angry.

'It's always like this! You can't go for a walk around this town without someone treading on your feet! If it carries on, I'm going to leave here and live in the woods!'

'T-woooooo,' said the owl.

'I know, I'll go and live in a ruined castle, said George. 'But an old castle might be haunted, and I don't think I'd like that!'

'T-woooo! You do make me laugh, George! Have you forgotten that you're a ghost?'

chuckled the owl. 'You're supposed to be the one that scares people, you silly thing!'

'Me? How could I frighten anyone? They can't even see me!' said George.

'My dear friend, ghosts were invented to frighten people,' said the owl. 'It's always been like that. If you don't want visitors treading on your feet, you shouldn't go out and about barefoot.'

'I don't like wearing shoes,' whinged George.

'You can get really comfy ones, you know,' smiled the owl.

'Thanks for your advice. I'll think about it,' said George.

Ever since then, during the rush hour in town, many people have sworn that they have seen a pair of comfy sneakers walking all by themselves through the town. If only they knew!

The chilly tree

icola watched as the snow fell outside. 'Can I go and play in the snow, please?' she asked her mother.

'Yes, but make sure you dress up warmly and don't stay out for too long,' said her mother.

Nicola put on her big red hat and the scarf her grandma had knitted. Then, she ran around the flower beds trying to catch snowflakes. Puffing and panting, she leaned against a tree. A few months ago, this tree had been covered in leaves, but now it was completely bare.

Nicola started talking to the tree, just as she often talked to her cat and her hamster.

'Why are you so bare now?' she asked the tree.

'Because it's winter,' said a rough voice.

Nicola was astounded to hear the tree speak and asked, 'Aren't you cold, you poor thing?'

'Oh yes, especially when there's a strong wind like there was today,' the tree shivered.

'Can't you just grow some more leaves?' asked Nicola.

'No, I can't. I have to wait until next spring,' said the tree.

Nicola removed her scarf and tied it round the trunk. 'Maybe that will stop you catching a cold,' she smiled. 'I would loan you my hat, but it won't fit you.'

'Oh, thank you for being so kind,' said the tree. 'Next spring I will grow lots of pretty blossom flowers just for you.'

It's raining! It's pouring!

t's really unlucky if an umbrella doesn't like the rain. Little Marcus is the only one in the umbrella family who doesn't like cold wet drizzly rain. His father loves to hear the rain tapping on his head. His mother, the flowery umbrella, says that rain makes her shine.

Poor Marcus. He's the one that's always taken out whenever the family go to the stores. And quite often, they leave him by the store entrance and forget all about him!

This morning, although he was soaking wet, Marcus was shoved back into the umbrella stand by his owner.

'Move up,' shouted a battered old umbrella. 'You're dripping all over me.'

'Sorry, sir,' said Marcus. 'I can't move. The lady umbrella next to me is perfumed and I'm allergic to it. *A-A-aaatchooo!* And to my other side, there's an umbrella sticking into my back. I'm sorry, but I can't move.'

'That's not good enough, you silly little umbrella!'

Then, a voice piped up, 'Hey, leave the kid alone! It's not his fault. He is always made to go out when it's pouring with rain. I'd like to see you put up with those downpours without a fuss, old timer!'

Soon all the other umbrellas were agreeing that Marcus did more than his share of the work.

Young Marcus smiled with pride when he discovered that the other umbrellas respected him and understood how hard he worked. That's when he decided the rain couldn't be that bad if it won you this much respect.

The brave little mice

Every day Tilly and Tiny, the two little mice, set off to go to the market. They have to creep out of their mouse hole without a sound and make sure there are no cats about. The worst part of the trip is getting past Gruff, the neighbour's dog. He's a real monster, who thinks it's great fun chasing cats and mice. Right now, he's lying by the door, his nose on his paws.

Tilly, the braver of the two mice, hides behind the dustbins and calls to her sister. 'Hurry, Tiny! Come on! It's safe, Gruff can't get us from here!' she squeaks.

'I think Gruff is sleeping,' whispered Tiny. 'I think he must be getting too old to chase after us!'

But Gruff wasn't sleeping, he was feeling ill because he had eaten too much for breakfast. He had seen the mice coming out of their hole, but couldn't be bothered to get up and chase them. Opening his eyes and moving just the tiniest bit, made Gruff feel quite unwell!

So, Tilly and Tiny scuttled past, right under his whiskers and he didn't even flinch.

The little mice braced themselves. 'On the count of three, we'll cross the corridor,' says Tilly. 'He won't have time to catch us. One...two...three!'

The mice reach the other side and Tiny says bravely, 'That was too easy. Gruff can't chase us because he's too old! We can do the same thing tomorrow and every day.'

Oh dear! What if Gruff is feeling better tomorrow? Perhaps the two little mice should be very, very careful!

Martyn, the tooth fairy

oday Martyn is going to the dentist for the very first time. He hasn't been worried about it because all his friends had been before. Some of them had braces and bands fitted to help straighten their teeth, and none of them had complained about going to the dentist. But this morning, Martyn is worried, and it's all his dad's fault.

When he came home from work last night, Martyn's dad was was in a bad mood. Holding a hand against his jaw, he mumbled, 'Ooh, I've got a really awful toothache!'

'Well, that's because you never go to the dentist,' said Martyn's mother. 'You probably need a filling.'

'I don't like dentists,' Dad muttered.

Martyn didn't hear the rest of what his dad had said because he was sent to bed. His dad said it was way past his bed time, but Martyn understood what was going on. His dad had nearly let slip the reason why dentists are so scary!

When his mother came to say good night, she said, 'Martyn, your dad's frightened of going to the dentist because he's left it too late. His teeth are in a mess because they weren't sorted out when he was young. Tomorrow, the dentist will check that your teeth are clean and growing straight, that's all.'

Martyn thought for a while then said, 'Dad can come to the dentist with me tomorrow and I'll show him it isn't scary. I'll be a sort of tooth fairy!'

'Good idea,' smiled his mother. You see, adults sometimes need a good example, too!

First flight nerves

I t's not always easy being an eagle, especially if you were born on a mountain top and you are afraid of heights!

Amra, the royal eagle and his wife, Princess Kutu, had two little eaglets. The eldest, East Wind was very brave. He had barely all his feathers when he had started flying. White Feather, his little brother was different. As soon as he neared the edge of the nest, he would feel sick and turn back.

White Feather's mother said it wasn't serious because he still had time to learn, but she was a little worried.

'You're grown-up now,' she said gently. 'Try and fly, just for me.'

'I'm frightened,' cried White Feather. 'It's too high. When I look down, I feel dizzy.'

'If you keep fussing him like that, he'll always be a coward,' grumbled Amra.

This morning at sunrise, when the wind had just started to blow, Amra announced, 'Today, you are going to make your first flight, White Feather. Now, go to the edge of the nest.'

Trembling, White Feather slowly made his way to the edge.

'Jump!' shouted Amra. 'All the animals on the mountain are watching. Jump now!'

White Feather closed his eyes, took a deep breath, and let himself fall into space. His huge wings opened easily and he was carried by the wind.

'I'm flying! I'm flying!'

'Of course you are!' said his mother, proudly.

Mrs Weatherby

Mrs Weatherby was a strange woman. She dressed in a very odd way and often seemed to be talking to herself. Her crooked hat and her big coat made her look like a witch. But she wasn't a witch, at least, I didn't think she was.

I first met Mrs Weatherby in a field. I knew I wasn't supposed to walk across the field, but I wanted to look at the beautiful wild flowers growing there. Mrs Weatherby told me the names of the plants. She knew so much about everything!

But there's no getting away from it, Mrs Weatherby did act quite oddly at times.

For a start, she never bought food from shops. She used vegetables and wild herbs from her garden and other bits and pieces to make soup. I tasted it once because she asked me, and it was really scrummy.

Mrs Weatherby lives in a tiny old hut with her cat, Charlie. There were books in boxes all over the place, but there was no tap, no television, no electric lights. She cooked her soup over a fire in the hearth.

When I once asked Mrs Weatherby if she would prefer to live in town she laughed, 'No, my dear. I love being in the country. I have nature as my surroundings, the wind and the birds for music, and then I have my books! What else do I need?'

Thanks to Mrs Weatherby, I always eat my vegetables, and sometimes ask for more, and I know more than anyone else at school about wild flowers.

Tiny turtles

The moon was shining on the sea and Meena the turtle decided it was time to take her eggs up to the beach. She had been waiting for this moment so that the lizards wouldn't see her coming and steal her precious eggs.

Meena was in a hurry because she needed to dig a big hole in the sand in which to lay her eggs. When she was sure it was deep enough, Meena carefully dropped the eggs into the hole, and then covered them with sand. The sun would keep her eggs nice and warm until they were ready to hatch.

When she was finished, Meena crawled back to the sea, leaving her babies behind. That's what turtles do, you see.

The babies hatch all on their own. Now, you might be wondering how they survive, but don't worry, I'll explain.

When Meena's babies hatch, they clamber out of their shells. Then, they clumsily scratch and scramble out of the hole and onto the sand. The babies then head for the sea because, even though they have never seen it before, they know that is where they need to go.

The baby turtles have to make a running dash across the sand to the water to avoid becoming a meal for the gulls, who swoop, dive, and cry overhead. The baby turtles also have to avoid the lizards who hide in the rocks edging the beach.

If you have ever seen a turtle running, you'll know that it's not exactly speedy! So, it is quite difficult for these tiny creatures to get to the water safely. But, when they eventually splash into the sea, they are off and swimming, criss-crossing the warm seas in search of wonderful turtle adventures.

Aunt Jemima's friends

Katie loved staying at Aunt Jemima's farm because there were cows, chickens, and a lovely horse to ride. Like many farms, there were lots of flies buzzing around in the summer. Even though Aunt Jemima closed the windows and curtains, the little pests still managed to get in.

Katie's mother thought they were dirty, and told Aunt Jemima to spray the flies with an insecticide. But Jemima didn't agree. 'I'm not going to poison the whole family with pesticides just because of a few flies,' she said. 'There are enough spiders in the house to kill them without causing pollution!'

'Oh, stop it!' said Katie's mother. 'You know I hate spiders. Ooh, those long, hairy legs make me feel all shivery!'

Katie's mother had always been afraid of spiders, but not Katie. Aunt Jemima had explained to her that spiders were very useful and not at all dangerous.

'There are some poisonous spiders, but as long as you leave them in peace they won't hurt you,' she said.

Aunt Jemima said that you should never break a spider's web because they take a long time to weave and they're very useful because they catch flies.

In Jemima's house there were a few spiders' webs in corners. Aunt Jemima didn't want to frighten anyone who didn't understand about spiders, so when Katie's mother came to stay, she would catch all the spiders in the house and put them outside.

Wonderful Aunt Jemima!

The honey hives

ouise went to stay with her grandma for a few days last summer. Grandma's was the most wonderful place on earth, thought Louise. There were fruit orchards, and thousands of bees lived in the hives behind the barn. Grandma warned Louise never to visit the hives alone.

'Why?' asked Louise.

'Because it's dangerous,' said her grandma. 'The bees might surround you and sting you if you annoy them. If it's a nice day tomorrow, I'll go and ask them for some honey for our breakfast.'

'Can I come with you to the hives? Please, Grandma, please?' begged Louise.

'Yes, but you must keep very quiet and stand right next to me,' said Grandma.

The next morning, Grandma made Louise wear netting over her head and special gloves on her hands, and then helped her into a big jacket. Grandma also tucked Louise's trousers into her socks, so there was no gap where a bee could sting her. When they were both ready, Louise and her grandma looked like two peculiar astronauts!

Grandma lit a special little pipe, which she used to blow a couple of puffs of smoke into the hive. Then, she carefully lifted the roof from one of the hives. The bees flew out in all directions. Louise couldn't believe how many bees there were! Grandma picked up a jar of honey from the hive, and put an empty jar in its place. Then, she replaced the roof very carefully. They hurried back to the farmhouse and enjoyed lashings of honey on a warm, home-made bread.

Brave Mali

One morning, Mali the cat woke up in an excellent mood. His feet felt like going for a run in the jungle and his whiskers were tingling with the wild smells of the air. He couldn't wait to dash outside. Cats don't always think before they act, as you will see!

Ah! It was wonderful outside, but Mali was a little worried, not a lot but just a little. He was all alone, outside without his mother for the first time. What if there was danger or something unexpected happened?

'Nothing frightens me. I'm a big cat now,' Mali said to himself.

Just then, Mali saw it! There in the stream – a tiger! Huge, scary and stripy, with its green eyes flashing. Mali jumped back and the tiger disappeared. Where had it gone? Mali spun around to face his enemy but there was no one behind him. Ha! What a brave cat he was. When the tiger saw his whiskers, he must have been frightened away.

Perhaps the tiger was at the bottom of the stream? Mali crept to the water's edge. The tiger was still there, but he looked just the tiniest bit scared now. Nervously, Mali held out his paw to the tiger. When his paw touched the water, the tiger trembled from head to toe!

'Well,' said Mali to himself, 'I have frightened a huge tiger away, but I should go home now because I don't know what other scary creatures might be lurking around the corner!'

Silly Mali! He didn't know that the tiger he had frightened away was his own reflection.

The dancing butterfly

Rupert was a young blue butterfly. He was very curious and would spend all day exploring the walled garden where he was born. He liked to let himself be carried by the wind like a glider. He also liked to try out all the flowers in the garden bed. He tasted the insides of the flowers with his long tongue. He would use his wings to test how soft they were. Rupert loved to admire their pretty shades of pink and yellow.

Sometimes Rupert would go inside the house. Most of all, Rupert loved playing with the children's cat. He did, though, have to be very careful not to get caught by its sharp claws.

Rupert was the happiest butterfly in the world! His only regret was that he didn't know how to dance. He had tried spins, leaps, and twirls, but he just couldn't do any of them very well. His feet would get twisted, his wings would get in the way, and his body was far too stiff. Poor Rupert was desperate to dance!

Silently, the butterfly fluttered around the children who were chatting to each other. They were talking about their school concert because the little girl was going to perform in a special dance. Once girl was saying that because the most gracious and beautiful creatures of all are butterflies, the children were going to perform the dance dressed as butterflies.

Rupert was so pleased when he heard this news he danced. For the time ever, he performed a perfect twirl.

'How wonderful it is to be a butterfly!' he thought.

Grandpa Ri-ri

eil was spending his holiday at Ri-ri's house in the mountains. Ri-ri was his friend Jane's grandpa. Neil thought Ri-ri was a strange name and he often wondered where it came from.

'Ri-ri,' asked Neil. 'Why are you called Ri-ri? It's a strange name for a grandpa, isn't it? Why aren't you called Grandad, or Thomas, which is your real name, isn't it?'

'Well there is a reason,' said Ri-ri, smiling at Jane. 'Can you guess what it is?'

'Is it because 'grandpa' is too hard to spell? asked Neil.

'No, no,' chuckled Ri-ri, 'that is not the reason.'

When they had all stopped laughing, Ri-ri explained why he was known by such a strange and unusual name.

'Ever since Jane was born, I've told her stories,' he said. 'As soon as she could pick up a book, she would give it to me and say 'Ri, ri'. 'Ri-ri', you see, was one of Jane's first words and she couldn't say 'read' properly. So that is why the family gave me this name 'Ri-ri'.'

Neil thought that was a neat story to explain the name.

'I know Ri-ri isn't a very normal name for a grandpa, but I was proud that I'd passed on my love of books to Jane,' Grandpa smiled. 'Anyway, who would like me to 'ri-ri' another story to them?'

'Oh yes, please!' cried Jane and Neil, who could both hardly talk for laughing!

Mad cows!

It was a perfect day for a trip to the lake. Ollie and Zoe loved paddling in its shallows. First, they followed a path into the woods. Then, they walked around the little hills and followed the stream until they came to the glorious lake.

They had just reached the stream when the children decided to stop for a moment and wait for Uncle George to catch them up. Walking past the cows in the fields was always a bit scary, even when the cows were grazing peacefully. As Ollie and Zoe were watching, one of the cows started bucking and making a very strange noise.

'I wonder why that cow is doing that?' said Zoe, nervously looking back for their uncle.

'Uncle George, there's a cow making horrible noises and running all over the place!' called Ollie.

'Maybe it's a bad-tempered cow,' said Uncle George. 'Most cows are harmless, but there's always the odd one that likes to be a bit grumpy.'

Hearing that, Mabel the cow turned to her friends and said, 'Come on, let's show those humans how grumpy we can really be!'

Suddenly, all the cows began running around and making grunting noises.

'Quick! Let's get back into the woods, these cows have gone crackers!' called Uncle George.

As soon as Uncle George and the children had gone, the cows rolled about laughing.

'I don't think they'll be back again,' chuckled Mabel.

Tadpole rescue

ason and Michelle were on a long hike in the mountains. They had climbed to the top of Streams Valley.

'This is called the Streams Valley because of all the little streams running through the rocks. They come from that glacier over there,' explained their dad. 'Come on, we're just about at the top.'

When they finally reached the summit, Jason, Michelle, and their parents were a little out of breath. They were glad to be walking on soft grass again after having walked on hard, sharp rocks for most of the hike. All the little streams had disappeared, but there were some large pools instead.

'Look,' said Jason. 'There are lots of tadpoles in this pool, but there's not enough water, they'll die soon!'

'Let's rescue them,' said Michelle, taking off her hat.

The two children filled the hat with tadpoles, and then ran to empty them into a bigger, deeper pool. Their parents weren't sure if this was such a good idea, but they helped out, running back and forth with the tiny wriggling tadpoles.

Jason and Michelle had a wonderful time and celebrated their rescue work by making up a frog song.

'Croak, croak,' sang Jason.

'Ribbet, ribbet,' sang Michelle.

'What's so funny?' asked their parents.

'We were just thinking of the thousands of frogs that we've rescued,' Jason said. 'Next year they will eat all the mosquitoes and stop them from biting us!'

Aaron's nightmare

It was getting late as Aaron ran through the storm. He was cold, alone, and very frightened. The sky lit up with forks of lightning and claps of thunder boomed loudly. Aaron felt like the sky was going to fall on top of him at any time! He ran and ran as fast as he could, leaping over stones and rocks that blocked his path.

Just as another fork of lightning flashed across the sky, Aaron tripped and fell. Looking up, he saw a horrible witch with long pointed fingers standing in front of him! She looked a bit like the dinner lady Mrs Miggins, and she was holding a big silver fork.

'Well, well,' she said, leaning over Aaron. 'Do you want to be struck by lightning?'

'NO!' screamed Aaron, terrified.

Suddenly, Aaron was blinded by a bright white light. Then, he felt his mother's hand on his forehead. Still trembling, he told his mother about his terrible nightmare.

'And the witch looked like Mrs Miggins? What did you have for lunch at school today?' asked his mother.

'I had sausages,' said Aaron. 'And I had second and third servings.'

'You always have nightmares after eating too much,' said his mother. 'Perhaps you won't be so greedy next time.'

As she was leaving Aaron's room his mother said, 'By the way, we're having sausages for dinner tomorrow night.'

'Oh no,' thought Aaron. 'I never want to see another sausage ever, ever again!'

Starry, starry friend

Ever since she was little, Sophie had loved looking up at the stars. During the summer, she would lie out every night on the patio to watch the sparkly show. She would often fall asleep and dream that she was talking to the stars.

One night, Sophie really thought that some of the stars had clustered together to form a face. It looked so real. A big mouth opened in the twinkling 'face' and said, 'Hello little girl. What's your name?'

'I'm Sophie. Do you have a name?' she asked.

'We don't have a name. But if you like, you could give us one,' said the stars.

'Oh, I know a perfect name, Sparkles. What do you think of that?' said Sophie.

'Oh yes, that's lovely, thank you! We have seen you looking up at us every night, you know,' smiled the starry face.

'Do you get bored up there?' asked Sophie.

'Yes, we do. Can we come and play with you?' said Sparkles.

Sophie thought for a while, then said, 'If you wanted, you could come and live on our planet.'

'But if we left space, the moon would be sad and the stars would miss us!' Sparkles replied.

'That would be a shame,' said Sophie. 'Well from now on, will you talk to me when I call you?'

The face of stars smiled, 'Of course! We'll always talk to you!'

'I'm going to talk to you every night, every month of every year, so that you never get bored again!"

Four-legged thief!

In Mr Smith's orchard the cherry tree was covered in big, juicy red cherries. They shone in the sun like baubles on a Christmas tree. Unfortunately, lots of animals had noticed the ripe cherries. The first thief was a squirrel. At nightfall, he went up to the tree and ate his fill from the upper branches.

The hedgehog family watched the greedy squirrel munching on the delicious cherries and tried their luck as soon as he padded away. But because they were so small they couldn't reach the fruit on the tree. Instead, the hedgehogs ate cherries that had fallen on the ground. Mr Smith didn't mind the hedgehogs eating the windfall cherries, but a squirrel stealing the fruit on the tree was another matter!

The next night, the squirrel climbed through the bushes to Mr Smith's orchard. He licked his lips as he thought about the juicy cherries. What a feast he was going to have!

The squirrel was padding stealthily across the orchard when he spotted a strange gentleman wearing a big hat.

'He must be the security guard for the orchard!' thought the squirrel, turning swiftly and quietly to escape unnoticed from the orchard.

The squirrel decided never to return to the orchard again. It's a shame that the squirrel didn't go a little closer to the strange gentleman. He would then have seen that it was only an old scarecrow that Mr Smith put up every year.

But it was lucky for Mr Smith because it means that his cherries are safe from four-legged thieves!

The last leaves

It was winter and all of the forest trees had lost their orange-red foliage a long time ago. All, that is, except one. The big blackberry bush on the edge of the forest was still covered in its coat of beautiful golden leaves.

The north wind started to whistle through the forest. Harder and harder it blew, tearing off twigs and snapping the branches of the poor trees. The blackberry bush was battered by the wind and lost most of its leaves.

Then, rain started to fall in sheets, sweeping across the forest and washing all the blackberry bush's leaves away. All of them? Well, all except two large leaves that clung to a branch at the top of the bush.

The weather became calm. The sky was white and the cold set in. A few lazy snowflakes danced through the branches and landed on the ground. Soon more snowflakes fell and the carpet of dead leaves became covered in white.

At the top of the bush, the two leaves felt lonely because they wanted to dance, too. One of the leaves let a little gust of wind catch it and it waltzed and somersaulted with the snowflakes. The leaf landed softly on the glistening ground.

Then, finally last leaf came off the bush and floated all alone in the sky. It twisted and turned, then gently fell and landed next to its friend.

On the perfect white snow, these fallen leaves looked like two golden crowns.

A new home for the voles

The vole family were very unhappy. Yesterday, a big bad badger drove them out of their cosy little home.

Early this morning, Mr Vole went off to look for food, while Mrs Vole stayed with the children. They were huddled under a rose bush when it started to snow.

Mrs Vole began chasing the snowflakes away and dusting them off the little ones. She didn't want them to get cold and wet, so she worked hard to keep the ground dry. Mrs Vole raced around, hitting the snow with her tail and pushing it away with her paws.

To keep the snow away, Mrs Vole built a wall of twigs and leaves around her family. It was like a cabin without a roof. The snow kept falling and Mrs Vole got very tired. It was very difficult to keep her children warm and their new home dry.

At last the snow began to lessen and eventually it stopped. Suddenly, Mrs Vole felt a light breeze and she looked up. A beautiful leaf from the rose bush had fallen on top of her twig wall. A roof! They had a roof! The children squeaked with joy when a second leaf landed on top of the first, leaving just enough room for the vole family to get in and out.

The family made themselves at home under the rose bush. The little voles lay down and were just starting to feel really cosy when their father returned. He was pushing three golden acorns in front of him.

'Hooray!' called the children who knew that without food it would have been a very dangerous winter. This winter would be fine after all!

Springtime is the best time

The mice family spent the whole winter in their warm shelter in the chestnut tree. One beautiful morning, Mr Mouse was in a very good mood, 'Hurry up, children! This morning we are going out to welcome the spring,' he said.

'But Dad, how are we going to welcome something that we cannot really see?' asked the eldest mouse.

'Just be patient. We'll look at it, smell it, hear it, and taste it,' said dad.

The four little mice were a little confused, but were happy to go on a trip with their dad. They climbed up a steep hill. When they reached the top, they looked around. The young mice noticed that the oak tree looked different because it was covered in tiny buds.

Further on, they could hear soft music. The melting snow had formed a stream that was rushing joyfully down the mountain. The youngest mouse went up to a nearby birch tree, scratched the bark

with his claws and hungrily licked the sugary sap that seeped slowly out. Oh, it was delicious!

Suddenly, Mr Mouse gestured to his children to listen.

'Cuckoo, cuckoo,' sang a cuckoo from a tree branch above.

'Dad, let's go home and tell everyone that spring has arrived!' squeaked the baby mice.

Rushing indoors, the little mice cried, 'Mother! We've...'

Mrs Mouse smiled and put a dandelion salad on the table. 'Yes I know, spring has arrived. 'Long live the spring!'

Buttercup, the friendly cow

The vole family were happily settled in their summer home. It was on the edge of the forest in the shade of a hazelnut tree, facing a big meadow. The little voles played outside every day. They had friends everywhere, especially in the pasture. Moles, shrews, birds, and even sheep and cows were their friends.

The voles' best friend was a cow called Buttercup. Every morning they would go and greet her. Sometimes they would climb up onto her head and perch on her horns or dance on her broad back. Then they would slide all the way down her long tail.

Whenever Buttercup was lying down, the young voles would leave her alone because she was resting. But on the days when Buttercup looked like she was in a playful mood, they would clamber onto her neck and whisper jokes into her ears.

The little voles would climb onto Buttercup's back. Once they were up there, they would give her the signal to giddy-up just like a horse. Buttercup would let them ride her across the field. The little voles rocked from side to side, giggling with delight.

Buttercup would check they were holding on tight, then she would begin to canter. The bell round her neck would clang and the voles would sing along. The voles thought it was the best fun ever!

Buttercup the friendly cow really was a great friend!

Making a mountain

Once upon a time there were no fields or pastures, or plains, or meadows. There were no hollows or humps, not one hill or mountain, not even a little mound on the surface of the Earth. Everything was flat.

The people who lived at that time wanted to build a viewing tower so they could see farther across the land. They set about building it, but because they made it out of sand, the wind blew it away. They were all very sad to see their tower disappear in seconds.

The people started again, this time using straw. But the wind destroyed the new building as well. Then one night, a man called Mountain saw a shooting star. He made this wish: 'Please make the ground lift up to the sky so that we can look down onto the world,' he said.

The next day, one of the people woke up and noticed a strange shadow across the sun. He was very alarmed. He looked outside and saw that the landscape had changed. He cried out to wake the tribe.

'Look! Look! Over there!' he said.

'My wish came true!' said Mountain.

'What wish?' asked the tribe's chief.

'Last night I saw a shooting star and I wished that the ground would rise up to the sky!' said Mountain.

'I don't know how this has happened,' said the chief, 'but from now on, we will call these wonderful things 'mountains'.'

Now you know the myth of how mountains were created.

When you wish...

Hannah and her cousin Annie were snuggled up in their blankets, sitting in a tent under a starry sky. Every summer vacation, Hannah slept in the tent with one of her friends on the night of the shooting stars. They would check the news for weeks beforehand to find out the exact date.

Hannah's cousin was seven this year, so she was allowed to spend her first night under the stars. At first, she was bored because nothing had happened. Then, suddenly...

'Hannah, Hannah I saw a shooting star!' gasped Annie.

'Make a wish!' said Hannah.

It was fantastic to see the stars shooting across the sky one after the other. Annie was amazed to see so many.

'Are you alright, Annie?' asked Hannah.

But Annie didn't answer because she'd already fallen asleep.

Hannah gently picked up Annie and carried her into the tent. Then, she settled herself just inside the tent opening and got back to work. She had a lot of wishes to make. She promised to make wishes for all of her friends and family.

'Okay, that's my friends done, and my mother, my father, my sisters, my...*yawn*...'

She didn't finish her long list because she fell asleep, too.

High up in the sky, two stars were watching over them. They were Hannah and her cousin's special stars, and now they would go and try to make the children's wishes come true.

The special visitor

Kevin was a little boy who was always dreaming about Christmas. On Christmas Eve he crept out of bed to search for Father Christmas. Kevin crossed the landing and tiptoed past his parents' bedroom, down the stairs and all the way to the living room.

Kevin looked to see if there were any presents under the Christmas tree, but there was nothing there yet. While he was heading back toward his bedroom, Kevin heard a noise on the roof. Then, he saw some soot fall into the fireplace and then two black boots appeared!

It was Father Christmas! He squeezed himself out of the chimney coughing loudly and muttered, 'More parents who haven't thought of getting their chimney swept. I'm filthy! Ah well, best get to work.'

'Yes, yes deliver the presents!' squealed Kevin excitedly.

'What? Who's there?' said Father Christmas.

'My name is Kevin,' the little boy said shyly.

'Why aren't you in bed like everyone else?' asked Father Christmas.

'I-I wanted to see you,' answered Kevin.

'Well back to bed now!' smiled Father Christmas.

'Wait until I tell my friends about this!'

The next morning when Kevin's parents woke up, there were lots of presents beneath the tree. Kevin was already looking forward to seeing Santa again next year. His friends were going to be amazed, especially the ones who say that Father Christmas doesn't exist!

Jenny's special star

With her face pressed up against the window, Jenny looked very sad. It had been four months since she last visited her grandma. Grandma's house was in the countryside and Jenny loved going there.

At home, Jenny always felt like she was stuck indoors. When she wasn't at school, she was on the train or bus, or at home in the apartment! Jenny wished she was running about in the meadows, picking wild flowers with her grandma.

Jenny looked out at the busy road, the busy pavement, and the dull buildings. She sighed and looked up at the sky. It was a starry night. She always watched the stars out of the skylight in her grandma's house. Jenny's grandma knew the names of all of the stars.

On her last visit to grandma's, grandma told Jenny the names of some of the stars, galaxies, and constellations.

Grandma had told her that we each have our own star, and that if Jenny looked hard enough she would find hers. One night as she looked up at the sky with grandma, Jenny found her star!

Jenny looked up at the sky and found her star again! It hadn't stayed over her grandma's, it had followed her to the town. Jenny was happy because she knew that a lot of good things would happen.

Did you know that you also have your own special star? You just have to look very hard and you'll find it!

Moonlit mystery

Lauren and her cousins, Scott and Gareth were on holiday. One night they decided to sleep outside in their tent. They took blankets and torches and set themselves up in a meadow. The children played at being cowboys, looking after their herd on a ranch.

Lauren, Scott, and Gareth pretended that four cows grazing peacefully in the next field were their herd. The old carthorse and the donkey sleeping in the stables were their horses too.

It was a full moon that night. Lauren's dad had told the children that when there was a full moon the elves came out into the clearing in the forest. Of course, Lauren and her cousins didn't believe in his stories, but they decided to go and have a look all the same.

They crept between the trees on tiptoe, trying not to make any noise. They came to the edge of the clearing and saw strange shapes were moving in the dim light. What were they? Elves? Pixies?

Fairies? Suddenly, the moon went behind a cloud and the three friends found themselves plunged into darkness, unable to see anything. They weren't too happy about this. What if the shapes they had seen really were elves? Maybe it was time to head back to the field.

While they were deciding what to do, the moon came out again and flooded the clearing with light. The children saw that the clearing was full of rabbits scampering about! Then in a flash they vanished.

They wandered back to their tent, laughing about their discovery. But were they really rabbits? Lauren and her cousins weren't so sure.

Vincent's catch

incent was playing with his little sister when his dad said, 'Come on Vincent, we're going fishing!'
Vincent didn't need to be asked twice! He raced to the cupboard where he kept his fishing rod.

Half an hour later they strode purposefully across the fields toward the river. They waded through long reeds and rushes until they reached the river bank. Then they set themselves up at their special spot.

Vincent's dad was a very good fisherman and usually he caught lots of fish. But this time it looked as though Vincent was in luck. After just a few minutes, he called out, 'Something's on the end of my line, Dad!'

Just as his dad had taught him, Vincent wound in his line to pull up the big fish. He struggled with the weight and finally managed to reel in his catch. But what was this? An old pair of shoes tied together and covered in mud and silt!

'Great catch, son!' joked his dad. 'Those old boots will taste great roasted with some herbs!'

It turned out to be a lucky afternoon for the fish. Vincent's dad only caught two tiny fish that were so small he just threw them back into the river! But the two fishermen were quite happy. They sang all the way home at the tops of their voices.

It was lovely going back to their warm house when outside the night was closing in, a wind was blowing up, and it had started to get cold.

Vincent wished he could go fishing every day!

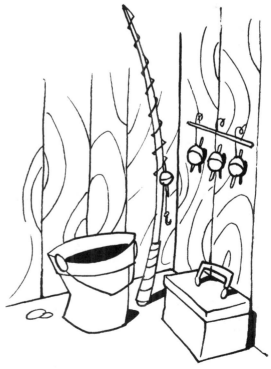

Cauliflower babies

Today, Claire had a lovely treat. Her Auntie Sandra had sent her a beautiful postcard from Africa for her birthday. On the front was a photograph that looked of a baby resting in the middle of a cauliflower.

'Paul, Paul! Look at the card that Auntie Sandra has sent me. You didn't believe me when I told you that boys were born in cauliflowers. Here's the proof! Look, it's written on the back!'

Paul wasn't very good at reading, but he was much better at it than his sister Claire. He turned over the card and worked out what it said. He burst out laughing.

'Yes, I remember!' Paul grinned. 'In Africa, boys are often born bundled in cotton!'

Claire looked confused and then cross as Paul read the card out loud.

'Bundles of cotton in Zanzibar. Wrapped in these green cotton cloths, which resemble big leaves, these baby boys look like giant cauliflowers!'

Feeling a little silly, Claire grabbed the card back from Paul and tried to understand the writing on the back of it. But she couldn't understand a word!

Claire decided that tonight she was going to ask her mother to teach her how to read properly!

Snowy fun

During the Christmas break, Richard and his family went on a winter sports holiday. There were so many fun things to do on the mountain. You could go sledging, ski down the snowy slopes or even build a snowman. As he didn't know how to ski or snowboard yet, Richard would be sledding with his little brother.

Firstly, they would catch the ski lift up to the slopes. It was really exciting, but a little scary if you looked out of the window at the ground far below! Once they reached the top of the mountain, Richard's parents would spend ages looking at the snowy scenery all around them. This often gave Richard and his brother the chance to have a snowball fight!

Today, the children were unlucky because the surface of ski run was rather bumpy and they kept falling off their sledge. But they safely reached the bottom in the end, even if they did have sore, wet bottoms!

They stood around waiting there for their parents who were coming down the slope very, very slowly!

To warm themselves up, the family went into a cafe and ordered mugs of hot chocolate with some delicious croissants. And guess who they saw?

A very famous skiing champion who they had seen on the television, was sat at the table behind them. Richard and his brother felt quite shy, but they went over and politely asked the man for his autograph. He was really nice and even wrote a little message after his signature.

Richard and his brother had the best holiday ever!

The tooth fairy mouse

Ellen was a charming little mouse dentist. She was very good at her work and loved her job. She doesn't only do dentistry, she does do-it-yourself, too. Every evening, Louisa reads her mail and plans the next day.

In the evening, Ellen crept into Lyn's house and tip-toed into her bedroom. Then, she silently climbed onto Lyn's bed and rummaged inside the little girl's pillow. She found what she wanted. It was a little milk tooth. Ellen took out a coin from her purse and swapped it with the tooth.

'Sweet dreams, Lyn,' whispered Ellen, blowing a kiss as she left.

Ellen worked all night, visiting different homes. When she arrived home in the morning, Ellen was exhausted. She just had time for a little rest and then back to work. She was a busy little mouse!

At nine o'clock, Ellen saw her first patient. It was an old dog with one tooth. Ellen searched in her bag and found four canine teeth, four molars, and four incisors. She took the lid off her pot of glue and stuck the teeth onto the old dog's gums.

'There! Now close your mouth and clamp your jaws together for ten minutes. Tonight you'll be able to eat a big, juicy steak,' she told the old dog.

Feeling very happy, the dog nodded his thanks to Ellen and went on his way.

A little later, Ellen was mending a labrador's chipped tooth. When the job was done she thought to herself, 'What a wonderful life I have, helping people and animals every day!'

Sweet tooth!

This evening, Natalie was determined to stay awake because she was hoping to get a visit from the tooth fairy. She had waited a whole week for her wobbly tooth to fall out. At last she could put it under her pillow and hope for a visit.

But what would happen to the tooth? Her mother had told her that the tooth fairy would come get the tooth and leave a present for Natalie. Last month, David lost a tooth and he got some money. But he hadn't been able to tell her where his tooth had gone. As Natalie thought about missing teeth she dropped off to sleep. Oh dear, she wasn't going to meet the tooth fairy this time!

The next morning, Natalie reached into her pillowcase and found a shiny coin!

'David, David! Look at the coin the tooth fairy has left for me!' she said, excitedly.

David turned over in his bed and reached into his pillowcase. He, too, found a coin.

'Look, the tooth fairy visited me too,' he laughed.

David looked at the coin, then sniffed it. It wasn't real money like Natalie's. His coin was made of chocolate!

The two children rushed into their parents' room to show them what they had found. They were pleased that tooth fairy had left money for Natalie, but where had the chocolate coin come from? They said that they hadn't put it there!

But because parents are supposed to know everything they said, 'Well, you're both very lucky.'

Fish tank blues

Poor Snapper! How had he ended up in a great big fish tank? He couldn't remember how it had happened, but he could remember life before the fish tank, when he lived in the warm Mediterranean Sea. He used to live in a comfy little cave in a coral reef. What a wonderful life! No one bothered him and he was happy in the clear blue water. The sun's rays would light up the bright scales of the fish swimming among the rocks and everything was very beautiful.

Poor Snapper! It was not much fun being stuck inside a fish tank, particularly when you don't get on too well with the other inhabitants. Some of the creatures in the tank were very odd indeed. In the sea you could always move on if the company wasn't very nice, unlike in here!

The worst thing of all was lunchtime, because you couldn't choose what you wanted to eat. You had to barge your way through all the other creatures to get any food when it was thrown in. The biggest or fiercest always got to eat first. Poor Snapper wasn't very big or very fierce, so often he got nothing but leftovers.

The people who looked after the aquarium had noticed that Snapper seemed very unhappy and that he wasn't eating enough, so they decided to return him to the sea. They caught Snapper and put him into a big container of water. Then, they drove to the coast and poured Snapper and the water back into the sea.

Snapper was delighted to be back in his natural habitat and couldn't wait to see his old friends again!

Sandcastle attack!

Suzi and Luke were at the beach. They had brought their buckets, pails, spades, and shovels and were ready to build the best sandcastle ever!

They soon found a good spot for their sandcastle. It wasn't too close to the water and it wasn't too far away either.

Suzi and Luke set to work and built a fantastic sandcastle with lots of towers. They used reeds, seaweed, and driftwood to build a bridge across the moat.

Soon, all that was left to do was to decorate their castle with pretty shells and pebbles they found on the beach. It was a really beautiful castle. The only things missing was a princess and prince.

'Dad, we've made the most beautiful castle in the world. Come and see!' called Suzi. 'It's the best sandcastle ever!

'Look even the crabs are coming to see it,' said Luke, excitedly.

The children watched as masses of crabs scuttled over their little bridge. Suzi and Luke started to cry out against the castle's visitors as the crabs began to trample over the castle, making the sand towers crumble and fall.

In a few minutes, there were no walls or towers left and their castle was destroyed. Suzi and Luke turned tearfully to their dad who had watched the disaster, too.

'Well that was quite an attack!' said their dad. 'I took some photos of your wonderful sandcastle, and we can build another one, can't we. We've got the whole summer ahead of us to design improved sandcastles with better crab defences.'

The happy holiday

Last summer, Jo and Becky's parents had a great idea for a holiday. They rented a lovely old caravan pulled by a chestnut horse called Fifi and set off on holiday.

Under the caravan was a big cage carrying two chickens. Next to that was a large sack full of horse food, and a tank in which drinking water was stored. On the roof there was another water tank that was heated by the sun, and a big mattress that you could sleep on if it was too hot and stuffy inside the caravan.

The caravan was fitted out with enough seats for the whole family. At night the seats turned into a double bed for the parents to sleep in.

During the day the family slowly trundled along so that the children could walk alongside if they wanted to or run ahead to find a good spot for lunch.

When they stopped for the evening, Jo and Becky would unharness Fifi and open up the chicken cage. But they had to remember to get the chickens back in before dark! Then, they would gather firewood, light the campfire, and cooked sausages and beans. It was all so exciting!

By the light of a gas lamp, the family would study the map and discuss plans for the next day. Sometimes, their mother would sing a song, but usually dad would tell them a story and they would fall sound asleep before the end.

Every day was an adventure! What a wonderful holiday they all had!

Down on the farm

dam had just spent the Easter holidays with his Uncle Bill. At this time of year most of his friends went on fantastic holidays to foreign countries with their parents, but nothing would tempt Adam to miss out on a trip to his Uncle Bill's farm.

Adam woke up, rubbed his eyes, then quickly pulled a coat on over his shorts and went down to the goat pen. Brrr! It was very cold in the early morning!

Uncle Bill was there already, feeding the goats and putting down fresh hay to keep them dry and warm.

'Animals are like us,' he said. 'They need to be comfortable when it's cold outside, especially at the moment.'

Why now, you ask? Well, because it's birthing time. During the night, two baby goats were born. They were white and smooth with tiny black hooves. By the time Adam got to the pen, the baby goats were already on their feet, feeding from their mother and wagging their little tails. He loved watching them play. They would stand on their back legs and play fight each other. Then they would leap and run around all over the place. All this and not even a day old!

The mother goat just chewed her food calmly, glancing over at her two babies from time to time. Sometimes she would bleat softly to call them and they would charge over to have a drink of milk before going back to play again.

'I wouldn't have missed this for the world!' thought Adam.

Roll up, roll up!

onight was going to be so much fun because Will and Chris were going to the circus. They could already see the big top in the distance.

'Dad, where are the animals?' asked Will, looking around.

'There aren't any. Come on, we're here. The show is about to begin,' smiled their dad.

Will was disappointed because he loved seeing animals. They could hear the sound of drums and music coming from off stage.

'Hmmph,' said Will, who wasn't at all impressed.

Suddenly, a drummer did three back flips onto the stage and jumped up onto a balcony. He began to climb higher and higher and then jumped off with his arms outstretched! Two singers ran about beneath him holding a

giant mattress. Bam! The man landed right on it!

'Wow!' said Will and Chris.

Then, the troupe started clowning around. They did a funny walk in single file toward three tall poles and climbed up them. Then, one by one, they threw themselves off, spinning headfirst at top speed and managing to land one on top of the other in a pyramid! The audience cheered.

Each trick was more amazing than the last, and the big top was filled with laughter and admiration. All too soon it was over. Will and Chris looked at their dad, they wouldn't forget this trip to the circus in a hurry!

Patrick's imaginary friend

 atrick had a wonderful imagination. He had invented a magical friend to play with, called Dougal. They had lots of adventures together. One day, Patrick said to his imaginary friend, 'I'd like you to come and spend a day at school with me.'

'Great!' said Dougal. 'I've always wanted to go to school.'

Next morning, Dougal followed Patrick to school and when they got into the classroom he said, 'Where shall I sit?'

'Just get a chair from the back of the room,' smiled Patrick.

'Sorry Patrick, what was that?' asked the teacher.

'Oh, nothing,' answered Patrick.

Kyle who was sitting next to Patrick, was quite confused by his friend's manner and said, 'What's going on Patrick?'

'Uh, nothing. Why do you ask?' said Patrick.
'Come on! I'm your friend,' said Kyle. 'You can tell me.'

'Oh, alright. I have an imaginary friend,' said Patrick.

'An imaginary friend? Is that why you keep talking to yourself?' said Kyle. 'I mean, keep talking to…'

'Dougal, he's called Dougal and he's very kind and funny, and he helps me with my homework!' said Patrick rather quickly.

'He sounds great!' said Kyle.

Patrick was beginning to wish he hadn't let Kyle know his secret. If Kyle told the rest of the class they would all laugh. But Kyle was a good friend so he kept Patrick's secret.

When school finished, Dougal said, 'School is boring. I'm going to stay at home from now on!'

No television!

Tess and Pippa were in a hurry to get home from school. They ran into the house, threw their coats on the floor and sat down in front of the television. They were just in time to watch their fave cartoon!

Pippa pressed the remote control, but no picture appeared.

'Oh, no, the telly's broken,' called Pippa to her mother.

'That's a nice way to say 'hello' to your mother. Yes, I know the TV isn't working and

the repairman will hopefully be here soon. So, hang up your coats and we'll have dinner,' said their mother.

The smell of butter and maple syrup was soon wafting through the air as their mother brought a huge batch of pancakes through to the table. Tess and Pippa wolfed down their pancakes while listening for the doorbell.

'We're going to miss all our programs if the repairman doesn't come soon,' whined Tess.

'Well there's nothing I can do. Why don't we play a game of snap?' suggested their mother

'Okay, we haven't played that for ages,' agreed Tess.

As the sky darkened outside, their mother said, 'Well, it looks like the repairman isn't coming tonight after all. But if you get into bed, I'll ask your dad to come up and read you a story.'

As dad read a story to them, their mother thought, 'Hmmm, I wonder what would happen if the television was broken for just a bit longer?'

The cheerful chestnuts

hessy, Leaf, and Conker were three chestnut sisters who were all born in the same case. They spent about a year hanging from their chestnut tree, and then in the autumn fall, they fell off.

Fortunately, they landed in some soft moss so their case didn't break. They stayed there for a long time, impatient to break out and explore the place where they had fallen. But they knew that their case was protecting them from harm.

Then, one day they had grown so big that the case could not hold them in any longer and it burst open with a loud crack!

The sisters really wanted to get out and roll around, but they remembered the golden chestnut rule: if you stay hidden in your case, in spring you'll come back to life!

Suddenly, they heard a snuffling sound. The chestnuts kept very still until the wild boar had trotted past. A few days went by as the sisters tried to avoid wild boars and chestnut pickers. Then, one morning the chestnut sisters woke up with nasty headaches.

'Oooh, I feel dizzy and sick,' said Chessy.

'I feel like my head is about to explode,' said Leaf.

'And I...look at Leaf! There's something coming out of her head!' gasped Conker.

With big grins, the sisters rolled out of their case and examined the green shoot coming out of Leaf's head. They were delighted!

'We've done it! We're going to grow into chestnut trees!'

Grandpa John's cabin

Sam and Alex had been pestering their grandad to build them a cabin. But Grandpa John knew what the boys were like. They changed their minds all the time. They'd be excited about one thing and then the next day it would be something completely different. If they stuck with this cabin idea for a bit longer, he might consider it. But not yet!

A few days later, the brothers tried again.

'Grandpa, did you say you were going to start building the cabin this weekend?' asked Sam.

Grandpa John sighed. It seemed that he wasn't going to be able to get out of this one, so he set to work. First, he found some trees that could act as beams. Then he asked the children to help him carry the sawn planks for the walls. Once the planks were in place, the cabin began to take shape. All it needed was a roof, a door, and a small window.

The next day when the boys got home they were amazed to see the door already in position. The door was closed, so the boys called, 'Grandpa John! Are you in there?'

Knocking at the door, Sam and Alex heard a strange husky voice say, 'Who's there?'

'W-Who are you? What are you doing in our cabin?' asked Alex.

Suddenly, the door flew open, and a grinning Grandpa John came running out!

'I'm a monster and I'm going to eat you!' he cried.

Life was never boring with Grandpa John!

The jungle taxi

n elephant was walking through the jungle when two monkeys loaded down with bags jumped onto his back.

'Could you take us home?' asked the monkeys. 'We've just been to the market and we're very tired.'

Then, three curious parrots flew down and landed next to the monkeys.

'We haven't spoken to anyone for five days. We've been going mad with the silence!' said the parrots and they began to chatter away.

The monkeys and the elephant were irritated by the noisy birds.

'We haven't eaten for seven hours. Three fat parrots would be just enough to fill us up!' said the monkeys, crossly.
But before the monkeys could say another word, the parrots flew off.

Two hours later, the tired elephant decided to rest under the shade of a coconut tree. He hit his trunk against the tree and nine ripe coconuts fell at his feet. He gave three to the first monkey, three to the second, and kept three for himself.

'Thanks Mr Elephant, this is where we're getting off!' said the two monkeys.

To thank the elephant, the monkeys gave him twenty green bananas, thirty ripe mangoes, forty cherry flowers, fifty berries, seventy beetle eggs, and eighty blades of grass. Then, they scampered away blowing a thousand big kisses to the friendly elephant.

Siesta time

When it's too hot in the savannah, all the animals take a nap. The lions and their young cubs like to sleep in the shade of an immense acacia tree. The lion chief always slept away from his cubs because they were too fidgety and stopped him falling to sleep.

A moment ago Lila, the oldest cub, had pins and needles in her legs. Sleeping is fine for an hour or so, but now she was restless and wanted to play. She tried to catch her mother's tail. Without looking up, the mother lion swished her tail moodily. Lila tried again, but this time she only managed to catch the fur on the end.

The mother lion tapped her lion cub's nose with enough force to show her that she should let her mother sleep in peace. So Lila jumped on her brother Louie's back. The two lion cubs rolled around in the dust, wrestling and shouting. Their mother slowly got to her feet and gave each of them a gentle slap, then went back to sleep.

Lila and Louie calmed down for about a quarter of a second and then forgot their punishment. They ran over to their father and jumped on his back.

What a mistake! The big lion shook his mane, opened his enormous jaws, and with a giant roar sent the two cubs scurrying away! They knew they had been told off, so they sloped back to their mother, where they lay down with their noses pressed to their paws. The cubs didn't dare move until the end of the day.

Lila and Louie learned an important lesson today: never disturb the king of the beasts during his afternoon nap!

The story of a raindrop

oday it rained all day on the mountain. The rain was warm because it was summer. Drip the raindrop, had just fallen onto the branch of a pine tree. She slipped along the scented pine branch. *Aaaarrgh*, too quick! Then, she plopped onto the rocks and into a cave.

'Is there anyone there?' called Drip, a little anxiously as it was very dark in the cave.

'Yes, we're down here! Come and join us, Drip!' replied a familiar sounding voice.

Drip let herself fall into the underground river where all the other raindrops had gathered. She felt herself being swept along and then there was light! Drip would have hated to have to stay underground for very long because she loved the sun. She and her friends made a lovely fresh water stream that trickled between the shiny stones.

'Where are we going?' asked Drip, at last.

The rest of the stream replied, 'We are going to meet the big stream that runs at the bottom of the valley and then we are all going to carry on to join the grand river.'

'And then?' asked Drip.

'Then, we are going to the sea, like we always do! Where have you come from?' asked the rest of the stream.

Just at that moment, Drip understood what was happening to her. She and her friends had been happy in the sea, but were now beginning to feel rather hot. The next thing she knew she was up in the clouds. A little while later, her cloud brushed against a mountain and Drip fell onto a pine tree and, well, you know the rest, don't you?

Kirstie and the silver streak

This morning, Kirstie saw a silver streak dash across the garden. Kirstie didn't know what it was. She wondered if it was a snake or something. Then, she saw it again, it was a very fast furry cat!

'Come and look!' Kirstie called to her mother. 'There's a silver cat in the yard. Can we give it some milk?'

'Alright,' said Kirstie's mother. 'But you will have to be quick because it's time for school.'

When Kirstie returned home, she rushed out into the garden to look for the cat. A little white rocket shot past, right under her nose! Kirstie was confused.

The saucer of milk was empty, so Kirstie filled it up again and waited behind a tree. After a few minutes she saw a little pink nose and two little eyes the shade of the sky appear on top of the garden wall. A tiny kitten crept slowly and cautiously toward the saucer.

'The cat has a little white kitten!' called Kirstie, excitedly.

The next morning, Kirstie rushed outside and the two fireballs of fluff dashed past her and into the garden! Noticing that the saucer of milk was empty, Kirstie filled it once again. Then, she tip-toed outside and saw the big silver cat stretched out on the patio. Curled up beside her were four little kittens, purring happily! There was one white kitten, two silvery kittens, and a black one with white paws!

Ninety-nine little mice

Slumber Grove was a rundown old house at the end of a very long and winding path. No one had been there for many years, but it wasn't quite as deserted as you might think!

A rather large family of mice had been living in Slumber Grove for a few years now. When they moved in there were only a few of them, but now there were so many, some of them lived in the garage!

Mr Mouse decided it was time for a count-up as he had long forgotten the number of children he had, let alone how many relatives there were! So, he put up posters all round the house asking the mice to attend a meeting that evening.

The mice started filing into the kitchen for the meeting. Gosh! What a lot of mice there were. There were mice on the floor, on the chairs, on top of the table! Mr Mouse carefully counted all of the mice. There were 99 little mice living at Slumber Grove!

Mr Mouse began to look around at their dilapidated home and thought, 'Ninety-nine mice! That means 99 pairs of hands could make this place spick and span!'

He told the mice of his plan for a spring clean of the Slumber Grove. All the mice clapped their hands with glee. Nobody, not even 99 mice, likes living in a messy house.

Soon, Slumber Grove was the prettiest cottage in the land. But don't tell anyone, or they might want to move in too!

Shooting stars

Oh, it was so hot! All day, Shimmer and Stella the two little stars, wished they were fish or swimmers playing down there in the cool water. How lucky they were! It must be wonderful to play and splash about in the cool water.

Every now and then, stars go on journeys. Sometimes they shoot and slide down toward the sea and are never seen again. Shimmer and Stella were very young, but they had already decided that the sea is where they would go if they ever got the chance.

Hanging in space, the two stars admired their silver reflections in the smooth sea. Then, one, two, three, go! The festival of shooting stars was like a fireworks display!

The sky was aglow! Shimmer and Stella did two perfect swoops and dived straight into the sea.

'How lovely, it's so refreshing here,' said Shimmer.

'And so cool,' said Stella.

The young star swam in the sea, enjoying this new experience. A big tuna fish swam over to welcome them and a shoal of tiny fish flashed past them at top speed. Three small sardines wriggled past winking at them.

Gradually, the stars sunk to the bottom of the sea and landed on the sand. They felt exhausted and so their star-light flickered and died.

Do you think the two stars have disappeared? Oh no, not at all. They simply became two magnificent starfish!

A hippo's life

My parents and I were happily living on the wide, open plains. But we had a big, big problem. It was the dry season and we had hardly any water left for drinking or bathing in. We hippos need to keep our skin wet, otherwise we get sunstroke, you know!

To help stay cool, we were lying still in the shade for as long as possible.

'When are we going to get some water? I'm so hot!' I asked my mother.

'Everyone is hot and everyone needs water. You will just have to learn to make the best of what we have!' she replied, rather crossly.

Gradually, the dry season came to an end and a few rain showers refreshed us. Later, the rainy season arrived. Big black clouds filled the sky, and it rained so hard and for so long that the river flooded all the plains. What were we going to eat? My ma was worried about the damage caused by the rain.

'We have nothing left!' mother cried, looking around.

'But we've got water, plenty of water!' I said, trying to cheer her up.

'Water?' she said in a desperate voice. 'That's the problem! We've got too much water and all our food has been swept away by the river.'

'But you said we have to make the best of what we have!' I reminded her and she smiled.

A few months later, the rainy season ended. The grass was long and green, and there was enough water for everyone.

Well, for the time being at least!

The playful puppets

 he show had just finished and Jeremy the puppeteer, was putting the puppets back into their trunk. Folding up their beautiful clothes, he talked to them like they were his children.

'Sleep well. You were all fantastic tonight. Pollyanna, your bonnet is a bit torn, but I'll mend it tomorrow. I also need to change the lace on your dress little Sarah. Good night!' he said.

The puppets lay as still as they could, but as soon as the lid of the trunk was closed they started to argue.

'Get your elbow out of my eye before I give you a hard poke!' said pretty little Sarah to the handsome young prince.

'Excuse me, my dear friend,' protested the prince. 'It's not my elbow, it's the thief's. He's elbowing you because he's trying to steal the lace hanky out of my pocket.'

'That's not true,' exclaimed the thief puppet. 'What exactly do you think I would do with your rotten hanky? Puppets don't sneeze or get a cold!'

At that moment the lid opened and Jeremy the puppeteer peered inside with a worried expression.

'I thought I heard someone shouting. I must have been dreaming,' he said.

Poor Jeremy! He had never really understood why even though he put the puppets away very carefully each night, he found them in a complete muddle the next day, with their hair messed and their clothes all creased.

Shhh! This is our secret!

All about acorns

The acorn is a wonderful fruit. It comes from a majestic tree, the oak. An acorn is beautiful and strange, and you can keep it for ages. But it is also very useful. You can do lots of things with an acorn.

One day, Milla the mouse was out for a walk. The wind was so strong she had to watch out for falling conkers!

'Hmm, I'm going to put on my acorn shell helmet to protect my head against falling conkers. I think I'll look quite cool!' Milla thought to herself.

The ants were fed up. The rain had formed a stream, separating the ants their anthill. Luckily, a big oak tree was dropping lots of acorns. The ants clambered into the shells and floated across the stream. They were back in their anthill in minutes.

Oscar the lion was going to a party. On the way, he noticed that a button was missing from his jacket! Such scruffiness is no good for the king of the beasts,

so he tried to think of a solution. Timmy the monkey had an idea. He found an acorn on the forest floor and sewed it onto Oscar's jacket. *Phew!*

Robbie the pig and Rosie the squirrel were hungry. By chance they walked under an oak tree and had a feast. One acorn was enough for Rosie, but Robbie ate about a hundred!

There are plenty of other uses for acorns. My grandma said that during the war her parents roasted acorns and ground them up to make coffee! I always carry one around in my pocket, because you never know when it might come in handy!

Free as a bird

esterday, Greg went for a walk in the woods with his parents.

On the way home, he found a little bird that had fallen out of its nest. Greg gently wrapped it in his jumper and showed it to his parents.

'Look, the poor bird is hurt! We need to look after it.' said Greg.

'We can make it a little bed next to the fire and you can give it some breadcrumbs in water,' said his mother.

The next morning, the little bird seemed to have completely recovered. Greg took him back to his nest and went to school feeling a little sad. He would have liked to have kept the bird at home in a cage.

'No,' Greg said to himself. 'It's better like this. The bird would have hated being in a cage. It needs to be free.'

After school, Greg went home in a thoughtful mood. To his surprise, there was the bird, sitting on the fence. Greg stopped, thinking the bird would fly away, but it didn't. The bird stayed where it was, twittering excitedly. Greg tiptoed toward it and then he had an idea. He had some leftover sandwiches in his bag, so he took them out and held out his hand. The bird hesitated for a moment, and then very quickly pecked one tiny crumb out of Greg's hand. Then, it flew off to a nearby tree.

Tomorrow he would take some birdseed because birds don't have a lot to eat in winter.

Doctor Nathan

athan had wanted to be a doctor for as long as he could remember. He looked after all of his stuffed toys and some of his sister's dolls too! The boys in the village sometimes teased Nathan for playing with dolls.

'Oooh,' they said. 'There goes Doctor Nathan. Off to play with girls' toys again, are we?'

Nathan ignored their silly taunts because he knew that one day he would be a real doctor.

Nathan's parents gave him a book about first aid for his birthday. He learned all sorts of interesting things about how to look after people who have hurt themselves.

One day, he was at a party at his friend Sam's house. There were lots of children there, playing musical chairs. Sam's mum played the music and everyone danced excitedly around the chairs. The music suddenly stopped and everyone jostled to get a chair to sit down on, when *crash* Gemma slipped and fell on the floor. The other children crowded round her as she started to cry. It looked like a nasty bruise was coming up on her elbow.

'Put a bandage on it!' a little boy shouted.

'No, that's not right,' a girl replied. 'You need to rub it with cream.'

'That isn't right either,' said Nathan as he applied a cold compress to the bruise. 'This will help the swelling go down,' he added.

Gemma and the other children were grateful to Nathan for his first aid skills and never teased him for 'playing doctor' again.

The mischievous magpie

trange things were
happening at home.
Things kept disappearing for
no reason. Yesterday morning,
dad searched the house but
couldn't find his cufflinks.
Later, grandpa got very cross
looking for his fish hooks.
In the evening, Max lost his
silver badge. The next morning,
Max's mother was racing about
searching for her gold earrings.

At lunchtime, it reached crisis
point when Kim started crying
about her missing red hairgrips.
Even grandma was hunting for
her scissors. It was chaos!

'Max,' said dad.'Have you
hidden my cufflinks?'

'Calm down,' said
grandma to grandpa.
'You must have left
your fish hooks
down by the river.'

'I'm sure someone's thrown
away my badge,' said Max.

'Cheer up Kim,' said her mother.
'Your hairgrips will turn up.
Did you leave them at school?'

'Yeah, right,' said Kim. 'And you
left your earrings somewhere, did
you? I think they've been stolen
by someone.'

'And my scissors,' said grandma.

Everyone started to accuse each
other of losing, throwing away,
or borrowing everything. Then,
a sudden movement made them
all look outside. At the top of a
tree was a nest and it was full of
all their things.

'Oh!' gasped the family. 'It's a
thieving magpie, so that's where
everything went!'

Pancake Day!

The girls were very excited because it was Pancake Day! Grandma gave Jenna and her little sister aprons to wear and the little bakers set to work.

First, they poured the flour into a big bowl and made a hole in the middle. Then, they broke the eggs into the bowl.

'Don't forget the milk, girls,' said grandma.

Then, they mixed and mixed, and stirred and stirred. They waited for half an hour while the mixture rested. Jenna and her sister didn't want to wait. They wanted to cook the yummy pancakes!

'Let's play a game while we wait,' suggested grandma.

The time flew by, and the children were surprised when grandma said, 'Right, it's ready. Let's go and cook!'

Grandma put the pan on the hob and poured some of the mixture into it.

'Watch carefully because it's your turn next, girls,' she said.

Hup! The pancake flew up into the air, turned over, and landed back in the middle of the pan.

'Now it's your turn, Jenna,' smiled grandma.

Jenna took the pan handle and flipped the pancake into the air. Oh dear! The pancake landed right in front of the dog who had come in to see what was cooking. He gobbled it up in a flash without needing to be asked! Everyone burst out laughing. Luckily, there was lots of mixture left.

Soon there was a lovely big pile of pancakes ready for tea!

Fearsome Fang

ne day, Fang the shark was hunting for a tooth he had lost in a battle. It was a magic tooth, and when he lost it, Fang lost all his strength and became very weak. Only Fang's reputation as a wicked hunter protected him. But for how long? He had to find his magic tooth quickly,

was a creature smiling at him. It was holding his magic tooth in its pincers. Fang swam up to collect his precious tooth, but the strange animal refused to give it to him.

'Please give my tooth back,' said Fang, politely.

because if the news got out, certain other creatures in the sea would come and get him. What could he do?

During the battle, Fang saw his tooth disappear into a hole in the seabed, so he went back to the battlefield. He found the hole and swam into it. When he reached the end of the hole, Fang discovered an amazing world full of extraordinary sea creatures. In one corner, there

'I'll give it back to you, but on one condition. In the future, you must only use your strength for good causes.

'But what will I eat?' asked Fang.

'Make the promise. If you don't, you'll stay as weak as a sardine forever!' replied the creature.

The shark agreed, and he was gentle for the rest of his life. He also found he liked seaweed!

The great race

The town was bustling with excitement. It was the day of the gala fete and this year, for the first time, there were quad-bikes for children to ride. Steve and Liam really wanted to ride them. They rushed over to the bikes, but they had already spent all of their money!

The boys stood by the barriers watching the other children having fun.

'Do you want a ride on the quads?' asked the man in charge.

'Oh, yes,' said the boys.

'If you can help me with a job, you can have a ride for free,' said Rob.

'Oh, yes!' they answered. 'What do you want us to do?'

'I'm about to close, so I'll let you have a good long ride, but then you'll have to wash and polish all the quads. They have to be ready for tomorrow,' Rob smiled.

Steve and Liam jumped onto the quads as Rob explained, 'The accelerator's on the right and the brakes are on the left.'

The boys skidded off and had a great race! At last, Rob beckoned them over. Steve and Liam stopped the engines and went to get the sponges and polish. The boys set to work. It wasn't exactly easy, but it was fun to work on the quads and polish them.

'That's great, boys. You've done a really good job. Come back tomorrow if you want,' said Rob, shaking their hands like real workers. 'You can have another free ride on the quads!'

A rainy day walk

Pip the poodle loved Wednesdays because Alex always took him for a walk in the park. If Alex put on his coat, Pip would get up and wag his tail. It was time to play!

Oh no, it was raining! Pip didn't like rain or snow.

'Oh come on, Pip,' laughed Alex. 'A few drops of rain can't put you off. What a wet blanket you are!'

'How dare he call me a wet blanket!' thought Pip to himself. 'I'm a pedigree dog. I'll show him who's a wet blanket!'

Pip ran outside and jumped about in the puddles. He ran about in the grass and jumped up at Alex, putting his wet paws all over Alex's clean jumper. Then, Pip ran off across the wet, muddy lawn chasing pigeons.

Before Alex knew what was happening, Pip ran back and shook the water off his coat. The wet spray went all over Alex. Pip was enjoying himself!

'That's enough, Pip!' cried Alex. 'Bad dog! I'm soaking wet now.'

Pip realised it was fun being wet, after all. He looked at Alex as if to say, 'Shall we do that again?'

But Alex didn't want to play anymore. He was cold and wet, and wanted to go home, much to Pip's dismay.

In a bad mood, Alex stormed off to the bathroom to get dry. But where was Pip? Well, Pip also needed to dry off, so he'd jumped onto Alex's bed and curled up on the warm quilt.

'Well,' thought Pip, with a twinkle in his eye. 'Why not?'

The lonely monster

Once there was a monster who lived in a huge cave. In the town nearby, the children were the only ones who believed in him. Nobody even knew where the cave was.

Early one morning, David and John were out exploring in the hills. As they were climbing over some rocks they discovered a hole. It was dark and looked scary.

David thought they should carry on walking, but John was curious.

'I want to explore the cave. I've got a torch in my bag,' he said.

Inside the cave the brothers came across two tunnels.

'Let's split up,' said John. 'I'll go right and you go left.'

'No way! We should never split up. Dad's always going on about that!' said David.

'Okay, follow me,' said John.

The tunnel seemed to go on and on, but eventually they reached a big empty room. They were just about to turn back when out of the shadows appeared a HUGE MONSTER! Terrified, the brothers ran toward the exit. Then a tiny voice whispered, 'Please don't go! I mean you no harm.'

The boys turned around and timidly approached the monster.

'I've been alone here for so long. I'd love to have some friends!' he sighed.

And that's how David and Jonathan made a new friend.

Thimble to the rescue!

Thimble loved living on the farm. Ever since the day Kiera picked him out at the rescue home, he had been her loyal pet. But there was a shadow cast over his happiness by the other farm animals, who didn't like him.

'Ever since that cat arrived, things have been different around here. Kiera never takes any notice of us!' said the other farm animals.

But one day, when the farmer and his family were away, Thimble heard frightened squawks coming from the hen house. He rushed outdoors to see animals shouting and running in all directions. They were terrified! Then Thimble saw black smoke billowing out of the hen house. Oh, no! The coop was on fire!

The pig hurriedly explained that a fire had started in the field next door and the wind had quickly blown it toward the hen house. The fire had taken hold in seconds, and they didn't know how to rescue the chickens.

'The poor things are going to burn to death!' sobbed the old cockerel. 'This is so awful! What can we do?'

Forgetting about his own safety, Thimble ran into the coop and gently picked up one of the hens in his mouth. He carried the hen outside, and ran back to rescue the others.

All the animals admired his courage and he became a hero. Ever since, they have been proud to have Thimble as a friend.

Home sweet home

oris the beaver was getting married, so he needed to build a new lodge for he and his wife to inhabit.

Boris went into the forest to choose the best building wood he could find. It needed to be solid, but not too thick. Using his sharp teeth he chewed all the way around a tree trunk until the tree fell into the snow. He then needed to get the tree down to the river, because that's where he was going to build his lodge.

Boris asked his friends to help him. They all came and helped to carry the wood to the place where the lodge was to be built. It was a perfect spot. It was not too near the water as the lodge needed to stay dry, and not too near the bank because of the wolves. He also made sure it was not too far from the other lodges, so that he could go fishing with the other beavers.

To make the walls and roof, Boris took the smallest twigs, wove them together and soaked them with water. When the wood was dry,

he added a layer of branches for extra protection. Then he collected some dry grass and spread it in the sleeping area to make a bed. The new home was ready.

But what about a door? He's forgotten the door!

'No need for a door,' said Boris. 'To get into our house, you simply swim underwater!'

Ping and Pong

Ping and Pong the kittens are so greedy that as soon as they finish their supper, they go next door where their friend Sukie lives. Ping and Pong then join her for their second supper.

Sukie's owner is an old lady who loves animals. But one day, when they went over to Sukie's, Ping and Pong saw a skinny white cat with thinning fur and a torn ear, timidly entering the kitchen.

'Who's that?' said Pong to his brother. 'What's he doing here?'

'He looks like a nasty piece of work,' said Ping. 'I think we should go and check him out. It's our duty to protect Sukie.'

So, the two kittens, both no bigger than little balls of knitting yarn, decided to take a closer look at the strange cat. Feeling very afraid, they jumped onto the window sill to get a better look before entering the house.

What a shock Ping and Pong had when they saw Sukie sharing her bowl of milk with the stranger! Annoyed, the two brothers marched into the house and bumped the poorly cat out of their way. The cat looked at them sadly.

'Stop that!' Sukie snapped at the two kittens. 'This is Geoffrey. He's going to live with me for a while. He's had some bad luck and hasn't been eating properly.'

'But you don't even know him!' protested Ping.

'That's true. But he's cold and hungry and needs our help,' Sukie replied.

'I suppose you're right,' said Pong, trying to imagine what being hungry must feel like. 'Enjoy your meal, Geoffrey!'

How do you get to school?

In towns, the country, and on mountains, islands and even in deserts all over the world, children go to school. In towns they go by foot, by train, by bike, by car, or even travel on the underground subway.

In the countryside, schools are sometimes very far away, so a coach collects the children. Sometimes, there is no set route.

Mateo canters across the hills on his horse, Francesca trots through the olive groves on her donkey, Malika goes across the desert on her camel, and Lanlan travels through the rice paddies on a cart pulled by two buffaloes.

Shirka is quite comfortable being taken to school on the back of a huge elephant!

Sometimes children travel to school by water. Paula holds onto her hat when she's in her dinghy, Chang weaves his junk in between the other boats on the river, and Ali glides through the water in his canoe, looking out for the rapids.

In some countries there is always snow on the ground. Every morning, Erik puts on his skis, Nanouk attaches six dogs to her sleigh, and Tatiana jumps onto her toboggan.

Maya lives on the top of a very high mountain where there are no paths or rivers. How does she get to school?

In her father's hot air balloon, of course! It is red with silver stars all over it and inside the woven wicker basket there are beautiful embroidered cushions.

How do you go to school?

Finding true love

Pompom the donkey was in love. Every day he would trot across his field to catch a glimpse of a pretty young donkey who lived in the next field. He would amble alongside the fence hoping that today she would come nearer so he could tell her how he felt. But each day he would wander back to his stable disappointed.

You see, this pretty young donkey, whose name was Pearl by the way, had another admirer. Prince, the stallion. Every day Pompom would watch forlornly as Prince marched about swishing his elegant tail as all the female donkeys giggled and blushed. He felt doubly sad when he saw how much attention Prince paid to Pearl.

'Oh,' he sighed. 'Pearl will never notice a clumsy donkey like me when a handsome horse like Prince is courting her. I may as well give up.'

Pompom was just turning away from the fence when he heard a timid cough.

'Excuse me, but isn't your name Pompom?' said a sweet voice. 'I've noticed you near the fence and wanted to talk to you, but I haven't been able to get away from that silly poser Prince! He's always hassling me and showing off, I do wish he'd leave me alone.'

Pompom shyly smiled at Pearl and they began to chat. Soon they became best of friends and it wasn't too long before they were married. Without a doubt, they were the happiest donkeys in the world.

Baby birds

I t was nearly summer. Finally, we could open the windows! Emily was very happy because she loved lying on her bed and reading while listening to birds singing in the garden.

Prrrssssh… What was that? It was a soft noise that sounded like tissue paper being crumpled. Emily went back to her reading, but then she heard it again. *Prrrrrssh…*

Puzzled, she got up and went to look out the window. Then, she heard the noise again. This time the sound came from above her head. Emily turned round and looked up at the ceiling.

It was a pretty bedroom at the top of her grandpa's very old house. There were big beams criss-crossing the ceiling and Emily could see that there was something up there. It looked like twigs or hay.

She climbed up onto a chair to get a better look. At that moment, something dived down toward her, skimmed the top of her head, and disappeared out the window!

A bird! Emily could see it now, perched in the big tree in front of the house. The little brown bird was looking round and tweeting madly. Emily ran downstairs to tell her grandad about it.

'A tiny bird making a lot of noise? That's the cave dweller,' smiled grandpa. 'She must have chosen your room to nest in this year. Sorry little one, we'll have to put you in a different room until her babies fly away. Is that alright with you?'

How could she say no to such a sweet little bird?

Let's go to the seaside!

arry is five years old. He still has lots of things to discover, and today his parents have decided to take him to the seaside.

'What is the sea?' asked Harry.

'The sea is like a huge lake with water as far as the eye can see,' said his mother.

'Does it go on forever?' asked Harry.

'No, it's just very big,' she said.

Harry was still sleepy as they all set off in the car. Just as the car stopped, Harry suddenly woke from his nap.

'Are we there? Is *that* the sea?' asked Harry, feeling a little disappointed. 'It looks like a car park.'

'Wait a minute. We have to walk for a bit,' his dad smiled.

They walked along a path and at the end Harry saw an enormous sandpit, lots of people, and a huge lake that went on forever! Harry's mother spread out a towel and handed Harry his swimming trunks.

'Now you can go swimming!' his mother said.

'But I'll get washed away by those rolls of water!' said Harry.

'Those rolls are called waves. Don't be scared,' said dad.

'Yuk! It tastes horrible!' Harry spluttered, after swallowing a mouthful of salty sea water. His parents both laughed as they paddled with him.

And that was how Harry found out about the sea. Have you been to the seaside?

The land of dreams

It's a magical land surrounded by mist, clouds, and bubbles; a land where things happen the moment you think of them. It is a beautiful country where everyone loves each other.

If you say 'hello', someone always appears to talk to you. It is a land where animals can talk and laugh.

If you want a hug, there is always someone to give you one. Everyone is kind and gentle and understands if you are upset, and laughs when you are happy.

In this magical land you can have a dog if you want one, or a cat, a bird, or even a leopard! You just have to wish for a pet and it will magically appear.

You can run with it in the fields and play with it all day long.

In this land, you only eat delicious things, you understand everything you learn at school, you dress as you want, and everyone else does too!

There are lots of children in this land and they are all very happy. They are all from different countries, but everyone can understand each other's language! The grown-ups never argue and they never shout at children.

You can go to this land if you like. All you have to do is go to sleep. As soon as you get there everything is wonderful, you'll see. But as we're not in the land of dreams yet, first you have to brush your teeth, say your prayers, and climb into bed!

A story about Jacob

This is a true story about a little boy named Jacob. He is a child of your age, who lives in Yaika.

Yaika is a little village in Africa. There are no elephants in Yaika, or lions or gazelles. Jacob's grandpa remembers that there used to be animals there long ago. They died because of poor weather and droughts.

Jacob doesn't go to school. The people of Yaika are very poor, so everyone works, even the children. Jacob collects water from the well and helps his parents every day in the fields. He doesn't mind and he has enough to eat, unlike some other children.

Jacob's parents would like to be able to afford to send him to school. They would like him to be educated so that one day he could be a doctor or a teacher. But unless the poverty crisis in his country is solved, Jacob will never be able to go to school. He won't learn how to read, he won't know how to write his name, and he won't know how to count.

So, you are luckier than Jacob and should work hard at school. Don't moan about getting up in the morning and you should always try your hardest in class. And when you grow up, perhaps you can do something to help children like Jacob in Africa.

The cleaner fish

There is a beautiful pink and white coral reef surrounding an island in the southern seas. The reef is a magnificent place, full of tiny fish. There are also lots of huge sharks and sting rays.

All of the mighty creatures wait in single file without fighting each other, or eating any of the fish. Now that's hard to believe, isn't it? The reason why they come to the reef is because there are some very special fish that live in this place. These fish are tiny, but very useful. They act like dentists for the larger animals.

Look at that big fat shark for example. You can tell that he's not usually so patient, but he floats there with his mouth open as if he were at the dentist. The tiny fish swim in and out of his mouth, right past those huge, terrifying teeth, and he doesn't move an inch.

Those tiny fish are doing some important repair work, nibbling off the itchy and ticklish parasites and fungus that the shark cannot get rid of himself. The parasites had been irritating the shark for ages, putting him in a very bad mood. But the tiny fish have solved his problem, at least for a while. Now while this work is going on, the other sharks patiently wait their turn.

When the little fish have finished their cleaning job, the sharks happily swim away. If you wait, some others will be along soon for their check-ups.

But beware of these sharks' terrible teeth and their very smelly breath!

The little liar

There once was a little boy called Luke. He was a happy, friendly little boy unless he had done something wrong. When that happened he would get terribly embarrassed and would pretend that whatever had happened was not his fault.

The trouble was that once he started lying, Luke would find it very difficult to stop. Also he sometimes got a little bit carried away with being naughty because he thought lies would get him out of trouble.

He blamed the cat for ruining his sister's painting by knocking water over it, forgetting that cats don't usually scribble lines and patterns all over paintings in felt-tip pens.

He told his teacher that he hadn't done his homework because he had to go to the dentist. But the next day he had to go to the dentist, so then he said he had a doctor's appointment. When his teacher asked him what was wrong, he forgot which lie he had told and said he needed a filling. She wasn't very impressed.

Soon Luke's lies began to catch up with him. He had to do lines for lying to his teacher, and his mother didn't let him watch TV for a week for ruining his sister's painting and lying about it.

Luke began to think that it really wasn't worthwhile lying any more. He decided to try to be nicer to his sister and to own up if he did something wrong. He soon discovered that people are much kinder to you if you admit your mistakes and so he never lied again.

Braces rule, okay!

Ian noticed that more and more children in his class had started wearing braces on their teeth. Every time one of his friends came to school with a mouth full of metal, he would tease them because they couldn't speak properly. Then, last week, Ian found out that he needed to wear a brace too! What a disaster!

'If you don't get braces for Ian, he will have very crooked teeth when he is older,' the dentist told Ian's parents.

Ian cried and refused to leave the house when he got his braces. He knew he was going to be teased, and he deserved it. Ian was finally going to get a taste of his own medicine.

Ian thought for a long while about this, and decided the only way to stop the others laughing at him, was to make them laugh with him!

So from now on, he would tell his friends to call him 'metal mouth'. And he was going to be proud of his braces.

He decided to start a club called 'The Metal Mouth Gang' that only boys and girls with braces could join.

It was a good idea and everyone stopped making fun of anyone with braces. In fact, it became quite cool at school. Each time a new child came in with braces, the members of the Metal Mouth Gang would give them a special little present.

All the children who wore glasses decided to make their own club, the 'Double Vision Club'.

Because of Ian and his wonderful idea, everyday at school is a lot more fun for everyone! Just ask anyone!

Hollywood or bust

 igzag the snake was very, very excited!

'I'm going to go to Hollywood and have a career in the movies!' said the snake. 'I'm very ugly and frightening, and I can be really scary.'

After packing his belongings, Zigzag set off. He had just gone past the hill when he met Poppy the dormouse.

'Where do you think you're going?' asked Poppy.

'To Hollywood!' said Zigzag.

'You're not going anywhere until you've given me back my potato masher,' said Poppy.

So Zigzag had to go back home to get the silly potato masher. But as Zigzag set off again, Bruno the bear blocked his path.

'Are you going away? You owe me money,' Bruno growled, so Zigzag had to retrace his steps to fetch Bruno's money.

'What's wrong with everyone today?' sighed Zigzag. 'A bear and a dormouse can't stop me!'

The snake had only slithered a short way when Crusty the rat came out of a hole and demanded his book be returned. On the way home to fetch the book, Zigzag bumped into Bobby the mole, who wanted his watch back. Then, it was Ariadne the spider's turn. She wanted her sewing box, and then Curly the sheep wanted her comb.

When he arrived home yet again, Zigzag looked at his little bundle of belongings and knew that he wasn't ready to go to Hollywood. He was just a little bit too busy at home!

Sleep magic

Peter was snuggled up in bed, reading a book with his teddy bear, when dad came into his room.

'Come on, Peter. It's time to go to sleep,' said dad.

'Can I just finish reading this page?' asked Peter.

'Five minutes!' smiled dad.

A little later, Peter's mother came upstairs to turn off Peter's light.

'Just a bit longer?' said Peter.

'No,' said dad, coming back into the room and switching off the light. 'It's time to go to sleep now, son! Sleep well.'

The bedroom was very dark. Peter wondered why every creak in the house seemed to be louder than usual.

'Dad, switch on the light! I'm scared!' Peter yelled.

'Come on, Peter,' said dad. 'You're a big boy now. You really don't need the light on.'

Suddenly, Peter felt a tiny breath on his ear. It was Seamus, the friendly leprechaun.

'Listen Peter, your dad is right. You're a big boy now. Just close your eyes and look for the light inside you instead. When you dream, you can be anywhere you want. You can fly, you can swim, you can be big or small, so just let yourself be rocked to sleep by the magic of it all. What do you think of that, eh?'

Peter didn't answer because he was already asleep in the land of dreams.

Frog in my throat!

When Olivia the famous singer tried to sing one day, she was in for nasty shock. Instead of sweet sound, only a squeak came out!

She needed to get through all her singing scales before that night's performance, so she asked her pianist to start again.

'Sorry about that. I don't know what happened,' she said. 'Do, re, mi, fa, so, la, ti… *eeeek!*'

Losing patience with herself, Olivia cried, 'What has happened to me? *Eeeek! Eeeek! Eeeek!* I've lost my voice!'

When the townspeople heard the sad news, it was as if the sky had fallen. Everyone was upset because each year the town held a little festival to celebrate their famous opera singer, Olivia.

'The next time people vote, I will lose the election because of this,' thought the mayor. 'What can we do to help Olivia?'

Someone suggested they call the village earthworm, Zip. Luckily he was delighted to help Olivia. Zip was so small, he was able to slide down and examine Olivia's poor throat.

'Slowly, let me down slowly,' said Zip, armed with a helmet and a torch. 'Ha! I can see something. Let me down a bit more. Easy does it now!'

A triumphant Zip reappeared just a few minutes later, holding a tiny frog.

'My dear Olivia, you had a frog in your throat. It shouldn't bother you any more,' said Zip.

And as quickly as that, Olivia's beautiful voice was back just in time for the show.

Night flight

It was nearly midnight. 'Wake up, Tweet! Why are you still sleeping?' called Mother Owl, urgently.

'Hmm? Why can't you leave me to sleep?' mumbled Tweet.

'Not now, lazy bones,' she said. 'We owls are supposed to hunt during the night and sleep during the day. Come on, get up and fly!'

Moments later, Tweet was perched, shivering on a branch of a tree. This was no kind of weather for owls or bats, she thought to herself as she looked at her friend, Majik the bat.

'Hey, Majik! It's freezing, isn't it?' called Tweet.

'Yes, but you should fly around for a bit. That will warm you up,' said Majik.

A little later, Tweet saw Spike the hedgehog. 'Hi, Spike! Have you caught anything?' asked Tweet.

'Just copy me and chase everything you can,' answered Spike.

'The winter months are hard, so we must stock up on food.'

'Maybe Ma Owl was right,' thought Tweet. 'There's a time for everything. A time for sleeping, a time for hunting, and a time for having fun.'

So Tweet flapped her wings and flew off into the night, in search of food.

'Hey, wait for me, you're not going to get all the good catches without me!' Tweet called to her friends.

Where's my bone?

Boxer the dog was annoyed because he had lost his bone. He was sure he had buried it under the apple tree, but when he tried to dig it up, he couldn't find anything. Boxer searched everywhere, but couldn't find a thing.

Boxer asked his friend the butterfly if he had seen the lost bone. But he said he couldn't help because he didn't know the area very well. Boxer walked away feeling very sad.

Then, Boxer decided to ask Tom the cat.

'Tom, wake up! It's me!' said Boxer, nudging the sleeping cat.

'What's going on?' asked Tom.

'I've lost my bone,' said Boxer. 'I buried it under the apple tree.'

'Well it's your silly fault then!' scolded Tom. 'That's the third time this week!'

Boxer set off toward the forest, where he bumped into Grizzly the bear. Grizzly said he hadn't seen the bone either, so Boxer continued on his way.

That day, Boxer saw Phillip the frog, Morris the mole and lots of other animals, but not one of them had seen his bone. Boxer began to give up hope and headed home.

He went to lie down in his basket in the kitchen. His owner was making a delicious pear tart.

'Yum! I love pear tart!' Boxer thought. 'Pear, pear... oh, but of course! I'm so silly!'

At last, Boxer remembered where he had buried his bone. It was under the pear tree, not the apple tree.

Some vacation!

 nna the ant was bored with work. She had never had a day off since the day she was born. She had to work in the anthill from dawn until dusk. One morning, Anna decided she was going to set off to spend a few days vacation with her ant aunt, way up in the mountains.

Anna spent all day walking and when evening came, she finally reached her aunt's house. The two of them had dinner together and caught up on the family news before going to sleep.

'Time to get up!' called Anna's aunt, early the next morning.

It was only just light outside and Anna had hoped she might have a few more minutes' sleep.

'Hurry up and have your breakfast. I need to pick an ear of corn to take out with us,' said her aunt.

Anna hurriedly ate some honey and joined her aunt outside.

'After this, we can rid the wild flowers of greenfly and when we've finished that we need to collect some water,' said Anna's aunt, pulling the ear of corn.

Anna helped her aunt all day. There was always something to do. That evening, Anna was exhausted and said she would go to bed early.

'Hey, this is not a modern anthill! You have to work hard to be healthy!' said her aunt.

The next day, Anna told her aunt that she had to leave to help an old friend, Simon the maybug. Anna and Simon had a lovely time doing nothing, except watching time go by. That was a proper vacation!

The terrible toothache

Carl the crocodile had very painful toothache, but he was too afraid to go to the dentist. As the day went on, Carl's toothache got worse, and he knew he couldn't put it off any longer. Feeling nervous, he walked over to Bucky the beaver's surgery.

Carl wasn't alone in Bucky's waiting room. Brutus the elephant was there with a broken tusk, Fruity the bat needed one of his fangs seen to, and Thistle the dog was there to have his teeth cleaned. When it was Carl's turn to go in, he was shaking with fear!

The dentist told Carl to climb up onto the couch.

'Oh dear. You're going to need lots of work on this tooth,' said Bucky, prodding Carl's aching gums. 'Open wide, I'll give you an injection before I pull it out.'

Carl was so scared that a big tear trickled down his cheek.

'Stop those crocodile tears, you're an adult!' said Bucky with a smile as he set to work.

Bucky had a bit of trouble getting to the bottom of the tooth, so Carl opened his mouth wider. Carl also started to feel very sleepy.

When the crocodile woke a little later, he was alone in the surgery. He sat up and looked around, but couldn't see anyone. His tooth didn't hurt anymore, but his belly felt amazingly full.

'Oh no,' Carl said to himself. 'I think I may have eaten the dentist! Poor Bucky! That always happens when I open my mouth too wide!'

Carl quickly scuttled out, hoping nobody would notice. He also hoped that he would never again have a toothache!

Blast off!

othing happened, not so much as a spark or a puff of smoke! Sammy the snail scratched his head. He had checked all the rocket engines and everything seemed fine. He wanted to be the first snail in space. To be the slowest animal on Earth in the fastest rocket in the world.

But the rocket wasn't ready to fly to the stars just yet. Sammy went through the technical checks again. Everything seemed to be fine. Was something jammed? Had he missed a wire?

Sammy looked sadly at the special helmet he had ordered and the stock of powdered food he had bought for the journey.

'Sammy, are you still going to the Moon?' asked Clara the tortoise. 'What are you doing? Lift-off is today, isn't it?'

'Are you leaving today, Sammy?' said Rex the dog.

'Can't you two just leave me alone! The rocket isn't working at the moment and your silly comments aren't helping me fix it!' Sammy snapped.

When he realised he had hurt his friends, Sammy said sorry for being mean.

'I may be a bit silly sometimes, but I've got a good nose,' said Rex. 'These machines usually have a very strong smell, but your rocket doesn't smell of anything at all. Why is that?'

'Of course! You are brilliant!' said Sammy. 'I am just plain silly. I've forgotten to put fuel in my rocket!'

An hour later, Sammy's rocket was just a tiny spot in the sky. He had become the fastest snail in the universe.

The ghost who couldn't scare

There once was an old castle. Anyone who had stayed there said they heard strange noises in the night. *'Whooo! Whooo!'* went the noise.

The noise was Noel the ghost, who lived in the castle. He was a young ghost who hadn't yet learned how to make proper ghostly noises. His parents were trying to teach him how to scare people the proper way.

'Tonight you are going to frighten the people who are staying in the castle,' said his dad.

So Noel flew around the corridors making the scariest noises he could.

'Did you hear that?' asked Michael, who was staying in the castle with his family.

'Yeah, I think it was a mosquito,' said his sister.

'A mosquito?! That does it. I'll show them!' muttered Noel.

Noel crept into the children's bedroom and in his spookiest voice cried, *'Wheeeee, wheeee!'*

As soon as the children saw Noel they said, 'Oh, he's so sweet! What's your name, little ghost?'

Noel was a bit shocked. After all, he was the one doing the scaring.

'We're Michael and Hannah. Do you want to play with us?' asked the children.

'Oh, yes please!' replied Noel.

They played games together all night, and by next morning they were friends.

The giant molehill

Jessica the mole whistled as she prepared for her journey. She had everything she needed: maps, a compass, a torch, and even a medical kit.

'I'm going to have a wonderful adventure!' she said, happily.

Jessica checked her compass, then started digging a tunnel towards the city. She dug and dug, and by the end of the day she could feel her whiskers' quiver. The city was near. She made her bed, ate a few tasty earthworms, then curled up and slept.

Suddenly, Jessica was woken by a terrible noise.

'What's going on?' she groaned. Jessica started digging again, and came face to face with a drill! Then, she saw a hole in an immense pipe. She attached a cord to the edge and lowered herself through the hole. She found herself in what appeared to be a gigantic molehill. At the bottom there were trains coming in and out of a tunnel. The trains were bristling with people!

Jessica went to a platform to take a better look at everything.

'How beautiful,' she thought.

But Jessica changed her mind when a big pair of shoes stopped in front of her.

'Ticket, please,' said a man, peering down at the little mole.

As Jessica scurried away she decided that perhaps she wouldn't go back there again.

'These humans are crazy,' she said. 'They have to pay to go into a molehill. I think I prefer the countryside!'

On land or sea?

s was usual, the two little dragons were arguing with each other.

'Come on, you must be joking,' said the flying dragon, Glider.

'I promise you, whales swim so quickly they look like flashes of lightning in the sea,' said the sea dragon, Scales.

'No, no, the fastest things in the world live in the air. Things like insects and birds and, the fastest of all, airplanes,' insisted Glider.

'Well, you've obviously never seen my fish then!' humphed Scales.

Glider and Scales used to spend all day squabbling like this, but after a while the dragon king decided he had had enough. He arranged for Glider to magically become a sea dragon, and for Scales to magically become a flying dragon for a day.

'Oooh, I'm really cold,' spluttered Glider finding himself splashing about in the waves. 'What am I doing in the water?'

''What am I doing up here?' said Scales. 'I'm flying in the air! This must be the work of the dragon king. He must be trying to stop our arguments by seeing each other's lives for ourselves.'

That day the two little dragons discovered wonderful worlds unknown to them and they were delighted. In fact, they even promised the dragon king they would stop squabbling and be more open minded about the world around them.

Battle for the beach!

nappy the crab had lived on the beach since he was born. He had lots of friends there, and Snappy was very happy. But he didn't like the summer because as soon as the first rays of sun broke through the wispy clouds, the beach was taken over by tourists.

'There are more and more people every year,' Snappy said to Bernard the hermit crab and Sarah the starfish. 'Remember those children who kept playing in our pools last year? They were always lifting up the rocks and searching for us.'

'Yes, I was put out to dry on someone's towel! Luckily, Bernard rescued me,' said Sarah.

'Right, so what can we do about it?' asked Snappy.

Snappy's question was met with silence. So he decided that he would have to come up with an idea. He would call on Bloater for advice.

Despite his extremely ugly appearance, Bloater was the gentlest fish in the world. He was only too happy to help Snappy. Together they worked out a way to trick the tourists.

One afternoon when the beach was crowded, Bloater launched himself out of the water, shouting *'Blaaaah!'* Bloater was so big and ugly, that all the tourists ran away believing they had seen a monster. At the same time an army of crabs, headed by Snappy, began nipping the heels of the tourists as they flee up the beach.

The beach was immediately closed. The beach creatures all agreed it was the best summer they had ever enjoyed.

Party politics

ach the earthworm and Jack the snail were opposing candidates for the leader of the vegetable patch!

'Vote for me and I will guarantee you sun all year round!' said Zach's poster.

'Vote for me and there will always be refreshing rain!' said Jack's poster.

Zach and Jack went round the vegetable patch explaining their plans. Zach told a row of pear trees that he would ensure that the trees would no longer be cold during winter. On the other side of the garden, Jack told the strawberries that they wouldn't need to live in fear of greedy birds, if they voted for him.

The rhubarb was considering who to vote for. On the right it heard, 'Carrots, you won't need to be afraid of rabbits any more if you vote for me.' On the left it heard, 'Onions! Vote for me and you won't make anyone cry ever, ever again!'

The tension rose throughout the day and the two candidates' scores were very close. When Zach and Jack crossed paths in a flowerbed they were furious, and neither would allow the other to pass.

'Go ahead, wormy!' said Jack. 'Pass me, if you dare!'

'Stupid snail! I could if I wanted to!' Zach retorted.

After all the fuss, the election was a draw! But the residents did reach one decision. They suggested that Zach and Jack leave politics alone for a while as their squabbling had proved that neither of them were fit for the job of leader!

The lamb who wanted a jumper

 very day, Merino the little lamb complained to his mother about the cold.

'*Brrr! Brrr!* I'm cold!' he shivered. '*Brrr,* I need a cover to keep me warm!'

'How can you be cold? If you were bald I would understand, but you've got a thick coat of wool on your back. I've never heard of a cold lamb before!' said his mother.

'Well I'm different,' said Merino.

A little later, Merino complained again. 'Brrr! Mother, I want a jumper! It's not fair. We sheep have to make all the wool and then humans get to wear the jumpers!' he bleated.

'Humans wear jumpers because they don't have fur, feathers, or wool to keep them warm,' Merino's mother explained.

'But they can choose to wear red, blue, pink, and green. I'm always wearing white!' sulked Merino.

'Oh, stop being so silly!' said his mother who was getting cross with her son's moaning, but she also wanted him to be happy, so she went to talk to Pete, the donkey. Together, they came up with an idea.

Pete found a can of paint in the barn and carried it up to the field.

'Now, close your eyes and don't open them again until I tell you,' Pete told Merino.

The donkey dipped his tail into the pot and painted some pretty patterns onto Merino's fleece. When he opened his eyes he was amazed!

'Now, I really am the brightest lamb of all,' smiled a very happy little lamb.

The love letter

Paul and Ben were in the same class and they were always playing together and sharing secrets. They thought they would be friends always. Their friendship was so strong that it made some people jealous.

There was a little boy in their class called Max, who didn't have many friends. He wished he could have a friendship like theirs.

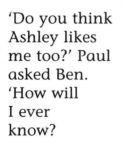

Paul liked a girl called Ashley, but had never dared to tell her how he felt.

'Do you think Ashley likes me too?' Paul asked Ben. 'How will I ever know?

Promise me you'll never tell anyone about it!'

'I promise,' said Ben.

Then, one day at breaktime, Paul saw Ashley coming over.

'Hi Paul.' said Ashley. 'Why didn't you tell me yourself?'

'Tell you what?' asked Paul.

'That you liked me. Ben wrote to tell me!' she replied.

Paul was very cross and didn't speak to Ben all that day.

'Can you tell me what I've done?' Ben asked Paul.

'How can you call yourself my friend? Why did you tell Ashley that I liked her?' asked Paul.

Suddenly, Ashley ran up. 'Max just told me that *he* wrote that letter and signed it from Ben,' she said.

So, Paul and Ben made friends again. Paul even forgave Max because he'd finally found out that Ashley liked him, too!

Magic painting

Once upon a time, a poor girl called Abigail lived in a small village. She lived all alone and her only hobby was painting. She painted whatever she saw around her: the fields, the animals, and the flowers. Her paintings were so good they almost looked like photographs.

One day, a boy came to the village. He was thin, tired, and looked like he was very hungry. When he said he needed somewhere to stay, Abigail felt sorry for him and invited him to stay at her house.

She fed the boy as well as she could, and by the end of the week he started to look and feel much better. They soon got to know each other and one day Abigail showed her new friend her paintings.

'You are a fantastic painter!' said the boy, excitedly. 'I own some magic paint. Anything you paint with it will become real. I've never used it myself, because I can't paint and it only works if the painting looks like the real thing. Go on, paint something nice... perhaps a delicious meal!'

Abigail started painting slices of ham, thick chunks of bread, creamy cakes, and a bottle of strawberry juice. It all looked delicious and as soon as the painting was finished, the food and drink appeared!

The two friends shared the food, and then Abigail painted a beautiful house with a vegetable patch, a herd of cows, and an orchard full of fruit trees. By the time she had finished, there was no paint left, but it didn't matter because they had more than enough to be happy always!

The candy tree

ver since Anthony had first tasted candies and sweets, he had always asked the same question, 'Where do they come from? Eggs come from chickens, cherries come from cherry trees, and lettuce comes from the vegetable patch. But sweets?Who would know where they come from?

Anthony thought that the only person who might know was Mr Toffee.

'Mr Toffee, can you tell me where all the candies come from?' Anthony asked one day.

'They come from the candy tree, of course. Didn't you know that I have just such a tree? smiled the shopkeeper. 'I just pick the sweet treats and fill all the jars in my store.'

Wow! A candy tree! Anthony never knew there was such a fantastic thing. He just had to see it.

The little wall around Mr Toffee's house wasn't very high, so one afternoon Anthony scrambled onto a box, trying to spot the candy tree. But Mr Toffee came home and caught him!

'Anthony! What are you doing?'

'Um, well, Mr Toffee, I wanted to see your candy tree,' said Anthony.

'I was teasing. you. There's no such thing as a sweet tree,' laughed Mr Toffee. Mr Toffee explained that the candy and sweets were delivered from a factory. Anthony's question was finally answered!

The sparkly herring

Henry the herring thought he was more handsome and intelligent than any other species of fish.

'You are all so ugly. You are dull and brown, and you all look the same!' said Henry, as he swam past another herring.

'Why do you think you're better than everyone else? You have the same scales as us, you know,' said the herring.

'That's the only way that I'm like you. I'm far more intelligent than you, and I shall be the most beautiful and the most unusual fish, too.'

That very day, Henry started looking for things to help make himself more attractive. He found some pink and orange coral and lots of shiny shells.

'Look at me,' said Henry. 'I am the star of the ocean!'

'What a show-off!' said the other fish.

One day, a huge shark appeared. He swam among the little fish and they fled in all directions to hide under the rocks. But one little fish couldn't hide! With his shiny decorations and his twinkly shells, the shark could easily see Henry. Another herring called, 'Quick! Take off your shells, Henry!'

Henry swiftly rubbed up against a rock to get the shells off, then darted under a rock so the shark couldn't see him.

'We hope that teaches you a lesson, Henry,' said the other fish when the shark had gone.

'Oh, yes it has! From now on, I'll just have to be happy with being the cleverest fish in the sea,' said Henry.

Will Henry ever learn anything?

The moving statue

 t was the second time that a statue had been stolen from the museum, so the director decided to call the best detective in town, Mr Switch.

'This is a difficult case,' said Mr Switch. 'Perhaps the burglar will strike again tonight!'

And he did! The burglar broke into the museum and stole yet another statue.

'One more for my collection!' he sniggered, sneaking away.

Once the burglar got the statue home, he looked at it and said, 'It's amazing! The statue is so life-like, it almost looks alive!'

'How right you are!' answered the statue.

The burglar fainted on the spot when he saw the statue moving and talking. You see, it wasn't really a statue; it was the detective disguised as one.

'I think I've caught you red-handed,' said the detective.

'I'm so sorry,' said the thief, through his tears. 'I just love statues more than anything else in the world. But I don't have any money to buy my own.'

'That's no excuse for stealing!' said Mr Switch. But he felt a bit sorry for the weeping burglar. 'Listen, if you promise you'll behave and never steal again, I could give you the chance to work and see statues every day.'

The next day, Mr Switch asked the museum's director to give the burglar a job as a security guard. The man loved his job, and there were no more thefts.

The brave old lion king

n deepest Africa, the old lion king looked very tired. The lord of the jungle was not a young lion any more. Ah, how powerful he used to be. But now he was too tired to do anything.

'I'm an old man,' he said to himself. 'I'm not fit to be king any longer. I don't have enough power left to rule.'

At the animals' council meeting, the old lion announced his decision to give up the crown.

'But you are our king,' said the elephant.'Who would rule over us in your place?

'You must choose one of the young lions,' said the old lion.

'But none of them are wise enough," said the hyena.

'What's the point of having an old king who is unable to protect you all?' said the lion. I'm retiring!'

The animals watched sadly as the king padded away.

The next day, there was a great disturbance in the savannah. It was hunters! They stalked through the jungle trying to find the best catch. The animals were terrified and went to find the lion. As soon as he heard what was happening his blood boiled. Without a moment's hesitation, the old lion rushed out to face them. Ignoring his weariness, the lion charged at the men with such a ferocious roar that they ran off.

A loud 'hooray!' boomed across the savannah. The old lion walked proudly home with the cheers ringing in his ears. He had found his strength again.

'Long live the king!' shouted the animals.

The mysterious old man

On the other side of the playground wall there was a little house. People used to say that an old man lived there, but very few people ever saw him, and those who did, said he never spoke to anyone. No one even knew what he did. All the school children were afraid of him.

One day, as the children were playing in the playground, a ball went over the wall. No one was brave enough to go and get it because it had fallen into the old man's yard. In the end, the teacher rang the doorbell and the old man came to the door.

'What do you want?' he asked, grumpily.

'Um, well, the children's ball has landed in your garden,' said the teacher, nervously. 'May I get it for them, please?'

'Follow me,' mumbled the man.

To reach the garden, they had to walk through the house. When they entered the sitting room, the old man asked the teacher to wait. She looked around and saw that the room was full of beautiful wooden puppets.

'Your puppets are beautiful, where did you buy them?' asked the teacher when the man returned with the ball.

'I didn't buy them,' said the old man, gruffly. 'I made them myself. Many years ago, I used to put on puppet shows.'

'Well you must come and do a show for the children at school!' smiled the teacher.

So they organised a puppet show and all the children thought it was wonderful. Now the old man teaches the children how to make beautiful puppets.

Can you do this?

Today the elephant family is going to have a picnic by the river. Bobo the baby elephant loves playing in the water. All the elephants spray each other with their trunks and roll in the mud.

When the elephants reach the river it is already busy. On a hot day like this, all the animals in the savannah gather at the river to cool down. Bobo is happy because his friend Naomi the giraffe is there too.

Bobo likes playing a game they made up called "Can you do this?" with Naomi. He sprays water with his trunk and says, 'Can you do this, Naomi?'

Naomi doesn't have a trunk, so she can't do it.

But Naomi is very good at doing other things! She can hide behind a tree and you won't see her because the marks on her skin merge with the shadows of the leaves.

'Can you do this?' she asks.

Bobo tries to hide, but he's so big that there's always quite a lot of him sticking out either side of the tree.

So Bobo wraps his trunk around a tree and pulls it right out of the ground. 'Can you do this?' he asks Naomi.

Naomi spreads her feet apart and cranes her long neck down to the ground. Then she tries to push the trunk with her head, but it won't move.

'Can you do this?' says Bobo, plucking a leaf from the tree.

Naomi doesn't even need to stretch to do that. At last! There's something both of them can do!

The storyteller's secret

*J*oseph the shepherd had never learned to read, even though he loved stories. Sometimes an old man from the mountain would come down to Joseph's village. He was a story teller and was very popular with the villagers, who never tired of his wonderful tales.

'His stories are so beautiful,' thought Joseph.

While he was grazing his herd on the mountain top one day, Joseph stood in front of the storyteller's little house. Joseph often wondered whether this was where the secrets of the storyteller were kept. He went past the house so often that one day the storyteller asked him, 'Why are you always prowling around here?'

'I'm just looking,' said Joseph.

'What are you looking for?' asked the storyteller.

'Looking for where your stories come from,' answered Joseph.

'My stories?' said the man with a smile. 'Come here. I'll show you.'

The man invited Joseph into his home. 'This is where my stories come from,' he said, pointing to a library full of books. Joseph had never seen anything like it.

'I've read a lot of books,' said the man. 'I've discovered amazing stories and fantastic worlds. These stories have inspired my imagination and now I create my own tales.'

Joseph was so impressed that he decided to learn how to read. As soon as he had learned, he read as many books as he could. Joseph is now a very famous writer and his stories entertain children all over the world.

The fashion show

 homas had a passion. He loved sewing. None of the other boys could understand how a boy could like sewing.

'It's a girl's hobby,' they said.

Thomas often remembered the day when his teacher asked about the pupils' hobbies. The boys said football, cycling or chess, but Thomas said sewing. Everyone burst out laughing and Thomas wanted to crawl under the desk. He really did love sewing. He made lovely clothes for his sister's dolls.

One day, his teacher asked if he could see some of Thomas's designs. Thomas was a little shy at first, but he showed the teacher his exercise book, which was full of pictures of wonderful dresses and beautiful costumes.

The teacher was very impressed and said, 'You really are very talented Thomas, and you've given me an idea.'

With Thomas's help, the teacher decided to arrange a fashion show for the end of the year. All the outfits would be designed by Thomas and the pupils were going to be the models.

At last, the big day arrived and the children's parents came to watch. Thomas was nervous and hoped the show was a success.

And it was! All the girls loved wearing the beautiful dresses that Thomas had designed. As they walked up and down the stage, everyone applauded and even the boys were very impressed.

That day, Thomas knew that it wouldn't be too long before he was a world famous fashion designer.

Two's a crowd

One day in the vegetable patch Speedy found a lettuce to eat. Yum! It looked like a delicious lettuce with crisp, green leaves. Speedy licked his lips at the thought of munching into it. But his mood quickly changed when he saw that Slimer the slug was already munching the lettuce and seemed to be really enjoying it.

Speedy was furious. He hated slugs. 'I'm hungry, let me have some!' he yelled.

'You're very rude. You could at least say 'hello'!' said the slug.

'Hello,' said Speedy through gritted teeth. 'Now go away and let me eat!'

'Hello, Mr Snail. I think there's enough lettuce here for both of us, don't you?' said Slimer.

'I'm not going to have any sort of discussion with a slug!' shouted Speedy.

'And why not?' asked Slimer.

'Because you are stupid animals. You slime around without any clothes on. You're not even clever enough to think of taking your home around on your back. No snail would be so dumb!' said Speedy.

Just as Slimer was about to reply, the gardener and a friend walked into the garden.

'I love snails,' said the gardener.

The snail looked about proudly. 'You see, Slimer, everyone loves snails! Who loves slugs? No one!' he sneered.

But the gardener continued, 'Yes, I love snails. They're delicious! Cooked in butter and garlic, they make a real feast!'

Speedy suddenly went very quiet. Then, he fled as quickly as he could while Slimer contentedly returned to munching the lettuce.

Sweet tooth!

Elizabeth's best friend in the world was Amber, the baker's daughter. Elizabeth was rather jealous of Amber.

'You are so lucky! You can eat as many cakes and sweets as you like,' sighed Elizabeth. 'I wish I could do that, but my parents won't let me eat anything sugary. They think it's bad for you. You can do whatever you want. That must be brilliant!'

'But I've eaten so many cakes that I don't even like them much any more,' said Amber.

'I'd never get sick of eating cakes!' said Elizabeth.

At the end of term and the beginning of the summer holiday, Amber had an idea.

'You know that during the holidays I help my parents in the bakery. Would you like to work there for a week instead of me, Elizabeth?' she said.

'Oh, yes please! Cakes and chocolate and toffee for me!' Elizabeth excitedly said.

The next day, she was up bright and early. Wearing a little white apron, she stood proudly behind the counter.

'Can I help you?' she asked, as the customers came into the shop. When the bakery was empty, Elizabeth would eat a chocolate or a cake. She couldn't help herself!

By the end of the day, Elizabeth had eaten so much she felt very ill. That evening, when Amber came to see her, Elizabeth was in bed with a very upset tummy.

'Are you going to work at the bakery tomorrow?' asked Amber.

'No way!' groaned Elizabeth.

A *hiss*-tory lesson

ong ago, snakes had feet! They had four little feet that they used to scramble up walls. They would have been perfectly happy had it not been for the lizards. Lizards and snakes were at war, you see. At that time, lizards didn't have any feet, and slithered around like the snakes we see today.

One day, the snake king called all his snakes together. 'My dear snakes, it is time we put an end to these evil lizards,' he hissed. 'We will do battle and get rid of them once and for all! I ask you all to help with this final fight against our enemies!'

On the other side of the desert, the lizard king was saying the same thing to his followers.

The armies assembled and they started a terrible war! The snakes seemed to be winning when the lizards captured the snake king. They took him to the lizard king who said, 'Snake, you are our prisoner. You have a choice: we can kill all of your snakes in battle or you can make peace. If you choose the second option, we will free you. But you must give us something in return.'

'What would I have to give you in exchange for peace?' asked the snake king looking quite puzzled.

'You can give us your feet and all the other snakes' feet!' said the lizard king.

'I accept,' said the snake, because he wanted to end the war between snakes and lizards.

Ever since that day, the snakes have slithered and the lizards have had feet!

Best of enemies

ily and Courtney were enemies. Nobody knew why, but the two little girls just could not get on. They were in the same class, but never said a word to each other. When anyone asked Lily why she disliked Courtney she would say, 'Because I do!'

When anyone asked Courtney why she disliked Lily she would say, 'Because I do!'

Everyone thought it was really silly, but the two girls wouldn't change their minds.

'She's my worst enemy in the world!' said Lily.

'She's my worst enemy too!' said Courtney.

To celebrate the end of term there was a fancy dress party at school. Lily had spent ages working out what she was going to wear.

'All the other girls will come as fairies or witches, so I'm going to go as a ghost!' Lily decided.

With her white sheet and a ball and chain, Lily made a perfect ghost. When she got to the ball, she saw that someone else had had the same idea.

Lily went up to the other little ghost to have a chat. They found they had a lot in common and laughed at the same things. When they talked about what they disliked most, Lily said, 'I can't stand Courtney.'

'I can't stand Lily,' said Courtney.

Lily couldn't believe it! She took off her sheet, then pulled the sheet off the other ghost. It was Courtney! The two girls burst out laughing, and have been best friends ever since!

Confused conversations

The king was so sure that he was more important than everyone else that he never spoke to anyone directly. The only person he talked to was his servant, who was employed to carry messages to everyone else. When the king was eating a meal and wanted some bread, he would ask his servant to ask the queen to pass it to him.

As he got older, the servant became hard of hearing and kept getting the messages wrong. For example, instead of asking for the marmalade, the servant would say, 'Pass me the garden spade,'... and the queen would rush outside and get the gardener to bring a spade into the dining room.

'This is ridiculous, I never get what I want any more!' said the king. 'This servant is making me so cross that one day I'm may throw him in the dungeon!

And if anyone doesn't like it, I'll throw them in too!'

Once the king asked his servant to order him a cheese omelette. When the dish arrived at the table, the king tasted it and spat it out. 'Yuck! This is disgusting! What on earth is it?' boomed the king.

'It-It's the flea omelette you asked for, your majesty!' said the servant.

'I've had enough,' said the king. 'From now on, I'm just going to have to ask for myself, then I'll know what I'm getting.'

The king tried, and straight away got what he wanted. It was so simple! He started to enjoy talking to people. He even made friends. Life was wonderful, and from then on, everyone wanted to be the king's best friend.

Happy birthday!

As soon as the bell rang for the end of school, Andrew rushed out of the classroom. He wanted to get home as quickly as possible because today was his birthday. His mother would have made a big cake for him, perhaps grandma would be there, and his cousins, Ethan and Dan. And then he would get lots of presents!

'Hello, darling. How was your day?' asked his mother, opening the door to him. Andrew was a bit surprised and stood still for a moment.

'You'd better go and do your homework, Andrew,' said his mother.

'She can't have forgotten, can she?' thought Andrew. He went to his room and tried for an hour to concentrate, but was just too upset.

'Has Grandma called?' asked Andrew.

'No, why would she? She doesn't call every day,' said his mother.

'Oh, nothing,' said Andrew. 'Um, has Ethan been round?'

'No,' she said.

'How about Dan? Perhaps he rang the bell and you didn't hear,' Andrew persisted.

'No, darling. Nobody has called,' said his mother.

'That's impossible!' said Andrew. 'Today is my...'

But before Andrew could finish his mother stopped him. 'Oh, I think there might be someone in the sitting room,' she said.

Andrew opened the sitting room door and standing round a table heaving with presents were grandma, dad, Ethan, all his classmates, and Dan! Happy birthday, they yelled!

Santa goes on strike!

There was panic in Father Christmas's town! It was nearly midnight and so time for the present delivery to begin, but there was no sign of Father Christmas.

'I'm going to look for him,' said Sparky the elf.

Sparky went to Santa's house and knocked

on the door, but there was no answer. So Sparky decided to go in. He found Father Christmas lying on the bed, fast asleep!

'Father Christmas! The children are waiting for you!' said Sparky, shaking him.

'Leave me alone,' answered Father Christmas. 'I'm very upset and I can't deliver presents again. Never, ever again!'

'But the children will be upset!' said Sparky.

'What about me? No one has ever bothered sending me a present!' said Father Christmas. 'I have been giving people joy for years, and in all that time, not one person has thought that I might like a gift.'

'Give me two minutes and I'll be back,' said Sparky.

A few minutes later, Sparky came back with a sack full of letters.

'Look at this,' he said as he emptied the sack onto the floor. 'These are all the thank you letters from children all over the world. Can there be any greater present than this?'

'You're right, Sparky. The children's smiles are my presents,' said Father Christmas. 'Let's go and deliver presents!'

Vegetarian vampires

Dracula and his wife Draculine, were the happiest vampires in the world. At last they had a child. He was an adorable little vampire who they named Draclet.

The little boy represented all his parents' hopes for the future. But before long, the vampires knew there was something strange about Draclet. He didn't like blood!

'We're cursed!' said his parents. 'Whoever heard of a vampire that doesn't like blood!'

Draclet didn't even have big teeth like his parents.

'All the better for sucking blood, little one,' they answered.

'Sucking blood? Yuck! Why would you want to do that?' asked Draclet. 'Blood tastes disgusting, I prefer juice. I also like tomato ketchup and mashed potato!' said Draclet, hungrily.

Late one night, Dracula caught Draculine searching around in the refrigerator. 'What are you doing, my dear?' asked Dracula, suspiciously.

'Um, nothing,' said Draculine.

'Oh, no! I must be dreaming!' said Dracula, when he saw that Draculine was about to eat mashed potato covered with tomato ketchup.

Dracula decided to taste the strange food. 'Mmm', he thought it really was delicious.

In fact, ketchup and mashed potato became the family's favourite meal. From then on, none of them ever drank a drop of blood again.

Albert's rescue mission

Paws the little farm cat loved exploring. She climbed onto the haystack, slid down the drainpipes and ran through the fields of corn. Oh, it was so much fun!

One day, Paws was perching on the edge of the well, but because it was the middle of winter, the surface was very icy. Paws wasn't being very careful and she slipped and fell down to the bottom of the well! She was stuck! What could she do?

Paws sat on a ledge and tried to climb out but the walls were too steep and slippery. The poor cat cried out as loudly as she could, hoping that someone would hear her. And they did! In a few minutes, the well was surrounded by farm animals. But how could they rescue her? None of them could climb down the deep well.

'We need to make a chain,' said Albert the donkey. 'Mr Rooster, you and the other hens can hang on to my tail and to each other. There are enough of you to reach the bottom.'

'Okay, let's go, chickens! We need to work as fast as we can!'

From the bottom of the well, Paws heard what was going on and was filled with hope.

'Hold tight!' called the rooster. 'We're on our way!'

All the chickens held onto each others' wings and formed a chain long enough to reach Paws. She grabbed the rooster's wing and Albert began to walk, pulling the chain of chickens up behind him. When they were all safely out everyone cheered.

Rat attack!

Winter was coming to the leprechaun village. The leprechauns had stocked up on grain to ensure they had enough to eat during the harsh months. They had hundreds of sacks of grain in their storehouse. But the evil rats planned to steal the grain.

Every evening, the leprechauns would take turns to guard the grain store.

'If only we could rid the country of these horrible thieving rats,' thought Lucky the leprechaun. He thought and thought, and eventually came up with a clever plan.

That evening, he told the guards to go home. When the chief rat saw that the entrance was unguarded, he shouted to his army, 'Attack! Steal and eat as much grain as you can!'

But as they rushed into the grain store, the rats saw that they were not alone. Lucky was already there, opening a big sack of grain.

'What are you doing here?' shouted the chief rat.

'I'm a thief, just like you, and I'm just opening a delicious sack of grain,' replied Lucky. Putting a couple of grains in his mouth, he suddenly choked, 'This grain has been poisoned!' and fell to the ground.

'Poisoned grain aagh!' cried the rats. 'Come on, let's get out of here!'

The rats fled, and when he was sure he was alone, Lucky got to his feet. 'Rats really are very stupid creatures,' he smiled.

Simon and the frog

imon was little boy who lived in a small village in Africa. As soon as he finished school each day, Simon loved to leave his village and go for a long walk. He would wander around the savannah, looking at the plants and playing with the animals. He felt so happy and free doing this.

One day, when he was walking near the swamps, Simon heard a strange noise. It sounded like a wounded animal. Simon knew a lot about animals and could recognise the different sounds they made. He went toward the direction of the sound, certain that it was a cry for help.

Simon couldn't see a thing at first. But as he crouched down by the edge of the swamp, he saw a little frog, struggling in the water. The poor thing was tangled in a branch and couldn't get out. Simon picked it up and gently untangled the frog's foot. The tiny creature was shaking from head to toe.

'Thank you,' croaked the frog. 'Please don't eat me now, will you, little boy?'

'Of course I won't eat you!' laughed Simon.

'Please don't keep me in a cage, either,' croaked the frog.

'Don't worry. I like my own freedom and I like others to be free too!' said Simon.

'I'll never forget what you have done for me today,' croaked the frog. 'One day I will repay you for your great kindness.'

'Goodbye, little friend. I hope I see you again soon.'

Beware of foxes... and chickens!

reddy the fox had fallen madly in love!

'I love you with all my heart!' he told Charlotte the chicken.

'This young fox must have lost his mind! How can he be in love with me?' snorted Charlotte.

It was impossible for a fox to be in love with a chicken. Foxes like chicken, but only roast chicken, barbecued chicken, chicken casserole, or cold chicken slices! So Charlotte was a bit troubled.

'Why on earth are you in love with me?' asked Charlotte.

'Because you are so beautiful with your red feathers and beady eyes, and you're so warm and plump,' said the fox.

'WHAT?' gasped Charlotte. 'Did you say PLUMP?'

The young fox tried to hide his face in his tail. 'Yes, plump. I want to marry you!'

All of the farm animals were shocked when Charlotte introduced the young fox to her parents and her terrified friends. And Charlotte was very proud to walk into church on the arm of the handsome fox. It was a strange but wonderful ceremony. Everyone was enchanted, except Charlotte's grandma, who whispered in her ear, 'You should be careful, my girl. A fox is always a fox, you know!'

Charlotte smiled as she got into the car that took them off on honeymoon. A few weeks later, Charlotte came home alone. Everyone was delighted to see her and no one asked about the young fox. Nor did anyone ask where she had purchased her new red fur cloak.

Red can be best

When Gilly the giraffe was born, she was a surprise to her parents and all the other giraffes. As you know, giraffes usually have brown markings, but Gilly was covered with red patches. What a strange little giraffe she looked!

'There must be something wrong with her! She must be ill!' said her aunt Lofty.

'Maybe she's cursed!' said her cousin Sally.

Even the other little giraffes laughed at Gilly. Poor Gilly was very upset. Why did they tease her like that? She thought the red rather smart.

One day, the king of the giraffes wanted his son Gino to get married. But none of the girls Gino saw took his fancy.

'Of course, they are all kind and pretty, but I want someone unusual!'

Gino told his father. So the giraffe king sent his servants to search the land for an unusual female giraffe.

One of the servants went to Gilly's village and as soon as he saw her, he knew she would be perfect. Gilly had red markings he had never seen before. The servant asked whether Gilly would like to meet the young prince. She thought he was joking, but agreed to meet the prince.

When Gilly and Gino met, they discovered that they had lots in common and fell in love instantly. Gilly became the princess of giraffes. No one ever laughed at her again. In fact it became the height of fashion in the giraffe kingdom to have red markings on your body instead of brown!

The wishful fairy

 lvira the little fairy was not happy!

'I've had enough! I don't want to be gentle any more!' she shouted. 'In fact, I've had more than enough! I always have good table manners, never say anything rude, and I'm always quiet and attentive. It just isn't any fun at all!'

'But that's the way you should be,' replied her mother.

'That's just the problem. Why do fairies have to act like perfect little girls all the time?' asked Elvira.

'Because that's the way it is,' her mother said patiently.

'Well if that's the way it is, then I don't want to be a fairy any more!' sulked Elvira.

'Any ideas what else you would like to be?' asked her mother a little later. 'Perhaps you would like to be an astronaut, or a dragon, or a fish!'

'That's just silly!' said Elvira. 'No, I would like to be a witch! Witches are so lucky! They can do whatever they want. They don't do their homework, they talk in class, they tell scary stories, they make magic potions by mixing loads of weird things in a pot, and they even play tricks on people. They're great!'

But being a witch isn't all fun, as Elvira soon discovered!

'Did you know that witches don't get Christmas or birthday presents? They are not allowed to taste anything sweet, they are only allowed to wear black clothes, and their mothers never ever give them a cuddle!' said her mother

'Oh, no! That's awful!' she cried. 'I want to be a fairy forever!'

Andy finds a friend

Andy was upset because all the children in the village had gone away for the winter holidays; all of them except him, that is! So Andy found himself all alone. He would have no one to play with for two whole weeks! How annoying! Luckily, it was snowing. Andy loved playing in the snow.

'I know, I'll build myself a snowman,' thought Andy. He started by rolling a huge snowball to make the body, a smaller one for the head. Then he added two pieces of coal for the eyes, a carrot for a nose, twigs for arms and hands, and there it was! A magnificent snowman!

The snowman was nearly as tall as Andy himself. But what could he do with him now? The snowman, however wonderful, couldn't replace his friends.

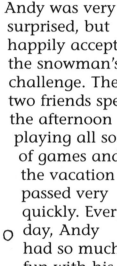

Suddenly, the snowman moved. Andy couldn't believe his eyes!

'*Brr!* It's so cold here!' said the snowman, rubbing his hands. 'Shall we have a race?'

Andy was very surprised, but happily accepted the snowman's challenge. The two friends spent the afternoon playing all sorts of games and the vacation passed very quickly. Every day, Andy had so much fun with his new friend.

At the end of the vacation, the snowman said sadly, 'It's getting warmer now Andy, and you know I will melt soon. But you mustn't be sad, because if you like, you can rebuild me every winter and we'll be able to play together again!'

And that is exactly what young Andy did!

Alfonso's tasty stew

There never was an animal as evil or cruel as the king of the rats. He and his gang had recently invaded the kitchens and pantry of the mighty castle in which they lived.

The lord of the castle was famous for his wonderful parties and the delicious food made by his top chef, Alfonso. Every night the lord would enjoy a different dish for his dinner.

Alfonso commanded his kitchen staff like the general of an army. He would not allow mistakes, untidiness, or sloppiness. All the

dishes had to be piping hot and taste delicious. But one evening, just as Alfonso was turning off the lights in the kitchen, he saw a great big fat rat rush out in front of him! Alfonso jumped back and watched the rat king admiring his kitchen kingdom.

Alfonso cunningly said, 'Dear rat, welcome to my kitchen.'

'I'm the king of this kitchen now. You will not be able to withstand my power,' cried the rat.

'Of course not. Your majesty, I've made an excellent soup for you and your army. You see the big casserole dish behind me?' said Alfonso. 'Inside it there is a fabulous feast.'

'Well, get out of the way so we can have some!' snarled the rat. Suddenly, a hideous black hoard of rats rushed into the casserole pot. Alfonso quickly slammed the lid on top of them.

'What is in this tasty stew?' asked the lord after dinner.

'Oh, I never give away my secrets,' said Alfonso, smiling.

Cock-a-doodle tooth fairy

 nuggled up in her bed, Tina didn't feel very well. She tossed and turned and felt really ill.

Now this was very serious, because Tina was the tooth fairy and if she couldn't do her job none of the teeth would be collected. Children would cry and wouldn't want to lose a tooth as they wouldn't get a coin in exchange. Some of them might never brush their teeth again. What a disaster!

'Drink some tea, my dear Tina,' said Mary the mole. 'It will make you feel better.'

'Thank you, dear friend. What am I going to do? Can you help me?' asked Tina.

'I'm afraid not,' replied Mary. 'I'm terribly short sighted. If I had to find a tiny little tooth, I'd probably come back with a teddy bear instead!'

'Oh, who can I trust to do the job?' sighed Tina.

'Why not a hen?' said Mary.

'A hen?' said Tina.

'I know a hen who would be happy to help you,' said Mary.

'Do you think she'd be able to do my job?' Tina wondered.

Harriet the hen did Tina's job brilliantly! She crept silently into a child's bedroom and without disturbing the child lifted the corner of a pillow, knowing exactly where to find the tooth.

It didn't matter that a tradition had changed. Instead of a coin, Harriet put a tiny chocolate egg under the pillows instead!

When Tina felt better, she returned to work and delivered coins again, and Harriet was the happiest hen in the world.

A friend in need

In the African village where Simon lived, the summers were very hot. But this year had been a disaster! There hadn't been a drop of rain for months! The sun was scorching, the earth was dry and there was barely any water around. Every village was in a bad way. What could be done?

Every day, Simon went to collect water from the well. The well was quite far away and Simon had to walk a long distance. One day, Simon couldn't find any water and was so upset that he started crying. Suddenly, he heard a little croak nearby. It was the frog that he had saved from the swamp!

'Hello,' croaked the frog. 'Why are you crying?'

'There's no water left for us to drink,' said Simon.

'I can help you. Frogs know all the secrets about water. We even know how to make rain fall!' croaked the frog. 'Just go home and trust me,' he croaked.

Simon went home feeling hopeful. Without saying anything to the others, he waited, his fingers crossed.

Finally, night fell on the village. The first croaks came quietly, and then got louder and louder. It was the frogs; they were singing a rain song!

All night they sang, and in the early hours of the morning the rain started to fall. Big, fat raindrops plopped to the ground! Everyone came out of their houses and danced in the rain. The drought was over thanks to a friendly frog!

George, the giant mailman

George was quite an ordinary giant. He was tall, ugly, stupid, and had a huge appetite. But George had a delicate stomach. He still ate three cows, two sheep, and a hundred potatoes for lunch, just like other giants. But children for dinner, didn't agree with him.

As you know, children are an important part of a giant's diet. They usually have chilled children for pudding. But if George tasted the tiniest bit of a child, he would start to burp and couldn't stop! People could hear him burping from miles away. They were burps so huge that their vibrations would knock everyone off their feet!

The people of Puddleton were furious. They hated the giant because he ate their animals, then destroyed their trees to make toothpicks. Even though George hardly ever ate children, the people could smell his burps.

The mayor was sent to ask George to stop burping.

'How am I supposed to do that?' answered the giant.

'It's simple. Don't eat any more children!' said the mayor.

'I agree, but only if I can be the village mailman,' said George. 'Yes! I have such long legs that I can deliver the mail much faster than any other mailman, and the exercise will do me good,' smiled the giant.

If you go to Puddleton for the day, don't forget to visit the mail office because there you might see the world's only giant mailman!

Nuts about numbers

Alexis was having problems. "Come on, Alexis! You must be able to answer this question. It's easy. What is six add six?' asked her teacher.

Alexis couldn't answer her teacher. She hated addition, subtraction, multiplication, division. In fact, she hated all sums. She liked reading and writing, but not numbers.

One day, Alexis saw an advertisement in the newspaper about a company that could help you with your sums. All you had to do was pay some money each month. But exactly how much money was far too complicated for Alexis to work out. She already had enough sums to tackle. What could she do? Not much for now as it was nearly the end of term.

Alexis loved cycling, but one afternoon she realised she had gone too far and was lost.

'Do you know where Steventon is?' Alexis asked a boy walking past.

'Yes, just take the fourth road on the right, the second on the left, and then ride for about ten minutes,' said the boy. 'You'll go over two bridges. Cycle past the big clock and then it's straight on to Steventon. It's easy!'

'Do you like numbers or something?' asked Alexis.

'I love them,' replied the boy.

'Would you help me with my sums?' asked Alexis.

'Of course I will. It will only take about fifteen to twenty minutes!' teased the boy.

He was true to his word, and next term Alexis topped the sums tests!

D for cat!

iff was having problems! 'Grrr! Grrr!' he growled.

'No,' said Fluff. 'Say 'Miaow'! If you don't try, how are you ever going to become a real cat?'

'It's easy for you. You are a cat!' said Biff.

A few hours ago, Biff the dog had decided that he wanted to be a cat. So he asked for Fluff's help. Biff wanted a change in his life. He had had enough of burying bones, running after sticks, and wagging his tail. He wanted to be gracious and agile. He wanted to chase mice and climb trees. But it wasn't that easy. He had to learn how to sound like a cat first!

'Griaow, Griaow!' went Biff.

'No, Biff. Mia-ow, Mia-ow!' said Fluff. 'You're not doing very well at this. Let's try something else.

Let's look at the way a cat sits. Watch what I do and copy me.'

Fluff sat down elegantly, while looking straight ahead with her feet side by side, and her tail still. Her head was carefully tilted, and her eyes were half closed.

Biff sat with a hunched back, his legs far apart, his tail wagging, and his tongue hanging out.

'Biff, are you absolutely sure you really want to be a cat?' asked Fluff, frowning.

'Oh, I don't know. But I do know one thing, it's dinner time!' said Biff, sniffing the air.

Fluff watched Biff running back to the house looking absolutely nothing like a cat.

'Somehow, I think Biff's much better as a dog,' smiled Fluff.

Sleepyhead

rriiiing! Paul's alarm clock went off at seven o'clock, like it did every morning. Paul wanted to sleep for five minutes longer, but the stupid alarm clock kept ringing!

Paul buried his head under the pillow and snatched the alarm clock and hurled it across the room!

The alarm clock knocked over a chair, and the chair fell onto the cat's basket. The cat was so scared, it jumped up onto his desk and knocked over his lamp! The noise frightened the cat even more, so he jumped out of the window straight onto the head of the gardener, who was watering the plants!

The gardener was annoyed by whatever it was that had landed on him, but was even angrier when he saw that his wig was attached to the cat's claws! In his haste to get his wig back, he had left the garden hose spraying everyone who walked past!

A jet of water from the hose made a newspaper boy fall off his bike. All the newspapers flew out of his bag and blew down the street.

A sheet of newspaper blew into a boy's face just as he aimed to kick a football. He mis-kicked and the ball smashed through a window.

Then, there was calm. Paul, who had woken up by now, looked out of the window and called down to the gardener, 'You haven't seen my cat by any chance, have you?'

Dog's dinner

asper the dog was having a very long day. He couldn't understand why the hours between breakfast and lunch, and lunch and dinner seemed to last for so long. The minutes were crawling by slower than snails and his stomach was beginning to rumble again.

'Why did there have to be hours between meals?' he pondered. 'Surely it would make far more sense to have meals available whenever you wanted them. Like now for instance!'

Jasper started to think about roast chicken and potatoes, beef and gravy, and best of all, sausages! He licked his jowls as he dreamed about a dish full of delicious sausages. But then remembered, it was ages until dinnertime.

He looked enviously at Snuffles the cat, who was contentedly napping on the patio. Snuffles didn't seem to care when he got fed, in fact sometimes he didn't even bother to come home for dinner!

Jasper wished that he could forget about food and doze off for an hour or two, but his stomach was grumbling too loudly for that.

Just then, little Bobby ran into the kitchen and headed straight for the cookie jar. As he munched on his cookie, he noticed Jasper's hungry face and so he went and got him a dog biscuit from the cupboard.

Jasper happily chewed on his biscuit. He decided it was okay to wait for dinner when there were biscuits to be had.

The lonely beetle

yrtle the beetle was very lonely. No one came to visit her, except the little midges that sometimes flew into her cave. It was time she made some friends.

She wanted to befriend someone classy like a butterfly, a bee, or a dragonfly. She knew the well respected swift who lived in the tree above her cave, but she was too scared to talk to him because he was so big and important.

'Would you like to be my friend?' called Myrtle as a bee flew past her cave.

'No time and too much work to do,' replied the bee.

Then a butterfly with beautiful royal blue wings fluttered by. 'Hey, would you like to be my friend?' called Myrtle.

The butterfly didn't even look at the beetle as it flew past.

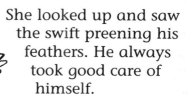

A dragonfly buzzed up to myrtle's cave and caused so much dust to fly into her face that she burst into tears.

Myrtle heard a voice from above her say, 'Life can sometimes be so unfair.'

She looked up and saw the swift preening his feathers. He always took good care of himself.

The swift glided down to the unhappy beetle and said, 'Come on, Myrtle, don't be sad. Climb onto my back and I'll take you for a ride. It will help you forget about what has just happened.'

With a *vroooooom*, the swift flapped its wings and off they went. Myrtle was flying.

It was Myrtle's first ever flight and Flash the swift soon became her first best friend, and a classy one at that!

Odd one out

It's always the same. Whenever Brandon wants to play with the older children they always say the same thing, 'No, you're too young.'

His big brother Leon is much nicer to him when it is just the two of them. But it's still not even worth asking to play computer games with him because he always says, 'You're too young!'

When the older children play hide-and-seek, they let Brandon join in as long as he always does the counting while they hide. Yesterday, the older kids had a football tournament. Well, a mini tournament, because there wasn't very many of them.

Brandon was hoping the children might let him play. But as usual they said, 'You're too young.'

So, Brandon sat down and watched the others play.

Suddenly, the football hit his brother's friend Jack, and knocked him over. Jack started to cry because he had grazed his knee and all the others ran away. They knew there was going to be trouble because they weren't supposed to play on the road.

Brandon went over and sat down next to Jack and asked, 'Have you hurt yourself?'

Jack didn't answer. He was sobbing too hard to speak. Brandon offered Jack a mint.

'They always make me feel better,' he said comfortingly. Jack looked at Brandon and smiled. Brandon may not have played football but he had made a new friend!

Ben's plan

oe the mole was very angry!

'This time it's war!' announced the mole.

'Don't you think that's a bit much?' said Ben the bear.

'No way!' replied Joe. 'We've all had enough of the hunters! Not only do they hunt, but they also ruin our beautiful forest by firing their guns and clomping all over the place. They stomp all over the plants, the grass, everywhere! They're not very bright, so I reckon we can easily chase them out of the forest!'

'But how do we do that?' asked Skip the dog.

Everyone was surprised to see Skip as he hunted in the forest with his owner.

'What are you doing here, Skip?' demanded Joe.

'Well, I love listening to your discussions, and I agree with you. I don't like hunting either,' said Skip. 'Do you think I like going out with my master in the middle of winter, running around in the muddy marshes, and being deafened by the loud bullets being fired nearby?'

'But the marshes are lovely,' protested Daisy the duck.

'Listen, I have a better idea,' said Ben. 'Skip can help us get rid of the hunters. When the hunters approach our forest, bark three times, then we'll know we must hide.'

Ben's plan worked perfectly, and Skip was delighted to be helping the other animals.

The hunters soon got bored with not finding any animals in the forest and went to look elsewhere, much to the joy of Skip and his new found friends.

Sam the sad skeleton

Sam the skeleton lived in a graveyard in the grounds of a castle. For company, Sam had spiders and some old skeletons, who played cricket using their arm bones as bats.

Sam was bored to death of life in the graveyard. One night, as he walked in the woods near the castle, he saw a light flickering in the distance. As Sam walked closer he saw a little fairy, who was in the process of turning a mushroom into a toad, and a toad into a mushroom.

'What are you doing here at this time of night?' asked Sam.

'I didn't do very well at fairy school today, so my teacher said that I had to turn five hundred mushrooms into toads, and five hundred toads into mushrooms,' replied the fairy.

'But that's impossible!' said Sam.

'Not really, fairies can do it pretty quickly. It's just very boring,' sighed the fairy. 'In fact, everything around here is boring. There are only elves and fairies to play with.'

'I'm bored too,' said Sam. 'Who would want to be friends with me? My bones clatter when I walk and it sounds like the wind whistling a sad tune when I laugh.'

'I think you're much more interesting than everyone else. You're not like the elves or the fairies,' smiled the fairy. 'We could play all kinds of fun games together!'

So, if you ever go to a fair, make sure you go on the ghost train, because there you will find Sam and his fairy friend making funny faces and creepy noises to amuse you.

The town cat

One day, an alley cat decided he'd had enough of living in the city.

'I wasn't meant to live in such poverty. I should run around in fields!' he said to himself. It took the cat a long time to reach the countryside! He had to cross many busy roads, then go through a dark forest full of creepy noises that almost scared him to death! Finally, he came upon fields of corn and beautiful wild flowers.

At the end of a path, the cat saw a little farm. Tired and hungry, he made his way toward the farm. He slipped under a fence and into a field.

'What are you doing here?' brayed a donkey.

'I've come a long way and I'm tired. Could you put me up for a while?' asked the cat.

'You are not a farm animal. There's no place for you here!' the donkey snorted. 'Be on your way, scruffy old cat!'

So, the sad little alley cat padded up to the pigsty to try his luck.

'I've come a long way. Could you put me up for a while?' the cat asked a pig.

'Certainly not,' grunted the pig. 'You are not a farm animal! Be on your way, mangy old cat!'

Feeling very unhappy, the cat was just about to leave when a little girl appeared in the porch. 'Daddy!' shouted the girl. 'Come and look! There is a cute little cat here! Can he stay with us.'

'I don't see why not,' said dad.

The little girl gently picked up the cat. Soon he was made to feel so welcome that he stayed there always.

Sophie and the salt marshes

During the summer vacation, Sophie often goes to stay with her Aunt Izzie in France. She loves it there because it's like being on an island. Aunt Izzie has a very unusual job. She works as a salt farmer in Brittany, and summer is harvest time.

This year Sophie went there in spring and helped to prepare the salt marshes.

The farmers need to make sure that the water flows through all the channels to gather the salt, before it flows down to the pans. On the pans, the sun and the wind make the water evaporate until nothing is left but a huge circle of dry salt.

It's very peaceful in the marshes. There are pools stretching out for miles. Aunt Izzie says that some people want to destroy this land and build houses on it, but she and the other salt farmers are not going to let them. At the moment, the marshes are protected because they are a haven for birds and flowers.

The first salt forms a sort of foam rather than a crust. The farmers call it the salt flower, and they believe it is the best type of salt.

Sophie always arrives after the harvest of the salt flowers because it is before her vacation starts, but collecting the second, bigger crop of salt is just as much fun.

At lunch, Sophie and her aunt have a picnic. After eating, Aunt Izzie tells Sophie wonderful stories.

During winter, Sophie always remembers these stories when she's tucked up in bed.

The fairy-witch

my had everything she needed to become a perfect little witch. Her father was a grand wizard and her mother was a famous witch. But Amy wasn't like the other witches. She couldn't hurt anything, not even a fly! Whenever she wanted to cast a bad spell on someone, she managed to make something good happen instead.

Once, Amy wanted to turn a little boy into an ugly toad, but she turned him into a prince!

'Will you stop this now!' said her mother. 'You must stop being so gentle and kind. It's not right.'

At witch school it was just the same. Amy was always ready to help people. Instead of copying her classmates' work, she would help them with their homework, and she was never, ever cross.

Amy's teachers didn't know what to do with her. If she carried on like this, she wouldn't get her witches' diploma.

One day, the head witch asked Amy into her office.

'No pupil has ever left this school without a diploma,' she said. 'Don't you care about the school's reputation? Can't you try to start being naughty?' she begged.

'But I only have good thoughts,' said Amy.

The head witch sighed. 'There's only one answer then,' she said. 'You will have to attend the fairy school!'

Amy's parents were not happy about this, but they agreed that she could go.

Amy was welcomed with open arms at fairy school. She soon became a star pupil and brought happiness and joy to everyone around her.

Sweet treats

Alice, Chris, and Tom loved eating chocolate. After school they would hurry to the store. Each time they went, they would taste something new. But one day, they arrived at the store to find it had closed.

'Where will we buy chocolate now?' asked Alice.

After the summer vacation, the three friends were walking home from school when they had a surprise. There, where the old chocolate shop used to be, was a new shop with a sign on the door saying: 'Sweet Heaven'.

They went in and gasped with wonder. The place was crammed with jars full of gorgeous treats. The strangest ones were the black ones that were so dark they looked like little pieces of night.

'Be very careful,' said the storekeeper. 'Don't eat too many of those ones, or you may get a shock.'

The children took no notice of him, and as soon as they got out of the store they started gobbling up the unusual candy.

Suddenly, they felt very strange. Everything around them started to change. The trees turned black and the sky grew dark. The whole town was plunged into deepest night.

Then, in a blink of an eye, everything went back to normal and the sun was shining again. The friends looked at each other and wondered whether it had all been a dream. The friends would never know.

But one thing was certain. Alice, Chris, and Tom never ate so many treats again!

The snake-flower

linky the snake is a small creature who is always in danger of being squashed .

'Sorry,' replied the rhino, 'I didn't see you down there.'

'This is the story of my life,' groaned the little snake. 'No one looks for anything that lives on the ground. Flowers are about the only thing that everyone is careful not to crush underfoot.'

With that, Slinky slithered under a bush and began to think. 'That's it! I'll become a flower!'

'Hey! You're ruining my web!' said a voice.

'Sorry to interrupt you Esme, but I heard that you caught a lot of butterflies this morning,' said the snake.

'Yes, but I didn't eat their wings. They give me indigestion,' replied Esme. 'I wish I could find some midges. They're much tastier.'

'Esme, could I use the butterfly wings? Could you to tie them round my head using your thread, please?' asked Slinky.

When the little snake-flower appeared with his head decorated with butterfly wings, all the other creatures came to admire him.

'Esme, why don't you weave a beautiful web to replace your broken one?' said the snake.

Before long, millions of midges appeared. So, Esme and Slinky had a real feast on the midges. trapped in snake-flower's web. After all, spider-artists are still spiders and snake-flowers are still snakes!

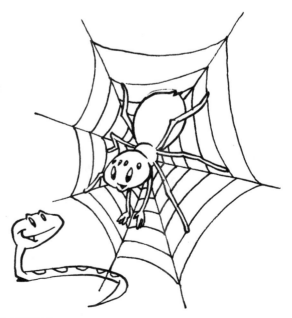

Toys, toys, toys!

When he closed his book, Nick was deep in thought. He had just read the story of two children who, one night, locked themselves in a toy store. All night they played with whatever toys and games they liked. For one whole night, all the toys were theirs!

'Oh, I wish I could do that,' Nick said to himself. 'Imagine being able to play with the latest toys!'

The next day after school, Nick went to the mall. He hid himself in a corner and waited for closing time. He was so worried that someone might find him, he could hardly breathe. Then he heard the announcement saying that the stores were closing. He was very excited. Soon he would be able to play with all toys.

But just when he was beginning to relax, Nick felt a hand on his shoulder! He looked up and saw his uncle Michael, who worked as a security guard.

'What are you doing here?' asked his uncle. 'You should be at home at this time of night.'

Nick was so surprised he burst into tears. Between sobs, he explained that he just wanted to have a look at all the toys.

'Well, come with me and I'll take you round the shop,' smiled Uncle Michael. 'I'll just call your parents and let them know you are here,' he added.

Nick couldn't believe it! He took his uncle's hand and together they looked at all the toys in the store. It was magical! Nick realised that all he needed to do was ask properly and his dreams could come true.

A sheep in wolf's clothing

Steven the sheep was fed up of his brothers and sisters being eaten by wolves. None of them would ever do anything to try to stop it because they were too frightened. Even the shepherd locked himself in his house, leaving the sheep to defend themselves.

One morning, Steven went to ask for help from the wise old owl. The owl said he could teach Steven wolf language in exchange for some of his wool.

'What are you going to do with my wool?' Steven asked.

'I'm going to give it to the birds so they can build their nests,' said the owl.

'Can we start the lesson now, then?' asked Steven.

The wise old owl was a good teacher, and Steven was a very good student.

When night fell, Steven went back to the meadow. His brothers and sisters wouldn't believe that he had learned wolf language. To show them, Steven went behind the shepherd's house and howled.

Suddenly, there was a sound of locking bolts, and the shepherd's terrified face peered through the window.

Steven howled again. In the distance, the other sheep could hear a howl in reply.

'What are the wolves saying?' asked one of the youngest sheep.

'That now they know the baddest wolf in the land has claimed this meadow, they'll never come back to our meadow again,' said Sandy.

All the sheep cheered and they lived in peace ever more.

The nightmare-eater!

Emma was very upset. The last few nights, every time she fell asleep she had horrible nightmares, full of scary people. She wanted to have some nice dreams again. But how can you stop nightmares? Emma didn't know what to do, so she decided to ask her big brother for some help.

Billy listened to his little sister, then thought hard for a while. After a couple of minutes his face lit up.

'I have an idea! We will make a nightmare-eater!' said Billy.

'What's a nightmare-eater?' asked Emma.

'A nightmare-eater is a creature that gobbles up your nightmares as soon as they begin. He's always hungry and never gets full,' explained Billy.

Billy went to get some paper and crayons and began drawing. He gave the picture to Emma.

It was a picture of a very strange animal. It was red with green wings, big eyes, a fat tummy, and a very long trunk.

'The trunk sucks up the nightmares,' said Billy. 'It works really well, you'll see. All you need to do is put the drawing under your pillow every night, and the nightmare-eater will eat up all of your bad dreams. You will be able to sleep peacefully from now on.'

Emma took the picture and went to bed. She put the picture under her pillow and she soon fast asleep. Not a single nightmare visited her that night!

Every night after that, Emma had lovely dreams. She didn't have anymore nightmares because the nightmare-eater gobbled them all up!

Mark's important letter

here was a new mailman in the forest, or should I say 'mailbadger' in charge of delivering all the letters throughout the woodland.

'Hello, I've got a letter for you!' called the badger, standing at Mark's mail box.

Mark the bear raised a sleepy eyelid and thought, 'Silly badger. Didn't he know it was rude to disturb animals that are trying to hibernate for the winter? Who was this badger anyway? Where had he come from? Bear could see that the badger was flapping a letter about excitedly.

'It has an "urgent" stamp on it,' said the badger.

'Let me sleep, you hairy fool, or you will get a very close look at my teeth!' the bear growled.

The badger was uneasy. He was new to the job, but that was no reason for the bear to speak to him like that.

But what was in the letter? What was important enough to disturb a hibernating bear? Should the young badger open it? His paws were already shaking with nerves. He quickly tore open the letter.

'Mark, Mark, wake up!' cried the badger, as he read the letter.

'Oh, not you again. I ought to...' began the bear. But when Mark saw the letter, he stopped. 'I'm so sorry, young badger.'

You see, the letter announced the arrival of spring. When spring arrives, it's time to get up. From that day on, Mark and the young badger were the best of friends.

The vegetarian wolf

 obert looked extremely confused and baffled.

'Emily, guess what? I've just seen a wolf in the vegetable patch, and it was eating carrots!' he said.

'Don't be so silly, Robert. Get the table ready for dinner, please. It was probably just a big rabbit or something,' said his wife.

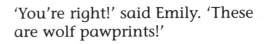

But Robert had not been mistaken. He had seen Felix, the wolf who ate vegetables. Felix was no ordinary wolf. Orphaned when he was only a baby, he had been brought up by rabbits and fed carrots and cabbages. This meant that Felix hardly ever ate meat. But a wolf is still a wolf, and by nature loves meat, so he persuaded the rabbits to try some meat.

'I definitely saw a wolf,' Robert insisted. 'Come and look.'

Leaving her cooking, Emily went to see what her husband was making so much fuss about.

'You're right!' said Emily. 'These are wolf pawprints!'

Not far from the garden, the wolf was carrying two carrots and a cabbage in his mouth. Suddenly, Robert and Emily heard a loud noise coming from the kitchen. Before they could stop it, a rabbit ran out with their dinner in its mouth! 'Well, I've never seen anything so strange before in my life!' gasped Robert.

That evening, a wolf and two rabbits shared a feast of roast chicken, carrots and cabbage!

Blinky's flight

 linky the mole was feeling very unhappy in his underground home.

'It's so dark and stuffy in here. I've really had enough of this place,' she sighed. 'I wish I could go outside and look at the sky and the lovely clouds and warm my fur in the sun! But if I go outside, the farmers and their dogs will try to catch me. What can I do?'

Just then, Blinky heard a noise above her head, *toc-toc-toc*! It was Feathers the crow.

'Oh, excuse me,' said Feathers, as he stopped pecking. 'I was looking for some earthworms, but it's so hot outside that they've all gone underground. I haven't eaten anything for two days and I'm beginning to get very hungry.'

Blinky wished she could go outside with the bird. 'Is it sunny out there?' she asked the crow.

'Yes,' replied Feathers, 'the weather is lovely. The sky is so blue, the clouds so few.'

'Feathers, if I get you a big tub of worms, would you do something for me?' she asked.

'For some tasty earthworms, I'll do whatever you like, Blinky!' joked the crow.

'I want to you take me to see the sky,' smiled the little mole.

So, Feathers took Blinky for a ride on his back.

'This is such an adventure!' said Blinky, as they soared higher and higher up to the clouds.

Since then, in exchange for a few worms, Blinky the mole flies up into the sky.

Horrible hiccups

Nina was a very greedy young witch. She loved gorging on pumpkins more than anything else. In fact, she ate so many that at Halloween, people in her town often found it impossible to find any to use as decorations.

One day, just as Nina had eaten a fourth pumpkin for breakfast, she hiccuped…once…twice…three times! The hiccups went on and on and made her very cross, so she went to see the witch doctor.

'Doctor–*hic*–help me–*hic*! I've had–*hic*–these hiccups for–*hic*–ages!' she complained.

The doctor looked at Nina's tongue, peered into her ears, tapped her on the head, and said, 'Well it looks like you are suffering from Pumpkinitus! You'll have to stop eating pumpkins for a while.'

Nina ignored the doctor's advice and kept on eating as much pumpkin as she could between hiccups. Sometimes, the hiccups were so huge, they would send her flying across the room. Soon, Nina's whole body turned green and she was covered in nasty spots! Then, Nina started getting smaller and smaller, until she was only the size of a toad!

'Yum, a toad! That will be perfect for my soup tonight,' said the witch doctor, picking it up by its foot.

'Help!' gasped Nina, falling out of her bed. 'What an awful nightmare–*hic*! I'm never–*hic*–eating pumpkins–*hic*–again!' said Nina.

And she never has!

When chickens had teeth

Did you know that long ago, chickens had teeth? Yes, beautiful white teeth! And they weren't the friendly, quiet birds that we know today. They were fantastic hunters, and many animals, even foxes, were afraid of them.

Humans, who looked like big monkeys in those days, used to live in fear of bumping into a fierce group of chickens. Back then chickens ruled most of the land. But one day when the chickens were pecking at some apples, disaster struck!

'Ouch!' cried a chicken. 'I've just bitten on a little stone.'

'You idiot,' said the others. 'There are no stones in apples.'

'This apple isn't ripe! I've just lost one of my teeth.'

'What?! Show us!' yelled the other chickens.

In those days, chickens kept all their teeth throughout life–losing one was almost unheard of. Horrified, they puffed up their feathers and strutted back to the flock to announce the news. By now, quite a few of the chickens had lost some teeth. Sobbing loudly, they carried the lost teeth in their wings. Eventually, the disease passed on to all chickens, even the proud cockerels.

This story may sound ridiculous, but that is the reason why chickens are toothless. Perhaps if they had toothbrushes and brushed their teeth every day, they would still be rulers of the world!

Prickly journey for Pickle

ickle was a hedgehog who wanted to visit the nearby town. After buying a train ticket for the journey, Pickle waited on the empty platform. But when the train arrived, he had a nasty shock. All the carriages were full to bursting! Pickle managed to squeeze onto the train, but finding a seat was going to be very difficult.

He tried to make his way through the crowd to find a free seat, but as he went, his sharp spines pricked all the passengers. As you can imagine, the passengers weren't happy about this and shouted at poor Pickle. What could he do? In the end, the passengers decided for him. They forced Pickle off the train!

Pickle waited patiently for the next train, but it was just as crowded as the first one, and Pickle was thrown out again!

'This is too much,' Pickle sighed. 'I may as well give up. I'm never going to get to town.'

The disappointed little hedgehog was about to leave the station when he heard the train driver calling his name.

Pickle walked to the front of the train and discovered that the train driver was his cousin, Bristles.

'Hello, Pickle! I haven't seen you for ages,' said his cousin. 'I'm going to town. Do you want to come along? Well, climb aboard and join me in the cab!'

Pickle happily climbed up next to his cousin in the front of the train. There was plenty of room next to the driver's seat and he wasn't in anyone's way. The train pulled out of the station and off he went to town.

No go in the snow!

ongo was warm and cosy in his basket, until...

'Pongo, come and look. It's snowing!' called Alex.

'Not again!' sighed Pongo.

All the other dogs seem to love rolling around in snowflakes, but not Pongo.

As far as he's concerned, snow is cold and it sticks to his fur, and even worse, it means that he will have to chase snowballs and look like a complete idiot.

'Why are children so different to dogs?' wondered Pongo. 'They always think we like the same things as them. Do I make Alex jump after sticks? Do I wake him up in the middle of a dream and make him go out for a walk? Do I ruffle his head? No!'

'Come on, Pongo, we're going out,' said Alex.

'Well I might as well say goodbye to this cosy moment,' thought Pongo, miserably.

When it's not snowing or raining, Pongo likes going out, especially with Alex, because he always has a treat for him in his pocket. They usually meet up with some friends, so while the children play, Pongo, Thistle, and Damson race up and down on the lawn. They're not allowed to, but dogs can't read notices, can they? And they don't understand what people say to them. Well, they only understand what they want to understand, if you know what I mean!

'Pongo! If you don't come here now, I'm going out on my own. There's lots of snow out there for us to play in,' cried Alex. Suddenly, the door slammed shut! Alex had left!

'At last I think we understand each other,' yawned Pongo.

The big baby bird

Mr and Mrs Blue Tit had just finished building their nest. At last, Mrs Blue Tit had somewhere to put the eggs she was about to lay. Soon there were three pretty eggs, warm and safe in the comfy nest. Mr and Mrs Blue Tit were so happy that they flew up to the top of the tree to sing for joy.

But what they didn't realise as they trilled and tweeted was that a cuckoo had landed in their nest. The cuckoo was much bigger than the blue tits and very lazy. She couldn't be bothered to waste time building a nest of her own and thought she might as well lay her egg in the blue tits' nest.

When they arrived home, the blue tits didn't notice anything. There was one extra egg, but as they didn't know how to count they didn't notice an extra one.

Finally, the eggs hatched. Mr and Mrs Blue Tit were a little surprised to see that one of the chicks was much bigger and didn't look like them at all, but how beautiful he was!

And what an appetite! All day long the poor birds exhausted themselves gathering enough food for their huge baby, who was always much hungrier than the others.

The day came when the birds were old enough to fly away.

'Bye, Dad! Bye, Mother!' they called .

'Cuckoo!' sang the little cuckoo. But his parents couldn't understand him, so they waved a sad farewell.

The following year, Mr and Mrs Blue Tit carefully prepared their nest for more babies. Hopefully, this time the cuckoo would lay her eggs in her own nest.

To the rescue!

There was a golden beach nestled in a cove on Westerly Island. Many creatures lived on the beach and even more came to visit in summer. All of these beach-goers were supervised by Mr Crab, the lifeguard. He was always looking out for everyone, ready to help if any trouble occurred.

It was a beautiful sunny day at the beach and that meant there would be lots of visitors. Mr Crab braced himself for a busy day, and busy he was!

There were so many families to watch out for and so many things to do that Mr Crab completely forgot to have any lunch. He gratefully accepted when his friend, Mr Starfish, offered to take over his post for an hour.

Although Mr Starfish tried to keep up the beach look-out, he was a dozy creature and soon dropped off to sleep.

Mr Crab was just tucking into a plate of seaweed salad when he sensed something wasn't right. He looked up from his lunch to see one of the mouse children struggling in the waves. The poor little one was splashing about and kept disappearing below the surface of the water.

Mr Crab leaped up and darted into the water. Within seconds he had towed the young mouse back to safety on the shore.

The mouse family thanked Mr Crab over and over again. That is when Mr Crab decided that he would train another crab to help with the beach look-out. Starfish may be friendly and helpful, but they don't make very alert lifeguards!

Secret agent 008

Whenever anyone asked Matthew what he wanted to do when he grew up he always said, 'I want to be a spy!' In fact, he already thought of himself as a spy and was always snooping around the house. He had even read his little sister's secret diary, which was a very naughty thing to do.

Matthew's parents thought his hobby was quite amusing, but they also thought it was a bit much sometimes. He was always hiding behind doors, listening to their conversations and taking notes.

'Matthew,' said his mother, 'people are allowed to have a few secrets, you know.'

'Nothing is secret from me. I'm secret agent 008!' said Matthew.

How could his parents make him understand that he shouldn't spy on people or listen into conversations and phone calls?

One day, Matthew's parents found a tape-recorder he had been using to record their conversations! Dad turned it on and said into the microphone, 'Matthew is being quite naughty at the moment. I think we'll have to send him to the countryside for a few years, perhaps to a farm miles away from here.'

When Matthew heard the recording he was very upset. He ran into his parents' bedroom and said, 'I don't want to go to live on a farm, I want to stay here!'

'Who said anything about going to a farm?' asked dad.

'Um, well… ' mumbled Matthew.

'Perhaps you shouldn't believe everything you hear!' said dad.

Matthew then realised that spying wasn't much fun when the joke was on him!

The hungry mice

Tina and Nina put on their jackets, picked up their tiny baskets and set off. They looked to the right and to the left, before coming out of their hole. For the moment it looked clear. There was no sign of Manx, the cat.

The two mice are very wary of Manx because he often pounces when they least expect it! But it was lunchtime and the crafty creature had probably gone to sleep after a big meal.

Tina and Nina were also always on the lookout for Harry, the next door's dog who loves chasing them. But Harry was nowhere to be seen either.

The mice took a deep breath. Now they faced the hardest task of all that of getting into the cheese store! The store is usually guarded by lots of big, dirty sewer rats. What chance would two little mice have against those monsters!

But there were no rats around either. How lucky! Tina crept behind her sister, trembling with fear.

'It's too quiet,' she whispered. 'I think we should go home.'

'No,' said Nina. 'I can smell a lovely, strong cheese nearby.'

The two little mice had barely managed to climb up onto the counter when a bright light made them freeze in terror. It was the storekeeper shining a torch all over the store to scare them away.

The mice grabbed a piece of cheese, jumped down and raced home. What a difficult life it is for mice. Imagine if you had to go through this when you wanted some dinner!

Trunk trouble

umper woke this morning with a blocked nose.

'Bubby, I can't breathe! I'm ill,' he honked.

'It's just a cold,' said his mother, feeling Bumper's clammy forehead with her trunk. 'It's your own fault. I've told you not to swim after dark! If only you'd stop having all those water fights with your brother.'

'But I didn't swim at all,' said Bumper. 'Can you check my trunk, I think there's something stuck up there. It's tickling me.'

Mrs Elephant gave her son a handkerchief so big you could use it as a curtain. 'Come on, blow hard!' she said.

Bumper blew as hard as he could. He turned bright red in the face and his eyes started watering. Now his mother was really worried. What could she do?

Suddenly, Bumper sneezed so loudly that all the animals in the savannah

thought it was the beginning of a storm. But what's that? A long, long way from the river, a fish was wriggling and squirming at Bumper's feet.

'Now where did that fish come from?' said Bumper's mother. Then it dawned on her. The fish had come from her son's nose!

Mrs Elephant grew very angry, and when an elephant gets angry there's a lot of noise.

'Bumper, you are nothing more than a fibber and a rascal!' she boomed. 'Not only did you go swimming last night, but you were spraying water with your trunk without checking what was in the water first. That's how this poor fish ended up in your trunk!'

Hungry hedgehogs

Hayley, Hamish, and Hattie were scurrying along one behind the other without looking behind them. When the little hedgehogs left home, their mother told them to look out for foxes, but they forgot her advice as soon as they left home.

Our three friends didn't glance behind themselves once. They were too eager to reach the orchard where big, juicy apples hung from the branches, ready to drop.

The moment the little hedgehogs reached the orchard they started eating the apples. Not once did they stop to look behind them. The apples were delicious, and soon their tummies were full.

Hamish, the greediest of the three, said to his sisters, 'I can't eat any more. What a shame we can't take some of these tasty apples home with us!'

'We can. Look!' said Hayley, rolling about on the fallen apples. When she stood up, a big, juicy apple was stuck to her spines.

The hedgehogs giggled as they rolled on the ground. When each of them had secured an apple, they started to walk home. But the hedgehogs really should have looked behind them, because a sly fox had been watching them the whole time!

Hungrily licking his lips, the fox waited patiently for the right moment. He was certain that he'd catch at least one hedgehog. The fox jumped and clamped down with his teeth! But he fell back with nothing in his mouth but an apple! By the time he realised what had happened, the three hedgehogs had fled, knowing they should take far more care in future.

Too many feet!

ince the beginning of winter in the forest, people heard strange shouts. '*Ay, ay, ay*' went the sound! But the strange thing was that the shouts came not once or twice, but ten times, a hundred times, a million times! After a week of this never-ending noise, nobody could bear it any longer.

Buzz the maybug was sent to find out what was making all the racket. After a while, he found what he had been looking for. The sound was coming from a creature crawling along just below him. Buzz flew down to take a closer look and discovered it was a centipede.

'Hello, centipede,' said Buzz.

'Hello–*ay*!–Mr–*ay*!– Maybug,' said the centipede.

'What's wrong?' asked Buzz.

'I've got–*ay*!–a terrible–*ay*! – pain in my feet,' groaned the centipede.

'Oh dear, that must really hurt,' said Buzz. 'I'll go and fetch a doctor.'

In a few moments, Buzz returned with Doctor Beetle.

'How long have you been in pain?' asked the doctor.

'Since the beginning of winter,' said the centipede.

'Just as I thought! Foot pains brought on by the cold,' said the doctor. 'Buzz, go and fetch Silky the spider.'

When Silky arrived, Doctor Beetle told her what he needed. The next day, the spider's work was finished. She had woven a hundred little socks. The centipede put them on one by one. His little feet soon warmed up, and he never suffered foot pains again.

Monster leapfrog

ave you ever played leapfrog? One child bends over and touches his or her toes, while another leaps over and then touches his or her toes. Then, the next player leaps over two people, and so on. The more people you have, the more fun you can have.

One day, six little monsters decided to play a game of leapfrog. Now these monsters are very silly. There is a little hairy monster, a little three-legged monster, a little red monster, a little fat monster, a little sticky monster, and a little invisible monster.

Before they even started playing, the six little monsters were fighting over which one of them the rest should jump over.

'Not me!' said the hairy monster. 'You'll snag my hairs with your claws.'

'Not me!' said the three-legged monster. 'You'll knock me over.'

'Not me!' said the red monster. 'Because... um...just BECAUSE!'

'Not me!' said the fat monster. 'My tummy is so big that I can't touch my toes.'

'Not me!' said the invisible monster. 'You would miss my back and fall flat on your faces!'

'Well, I'll do it!' said the little sticky monster.

'NO!' cried the other monsters.

'Why not?' asked the sticky monster.

'Because we'll all get stuck to you!' said the other monsters. They never did play leapfrog!

Duffy's scare

t was late at night and the house was calm. Curled up on the sofa, Duffy the cat had just nodded off to sleep. He purred for a while at first, just to soothe himself and then he started to dream.

Duffy had cat dreams of running through the long grass, chasing grasshoppers, and eating delicious strawberry yogurt.

Duffy felt a little hungry and woke with a start. Maybe it was time for a trip to the kitchen, he thought.

But when he opened his eyes, Duffy saw two red circles glinting at him. They looked strange and dangerous.

'What beast has such frightening eyes?' he shuddered.

There was nothing else for it, Duffy would have to take a closer look. Very cautiously, he approached the glowing eyes. Suddenly, something sprang out and Duffy leapt back.

'Ow!' he cried as something burned. Whatever it was, it was hot!

Duffy looked up to see there were more glowing eyes than there were before. Terrified, he fled from the room, knocking over a vase on his way. The sound of glass breaking woke his owner and a light went on in the hall.

'What's going on in here?' called a stern voice.

Cowering in the corner, Duffy quickly realised his mistake. The monster's eyes that had gleamed in the shadows were nothing more than the glowing embers in the fireplace.

'I'm a silly cat!' thought Duffy.

Sweet music

A guitar and a violin had been forgotten long ago and left at the bottom of a wardrobe. Nobody was interested in them anymore, and they were sad and lonely.

Then, one day the door of the wardrobe opened and the two instruments were blinded by bright light. A man gently took them out and brushed off the layers of dust.

'Wow! These must be worth a fortune! It's off to the museum with you, my pretties!' he greedily chuckled.

The guitar and the violin suspected that it might be the end of their quiet life. They were right. Three hours later, they were in a glass box being stared at by visitors.

That night, the guitar heard the violin calling, 'Guitar! Guitar!'

'Yes, violin. Stop crying, someone will hear you!' said the guitar.

'Why are we here?'

'It must be because of our age,' replied the guitar. 'We get more valuable with time.'

Just then, a voice said, 'Hello, my name is flute and you are..?'

'Guitar and violin! We're over here. Have you been here long?'

'Yes, I've been alone in here for ages. It's been such a long time since I've played with friends,' said the flute. 'Perhaps we could play music at night when there are no visitors around.'

And so, every evening the instruments talked and played to their hearts' content and nobody ever found out.

Precious pumpkins

Mr Lewis is a very good gardener. His tomatoes are the juiciest in the village and his strawberries are delicious. He used to be very grumpy and spent all his time worrying that people would steal his fruit and vegetables.

Last season, Mr Lewis's vegetable patch was full of huge, orange pumpkins. One evening, just as he was leaving his house, Mr Lewis noticed a fire-like glow coming from his vegetable patch. As fast as he could, he rushed back inside to call the fire station.

When the fire trucks arrived, Mr Lewis went outside to see what was happening. There among his cabbages, he saw several children. All around them were orange globes, lit from the inside by candles.

'Those are my pumpkins!' cried Mr Lewis.

The chief firefighter ran up to Mr Lewis.

'Calm down, Mr Lewis. There's no serious damage done,' said the fireman. 'It's Halloween today. The children were wrong to take your pumpkins, but if you give them a few treats, your pumpkins will be spared next year. What do you think?'

From that day on, Mr Lewis let the children help him in the garden. Together, they grew enough pumpkins to decorate the whole village for Halloween.

Stormy journey

A terrible storm raged and strong winds battered the garden. The cherry tree had terrible trouble protecting its delicate flowers. When the storm finally ended everything was a mess. A beetle, a few strange leaves, and a grain of sand had been blown inside the cherry flowers.

The little yellow grain of sand would have probably gone unnoticed had it not landed inside the tree's most beautiful flower. The grain of sand had journeyed all the way from the Sahara Desert. It had lived there peacefully until the storm had whirled it away.

While it was being carried along, the grain of sand had no idea where he was headed and now here he was.

'It smells lovely here. Where am I?' said the grain of sand.

'You are in a cherry tree flower,' said a grain of pollen who lived in the flower.

'I'm Zara, a yellow grain of sand from the desert.'

'Well Zara,' replied the pollen, 'I'm getting married today. You see the cherry tree in flower at the bottom of the garden? My fiancée is waiting there for me.'

'How are you going to get over there?' asked Zara.

'Oh, I just climb aboard a petal and float across! The perfect taxi!' said the pollen.

'Do you think the wind will carry me back to the desert one day?' asked the grain of sand.

'Maybe, you never know your luck,' said the pollen.

Ricky's thumb

Yesterday was Ricky's sixth birthday. He was given lots of presents, cards and a big cake. However his day wasn't perfect because his parents made him promise to stop sucking his thumb. Only babies did that!

They were always saying, 'Ricky, stop sucking your thumb. You'll ruin your teeth! You're a big boy now and big boys don't suck their thumbs!'

Ricky tried to explain that he didn't really want to be a big boy. He was quite happy as he was, thank you very much. But it didn't make any difference.

'Sucking your thumb is a really childish thing,' said his dad. 'Do you ever see me with my thumb in my mouth?'

'Haven't you ever tried it? It's brilliant! Try it!' said Ricky.

He couldn't believe his dad hadn't ever been tempted to try sucking his thumb. Poor old dad, he didn't know what he was missing out on!

Then Ricky had another idea. If he had to stop doing something he loved, then so should they. Perhaps they should give up watching so much television and play games with him instead? Maybe they should give up driving their car, and travel on foot or on the train. Ricky preferred going on a train any day! Much better than boring old cars!

When Ricky explained all of this to his parents, they looked at him and then burst out laughing.

Perhaps he was being the tiniest bit silly!

Faking it!

Tomorrow Ben's class has a times tables test. How can he get out of it? He could pretend to be ill, but he had tried that before and his mother caught him out. She'd take his temperature, and then he'd have to stay in bed for the whole day and only get vegetable soup to eat. Yuck!

'Test or thermometer?' Ben wondered, falling asleep.

When the alarm went off next morning, Ben quickly made his mind up.

'Ben,' called his mother, sticking her head around the door. 'Didn't you hear your alarm ring?'

'I feel ill,' groaned Ben.

His mother felt his forehead. 'You do feel a bit hot,' she said, 'let's take your temperature.'

'But I have to go to school today. There's a test this morning,' said Ben, pretending to be worried.

'I know,' said his mother. 'That's why I'm wondering whether you're fibbing. Maybe I should see your teacher. She can give me the test for you to do at home.'

Ben was beginning to wish he had never pretended to be ill. Then his mother added, 'I'll also call your friend Julie's parents. I don't think you should go to her party because whatever you've got might be catching!'

Oh, no! The party! Ben had forgotten about that. Now he'll get all the things he didn't want – the thermometer, the vegetable soup, and the test, but not the one thing he really wanted.

Pretending to be ill was really a dumb idea!

The magical bird

any years ago, there was an old man who lived in a little cottage miles away from anywhere. No relatives, friends or neighbours ever came to visit him. All day, the old man worked in his vegetable patch. In his poor home the old man had hardly any belongings. There were just a few pieces of furniture, a bed, a spoon, and a porcelain bowl from China.

The old man had found the bowl in the house when he moved in. It was decorated with a painting of a pale blue bird, and the old man would admire it for hours.

'Well,' said the old man, 'if someone did drop by and wanted to chat to me, I would ask them to tell me stories about what is going on in the world. It seems like years since I last heard someone's voice.'

One evening, the old man was looking at the bowl again.

'Oh pretty bird, where do you come from? Which artist painted you so beautifully?' he asked.

Suddenly as if by magic, the pale blue bird began to move. It came off the bowl and started flapping its wings and flying around the old man. He couldn't believe his eyes. The old man was even more surprised when the bird told him that it came from China, and that it was painted hundreds of years ago using magic paint.

Moved by the old man's loneliness, the bird decided to tell him what he had seen and where he had been during all those years. From that day on, the bird's magical stories brought enchantment and delight to the old man and he was never lonely again.

The wild flower

Once upon a time, there was a little wild flower that had grown up with lots of big yellow flowers in a garden nursery. The little flower felt very small and dull next to them. All alone she sighed, 'Ah, if only I could be grand like these lilies and roses that people admire so much. People come from far away to see them and to smell their perfumed scent. Wild flowers like me are just ignored. Life is so unfair.'

Just then, the wild flower saw the gardener approaching with a customer.

'These flowers are wonderful! Look at their shape and they have a lovely scent. They are quite magical,' the customer said.

'Here we go again,' groaned the wild flower. 'It's always the same story. People only come to see the big flowers.'

'So Madam, have you made your choice?' asked the gardener. The lady hesitated for a moment, then pointed to the roses. 'I want all of them, but today I'll just have the beautiful red ones,' she said.

The gardener cut off several rose stems. He made a bouquet and handed it to the lady.

'Oh, how could he just cut those rose stems like that?' gasped the little wild flower. 'Those poor roses must be in agony! I wouldn't change being a little wild flower for anything in the world.'

A little bird told me!

lan never listened in class and always received bad reports from his teachers.

'Try to be more interested in your lessons,' said his teacher.

But Alan was unable to concentrate in class. He was far too interested in watching the birds outside!

During lessons, he would gaze out of the window and admire the beautiful birds. If the windows were open, he would listen to their lovely melodies. The world of birds was far more interesting than whatever his teacher was saying.

'What can we do?' wondered his teachers.

Ricky carried on listening to nothing but birdsong.

Right up until the night before his tests, Alan couldn't remember any of the lessons he had been taught. He opened his school books and tried to take in all the information, but it was too late. Alan was worried but there was nothing he could do except try and get a good night's sleep.

As soon as he began to fall asleep Alan felt something hop onto his pillow. He opened his eyes and saw a little bird.

'Don't try to understand, just open your ears. Go to sleep and tomorrow you will remember everything I have told you,' said the little bird.

When Alan woke the next morning, he realised he knew all his lessons by heart! He could remember everything! He got excellent marks in the tests and found everything the bird had told him so interesting that he promised to pay attention in class.

The magic fish

Angela loved going fishing with her grandpa. One day at the river bank, he held out a brand new fishing rod and said, 'It's your turn now!'

Angela was thrilled! At last, a fishing rod of her own! She sat by the river and cast her line. After a few minutes she felt a tug at the end of it.

'I've caught something,' said Angela, turning to her grandpa. But he had fallen asleep! Angela pulled in the line and saw a beautiful rainbow fish on the end of it.

'If you throw me back into the river, I promise you the best day of your life,' said the fish.

Stunned, Angela dropped the fish back into the water.

'Now come and join me!' called the fish.

Angela hesitated for a moment and then dived into the river. As soon as she touched the water she turned into a fish!

The rainbow fish showed Angela an underwater world full of amazing creatures. The little girl had never imagined that the world underwater could be so beautiful. How wonderful it was to be able to swim like a fish!

But Angela knew she had to go back. So she said goodbye to the fish and hurried out of the water. When she reached the bank, Angela turned back to her normal self.

'Haven't you caught any fish?' asked her grandpa.

'It doesn't matter. I've had the best afternoon of my life!'

Snow flakes and ice flowers

Carlo lived in a country where it is always sunny and hot. One winter morning the sky seemed darker than usual. It looked like the night didn't want to let the day begin.

'Look at the sky, Grandpa,' said Carlo. 'There isn't any noise and there are no birds singing.'

'Come outside with me. You are about to see an amazing thing,' said his grandpa.

Carlo was looking up at the sky when a wind started to blow. It was so cold it made his eyes water. Then tiny white dots began falling. Holding out his hands, Carlo saw that these dots were tiny flowers of ice, shaped like little stars.

'Grandpa, it's snow!' said Carlo.

'Yes, it is snow, and you're lucky because it's very rare to see snow in this country,' said his grandpa. 'The first and last time I saw snow was when I was about your age.'

A thick white carpet of snow covered the ground and Carlo couldn't help running about and rolling in it. He was fascinated by the snowflakes. When he caught some in his hand, Carlo looked at them closely. They were all different shapes.

'Where do these ice flowers come from?' asked Carlo. 'They're so beautiful, they must have been made by a magician who cut them out of tiny diamonds.'

'No, they are made by three simple things: water, cold, and you. It is your longing to see snow that brought them here,' said grandpa.

The tired baker

Gavin was a baker who lived alone without a wife or children. He worked very hard in the bakery. Gavin had to wake up at four o'clock every morning to bake delicious fresh bread, croissants, and pastries for his customers.

After work, Gavin liked to wander in the wheat fields. He liked watching the wheat grow and ripen under the warm sun. Near the fields, a tree had been planted. It wasn't a very strong or tall tree, but Gavin liked it very much.

One day, Gavin was feeling tired so he took a nap under the tree. The baker soon fell into a deep sleep. But then a leaf fell on him and tickled his nose. As he pushed it away, he heard a shrill voice.

'My dear Gavin, look at yourself and look at me. You are heavy, while I am just small and fragile. You are leaning too heavily on me,' said the tree.

'I'm sorry,' said the baker. 'Is there anything I can do to make amends?'

'Well, I am quite lonely here in the fields, but if you come and keep me company for a while each day, I think I could grow bigger and stronger with your help,' said the little tree. 'Good friends and good company make all of us stronger and firmer.'

Gavin realised that the fragile tree could probably help him become stronger and happier.

'That sounds like a fine idea,' he told the little tree.

Gavin and the little tree see each other every day and have a little chat or two. Sometimes, you can even hear them laughing.

A time to sleep

inky the dormouse just never kept still!

'Sleeping is a waste of time! It's completely pointless. Time should be spent having fun even in winter,' he said when his sisters went to hibernate.

Pinky wanted to go and have fun with his friends in the mountain. He wanted to leap about with Ralph the hare, play hide-and-seek with the bearcubs, or play cards with Mr Hedgehog.

Pinky's sisters begged him to hibernate for the winter with them, but it was no use.

'Leave me alone! I have my own friends to play with,' he shouted.

Although they would have liked to play with him, Pinky's friends also needed to winter hibernate.

One by one, he watched Ralph, the bearcubs and Mr Hedgehog make their beds in the ground and go to sleep. Staying awake wasn't so much fun any more. The days grew shorter and it became bitterly cold outside.

One night, Pinky heard a cry from the forest that made his hair stand on end. There was danger nearby! He saw two big, red eyes come toward him and heard the crunch of heavy paws in the snow. It was a wolf!

'I don't want to be eaten by a wolf,' cried Pinky. 'I want to go to sleep underground where it's warm and safe!'

Pinky had learned his lesson. There is a time for having fun and a time for sleeping.

The firefighting dragon

Ah, if only you had known Alphonso when he was young. He was a handsome dragon who kidnapped beautiful princesses and could eat a knight and his horse in one mouthful. There was no other dragon as powerful as Alphonso who could raze a village to the ground or burn down a forest with one blast of his fiery breath!

But Alphonso was now old and he spent his time reading magazines that told stories of rich and beautiful princesses. Because Alphonso was old he easily caught colds. As he stood in a store one day, Alphonso felt a tickle in his nose.

'Atchoo!' he sneezed, causing all the newspapers to catch fire. He stepped outside and 'Atchooo!' The store became a barbecue!

The villagers were desperate to stop Alphonso setting fire to everything. Harry was particularly concerned about Alphonso. Harry was the village's only firefighter and each time the dragon created another fire, Harry had to go and put it out.

One evening, Harry went to talk to Alphonso. 'I've come to see you because life in the village is becoming impossible,' said Harry.

'I know,' replied Alphonso. 'But I'm old and I can't help sneezing.'

'That's why I've come to ask you if dragons can breathe water as well as fire,' said Harry.

'Of course we can but no one ever asks us to,' said Alphonso.

'I have an idea,' said Harry.

From that day onwards, there have been two firefighters in the village: Harry and Alphonso!

One wheel or two?

A bike and a wheelbarrow were in deep conversation by the roadside one day.

'You have been designed badly with your one wheel and your two long handles,' said the bike.

'But I'm very useful,' replied the wheelbarrow. 'People can use me to carry heavy things.'

'Of course, but you also have to be pushed like a donkey. And when you're not needed, people forget about you and leave you to get rusty. I don't envy you,' said the bike.

'With my two wheels, people can ride me like a horse and zoom around the countryside. My master cleans and polishes me, and in the evening I get put away in the warm garage.'

The bike was busy boasting about himself, he didn't notice a car driving up behind him.

'Get out of the way, you skinny little thing!' shouted the car as it knocked him off the road.

The injured bike squealed and began to cry. The wheelbarrow did its best to comfort the poor silly bike.

When the wheelbarrow's owner passed by, he took one look at the bike and said, 'You look like you need some work doing. I'll mend you, poor thing.'

The man put the bike into the wheelbarrow and wheeled it to his house. The wheelbarrow thought this was amusing.

'Poor old bike. Are you okay in there? Am I comfortable enough?' it laughed.

The bike was sulking and didn't reply, but it had learned that boasting wasn't very clever at all!

The little train

The little train was sad. Today would be his last journey through Daffodil Valley. The valley was small, but he loved it. As he trundled passed he said hello to the cows and rabbits with a joyful *'Choo-choo'*!

There weren't enough people living in the valley to make the little train's journeys worthwhile any more.

Little train picked up George the station master. He also had to leave the valley because if there were no trains, there would be no need for a station master.

'I'm sad too,' said George. 'I'm going to have to work in a big, cold, and horrible city station.'

The little train felt better when he saw that all the animals had come out to accompany him on his last journey. They all cheered him and threw flowers to him.

The animals really loved the little train and didn't want to see him leave. Last week they held a meeting and decided that they needed to get everyone in the valley together to prove there were enough customers for the train. The animals organised a show to attract more tourists.

So, that evening the cows performed a ballet, the rabbits juggled, and the stag did magic tricks. The dormice did a wonderful tap-dancing routine.

The show was a great success and quickly became a huge tourist attraction. The little train was put back to work and George returned to his old job.

Little train felt very proud as he went through Daffodil Valley. He saluted his friends with a thankful *'Choo-choo'*!

Naughty or nice?

Phillip was walking through the fields one afternoon with his dog. It was a lovely sunny day. Phillip wandered along, totally unaware of the argument going on just above his head between the Little Angel and the Little Devil.

'It's obvious that I'm Phillip's favourite,' snapped Little Devil. 'He loves playing tricks with me.'

'No, he prefers me. I give him wise advice,' replied Little Angel.

'Nonsense! He's bored because of you,' retorted Little Devil.

Little Angel and Little Devil were Phillip's conscience. They could make him naughty or nice.

Phillip started to play a hunting game by getting his dog to track animals. The dog loved it and before long a rabbit ran out of its burrow.

'Don't let your dog hurt the rabbit!' shouted Little Angel.

'Leave him,' said Little Devil. 'It's natural. Don't be so weak.'

Phillip listened to Little Angel and called his dog back to him. Little Devil was furious. He had boasted to Little Angel that he could always get Phillip to do naughty things.

Suddenly, a hand grabbed Little Devil and a voice said, 'Ha! I've found you, you little rascal! Go to your room at once!'

Even Little Devil and Little Angel have parents who they have to obey.

Dancing partners

The entire jungle was busy preparing for the New Year's Eve party. The monkeys were rehearsing their music, the zebras were cooking lots of food, and the porcupines were busy decorating the trees around the dance floor. Most importantly, the dance lessons were being held. In every family, the older brothers and sisters were teaching the younger ones how to dance, hoping they would win the dance contest.

Poor Nellie the elephant, didn't have any one to help her, so she went to see her cousin Momo the hippopotamus. But Momo said he had enough hippos to teach without her as well.

While Nellie was walking home she nearly trod on Compo the mole.

'Hey, look where you're putting your big feet!' he cried.

'Sorry Compo. I was so busy worrying about this party that I didn't look where I was going,' sighed Nellie.

'What's the matter? Everyone loves a party!' said Compo.

'But I don't have anyone to teach me to dance,' she sobbed.

'Why don't you ask Edgar to teach you?' suggested the kindly mole.

'Edgar the rhino or Edgar the lion?' asked Nellie. 'Oh, I hope you don't mean that nasty crocodile!'

'No, Edgar the butterfly!' said Compo.

On New Year's Eve, Nellie proudly stepped onto the dance floor with Edgar the butterfly. They made a fantastic dancing couple. Edgar flew around Nellie as she danced. Everyone admired them and they even won first prize.

Bath time blues!

 very evening, Mrs Bear had the same problem.

'Teddy, come on now. It's bath time!' she called.

'Oh, I haven't finished playing,' sighed Teddy, the little bear.

'I don't want to hear any more excuses! Hurry up before the water gets cold,' said his mother.

'Just give me five more minutes,' begged Teddy.

Teddy hated bath time and he couldn't understand why he had to wash *every* evening. Sometimes, Mr Bear would have to pick Teddy up and put him in the water to make him wash.

One day, when his mother asked him to get ready for his bath, Teddy appeared at the bathroom door and said, 'I'm ready for a bath, Mother.'

Mrs Bear raised her eyebrows in surprise, but didn't say anything. Closing the door behind her, she left the room.

Downstairs, Teddy's parents heard splashing water.

'Finally, he has realised that it is good to bathe,' said Mrs Bear.

'I think Teddy might be trying to make us believe he's washing by dipping his arm in the water and splashing about,' said Daddy Bear. 'Teddy's not a dirty bear, he just gets bored easily.'

'Maybe that's the problem,' said Mrs Bear.

She was right! Mrs Bear gave Teddy some lovely plastic boats to play with in the bath. Ever since, Teddy loves bath time and spends hours in the bath. Now, when Mrs Bear says, 'Time to get out of the bath!', Teddy says 'Five more minutes, please!'

Brave Casper

asper was a very shy little cat. So shy that he was always hiding behind his mother and never spoke to any of the other cats.

One evening, Casper heard sobs and saw Mollie the puppy with tears running down her face.

'What's wrong, Mollie?' Casper just about dared to ask.

'Casper, do you know Aldo the crow? Well, he's always picking on me. I can't even walk across the farmyard without him pecking my ears with his big beak. He does it every day,' cried Mollie.

'But why?' asked Casper. 'What does he do that for?'

'It's because my father doesn't like crows, so Aldo doesn't like me,' answered Mollie.

'That's not fair,' said Casper. 'We must do something!'

The following day, despite his shyness, Casper bravely went to see Aldo the crow. He explained that there was no point in picking on Mollie, and that he should talk to Mollie's father if he had a problem.

'Dogs and crows should stop fighting!' Casper said.

'Easier said than done,' replied Aldo. 'Dogs always behave badly towards us.'

Mollie's father said almost the same thing to Casper. 'Crows and dogs have always been enemies, so what can we do?'

Casper ended the dispute by making the dogs and crows talk to each other. It was that simple!

Kiko and the walrus

Kiko was an Inuit boy who lived all alone in a little igloo in the middle of an ice field. Kiko went fishing every day and he never saw any other people.

One morning Kiko set off to do some fishing. After catching some fish he started to pack up to go home. Suddenly, a big walrus appeared in the hole Kiko had carved in the ice.

'What are you doing here? This is my territory,' said the walrus.

'I thought the ice field belonged to everyone,' said Kiko.

'Well you were wrong,' replied the moody walrus. 'Go away, and don't fish here again!'

But Kiko knew that no one owned the ice field and he was very stubborn. So he went to the same place each day, and each day the walrus would chase him away.

One day, the walrus followed Kiko to his igloo,

ready to give him another telling-off. But when the walrus tried to go into the igloo, he got his head and tusks stuck in the doorway!

'See what you've done now!' said Kiko. 'Why are you so mean?'

'I'm not mean, I'm just alone and bored,' mumbled the walrus. 'Nothing happens around here, so when I see you I think it is quite fun to annoy you. Who are you, anyway?'

Kiko and the walrus talked for ages. If you go to the ice field in the early hours of the morning you might see a huge walrus playing chasing games ever so happily with a young Inuit boy.

Fish overboard!

hen Cathy's parents said they were all going on a cruise, Cathy was worried. She loved her goldfish Soapy more than anything else in the world and couldn't bear to be parted from him, even for the vacation of a lifetime.

'We can leave Soapy with friends,' said her mother.

'No way!' said Cathy. 'Either the two of us come on the cruise or I'm staying here.'

Cathy would not give in so her parents agreed that Soapy could join them.

On the big cruise ship Cathy kept her goldfish with her at all times. During dinner, she even put Soapy's bowl on the captain's table!

But one evening, just as Cathy was watching the sun set, a big wave rocked the ship. Thrown off balance, Cathy stumbled and dropped Soapy's fishbowl into the sea.

'Oh, no! Fish overboard!' cried Cathy at the top of her voice.

The crew and passengers couldn't stop laughing. 'Yes, dear. There are millions of fish overboard,' smiled a lady.

'No, I mean Soapy my little goldfish has fallen into the sea!' gasped Cathy. Then, Cathy did a very silly thing and dived into the water to rescue her Soapy.

'Girl overboard!' shouted the captain. In a split second, a lifeboat was dropped into the sea to rescue Cathy.

When the rescue team brought Cathy safely back onto the ship, she shivered and said, 'Look at my fishbowl. Now I've got two fish. Soapy has a friend!'

The brave firefighters

win brothers, Theo and Nick worked in a fire station. As they were still training, they weren't allowed to go on all the missions. They were only allowed to help the firefighters rescue cats that were stuck in trees or clean the fire trucks.

Theo and Nick stayed in the fire station for days at a time putting away hoses, cleaning the firefighters' boots, and sweeping the floors. They were hard working lads and they never complained, but they were beginning to get bored.

One day, all the firefighters were called out to a fire in the next town. Theo and Nick were left behind. They were worried that if someone needed their help they would not be sure what they should do.

Suddenly, a big car sped up to the fire station, screeched to a stop, and burst into flames! The driver, who was unhurt, fell onto his knees shouting, 'Fire! Fire!'

The brothers needed to act quickly before the fire station went up in flames!

Theo and Nick sprayed the big water jet onto the fire and in a few minutes the fire was out. People who lived nearby came out to applaud them.

A little later, when Theo and Nick told the chief fire officer what had happened, he congratulated them and said they had proved that they could do the job well. He said that as they were nearly at the end of their training they could now go on all of the missions too.

Horace has got the humpf

Kate had lots of dolls and cuddly toys that she played with every day. There was Princess the ballerina, William the woolly mammoth, a family of mice, and lots of others. Kate would make up stories about them all. It was wonderful to have so many imaginary friends! But Horace the stuffed teddy bear didn't think this was wonderful at all. Horace was jealous. He didn't want Kate to play with any of the other cuddly toys.

'I was her first teddy bear, but now Kate's forgotten all about me,' sighed Horace. How he missed the days when he was her only toy. Now, Horace had to put up with all these stupid rivals.

Every Christmas and every birthday Kate was given dolls or even worse other teddy bears. Each time Horace's heart sank a little more. Kate did love him, but Horace was so blinded by jealousy he just couldn't see it.

One day when Horace was under the bed, Kate thought she had lost him. She searched her bedroom from top to bottom but couldn't find him.

'Mother, Mother, I've lost Horace! He's my best ever teddy bear!' cried Kate, sobbing.

A little later, Kate spotted one of Horace's paws sticking out from under the bed. Rushing over, she picked him up and laughed, 'My wonderful teddy. I love you more than anything else in the world!'

At last, Horace realised he was a very silly bear and that Kate loved him more than ever. From then on, Horace forgot about being jealous and was happy to share her with the other toys.

The king's fortune

espite his huge fortune, the king was unhappy. He could not find anyone honest enough to be his treasure keeper. Each person he had employed to do this job had stolen some of his treasure.

'Are there no honest men in this kingdom?' he asked his wife Samira.

'I know how you can find the right person,' said Samira. 'Publish an advertisement for the job. I will do the rest.'

Two weeks later, the palace was filled with all the people who had replied to the king's advert.

'Now get them to come in one by one and make them wait in the drawing room for a few moments,' said Samira.

Samira had put a vase in the drawing room, filled with pieces of gold. One by one, the people waited in the room

before they were received by the king. When he had seen each of them, the king gathered them in the drawing room again.

'Ask them to show you their hands,' said Samira. 'I dipped the pieces of gold in a chemical that turns the skin blue.'

The king did as Samira said and among a hundred men, only one did not have blue hands.

'You miserable creatures!' shouted the king. 'Clear off the lot of you! Be happy that I'm not throwing you all into prison! But you,' he added, turning to the young man who didn't have blue hands, 'I think you are worthy of my trust and I will let you guard my vast treasures.'

The young man was honest and loyal, and the king never worried about his treasure ever again.

Sally's clever tricks

On the farm where Matthew lived, there was a very old horse called Sally. Everyone said that Sally was too old and that it was time for her to retire. Sally was Matthew's most-loved horse. He took her for rides every day.

One day, Matthew's father called him in and said, 'Listen, son. Sally is too old to keep any longer. She can't pull a cart nowadays, so we're going to have to sell her.'

'No, you can't sell Sally! She's the best horse in the world!' cried Matthew.

'I know it's difficult, but Sally is good for nothing except grazing in the field,' said Matthew's dad.

'That's not true, and I'll prove it!' said Matthew. 'Just give me a little more time with her and I'll show you that she's still useful.'

Rolling his eyes, Matthew's dad reluctantly agreed.

Matthew decided to train Sally. He taught her to stand on her hind feet, to dance, and do all sorts of clever tricks. The old horse enjoyed the exercise and after a short time Matthew arranged a show with Sally as the main attraction. People came from villages near and far to admire the horse and paid money to see her wonderful tricks.

Matthew had been right! Not only was Sally good for something, she earned the farm more money than she cost to keep. Matthew had won and his parents never mentioned selling his precious horse again.

Animals to the rescue

ne fine day the hens decided to go for a walk. They set off without a cockerel escort and this was against the hen house rules.

Walking through the woods they clucked and giggled about all sorts of things. Then suddenly a the fox appeared from behind a tree! The hens was so afraid, they were unable to move! They trembled under their feathers, afraid that the young fox would eat them.

'My little hens, your timing is good. I'm as hungry as a wolf!' said the fox, licking its lips.

As the other hens began to squawk in fear, Hilda the hen said, 'Mr Fox, since you're about to eat us would you do us one last favour before we die?'

'Anything you like,' answered the greedy fox.

'We would like to sing a prayer,' said Hilda.

'Okay,' said the fox, 'but make it quick, I'm absolutely starving!'

Hilda made a secret sign to the other hens and they began to sing at the top of their voices. What the fox didn't know was that the song was a message to alert the other animals.

In the blink of an eye, a pig, a donkey, a fierce bull, and lots of other farm animals were charging toward the fox.

The fox knew that he didn't stand chance against such a group, and ran away. The farmyard animals escorted the silly hens all the way home.

The not so wicked wolf

As soon as night fell, the people of Charnham were filled with dread. Every evening the horrible howls of a wolf could be heard from the forest. One day Timmy had gone out to pick some wild flowers for his mother and hadn't returned. It was getting late and his parents were growing anxious.

When he set off on his walk, Timmy had no idea the danger he was in until he came face to face with a wolf! Terrified, Timmy took a step back but instead of coming after him the wolf ran into the bushes, shaking with fear.

'Please don't hurt me,' begged the wolf. 'I'm not bad.'

Timmy held out his hand to the poor creature who was hiding his head in his paws.

'If you're so frightened of people, why do you roam around here?' asked Timmy.

'The other wolves elected me chief of the wolf pack! I have to pretend to be fierce or I will be laughed at,' sighed the wolf.

'There is no point pretending to be bad. If you're gentle, accept it,' smiled Timmy. 'It's the way you were made. Come with me. I think you would make an excellent sheepdog.'

Timmy went back to Charnham with the wolf. Everyone was afraid at first, but they soon saw that the wolf was as gentle as a lamb.

The young wolf became the best friend of the town and its flocks of sheep, and could often be seen roaming across the fields with Timmy by his side.

Rebecca's fairy secret

ebecca was always daydreaming. She imagined all sorts of things– wonderful worlds inhabited by princesses, princes, dragons, elves, and imps. Rebecca could imagine whatever she liked.

One day, when Rebecca was daydreaming, a little fairy appeared in her mind. It was a little fairy that she hadn't tried to imagine! Rebecca tried to chase it away, but the next day it appeared again. However hard she tried, Rebecca could not get rid of the annoying little creature.

'Go away!' said Rebecca. 'I don't want to imagine you so what are you doing in my head?'

'I think you're interesting,' replied the little fairy.

'What do you want? You're making me cross!' shouted Rebecca. 'When I want to dream of fairies I'll let you know!'

'You are a little girl with a big imagination and only you can help me and the other fairies,' said the fairy.

'How?' asked Rebecca.

'Well, perhaps you already know that fairies only exist in young children's imaginations,' said the fairy. 'At this very moment, hardly anybody is thinking of fairies, and that means we might die out. All you need to do is think of me once a day and in exchange I will grant you a wish. Is that a deal?'

The little girl accepted and took great pleasure in thinking of her little fairy friend once a day. As  for the wish she made, well I can't tell you. It's Rebecca's secret and if anyone finds out, it won't come true!

Tick-tock, perfect watch!

he little watch was very sad.

'I never get it right,' she sighed. 'It's too difficult!'

Poor little watch, she always tried her best, but she was never on time. People had tried to fix her, wind her up, shake her, but it didn't do any good. She had tried concentrating as hard as she could, but it didn't make any difference. The little watch's hands wouldn't turn correctly. In no time at all, she was late again.

The little watch's owner was getting cross.

'I'm always late for meetings,' he sighed. 'I need to buy a new watch.'

Each evening, the man wound up his watch and put it on the table, and each time the little watch thought she had been given up.

'I'm just a stupid, broken watch!' she cried. 'One of these days my master is going to throw me out and get a new watch, I'm certain of it!'

But one evening, the big clock in the hall heard the little watch crying. Taking pity on her, he said, 'Listen to me, little watch. Our job is to keep the exact time. You must be able to do it! I will give you lessons every evening.'

The little watch was delighted. Each night when everyone else was asleep, the little watch took time keeping lessons from the big grandfather clock. She learned very quickly, and by the end of the week she was keeping absolutely perfect time.

'How strange! My watch is working now,' said the little watch's owner. And the little watch never left his wrist again.

Injury on ice

oor Julie! The first time she went ice-skating she fell over and hurt her knee, which quickly turned a nasty purple colour. When Julie's mother took her to see the doctor, he said, 'You need to take her to hospital for an x-ray.'

The hospital? Oh, no! Julie tried to explain that her knee didn't hurt very much, but nobody believed her.

The ambulance came to collect Julie in the morning. She was put onto a bed and they drove through town with the siren blaring. *'Neeee-naaaar! Neeee-naaaar!'* went the siren, just like in a film! Julie would have thought it was quite funny if only her knee didn't hurt quite so much!

When they reached the hospital, a nurse took Julie into a room. Julie was a little frightened and asked her mother to stay.

'Do you promise you won't leave me?' asked Julie.

'Of course I won't. Don't worry, they're going to do an x-ray to check you haven't broken anything,' said her mother, gently. 'You'll be home by this evening.'

Luckily, Julie's knee wasn't seriously hurt. The doctor said she should rest it for a few days and everything would be fine.

In the end, Julie found that going to hospital wasn't so bad after all. The nurses and doctors were very kind and the parents were allowed to stay with their children for the whole time.

'Oh well, I guess I won't win any ice-skating trophies this year,' smiled Julie.

Bless you!

an had a question for his dad.

'When someone sneezes, why do you say 'bless you'?' he asked.

'I don't know,' said his dad.

His mother didn't know either. When Ian's grandma came to visit, he said, 'Do you know why you say 'bless you' to people when they sneeze?'

'It's because of the genie,' smiled Ian's grandma.

'What genie?' asked Ian.

'The genie in the oil lamp,' said grandma. 'Listen carefully and I'll tell you the story. Once upon a time, in a land far away, there lived a boy called Aladdin who found an oil lamp.'

'What's an oil lamp?' asked Ian.

'In the old days there was no electricity, so people put oil into a jug or a bowl with a piece of string that you lit. It was a bit like a candle,' explained grandma patiently.

'Was it cooking oil?' asked Ian.

'In a way,' said grandma. 'But if you keep interrupting me all the time...atchoo!'

'Bless you,' said Ian.

'So, Aladdin found a lamp and when it was opened...atchoo!' sneezed grandma.

'Bless you again!' said Ian.

'Thank you. I will tell you the story another time. I think I've caught...atchooo...a cold!'

So Ian still doesn't know why people say 'bless you'.

On safari

randpa Harold and
Grandma Martha had
been talking about taking their
grandchildren to a safari park
for ages.

'It's best to go when the weather
is cooler, otherwise we'll get
too hot in the car with all the
windows closed!' said Grandpa.

'Well, we can just open the
windows then!' said Grandma.

'We'll be attacked!' said
grandpa. 'You see, we would
drive right alongside the lions as
they walk around freely, so it's
best to keep the windows closed.'

At last, the cooler weather came
and the family set off. At the
start of the visit to the
park, they drove through
a huge bear enclosure.

'Close your windows
and don't get out
of the car,' said
a guard. 'The
bears may come
very close to
you. They look
cuddly but
they are
dangerous.'

What a shame they couldn't
stroke the big, furry bears,
especially when they nuzzled
up to the windows!

Finally, they reached the lion
park. The children were very
disappointed.

'Where are the lions?' they
asked. 'I can't see any!'

Grandpa drove a bit further and
parked under a tree. Close by a
lion and four lionesses with their
young were lying in the shade.
The lion opened his huge mouth
and yawned like a great big cat.

Everyone loved the safari park
and agreed it was the best day
out ever!

The puppets' party

nce upon a time there was a famous puppet show that criss-crossed the country putting on shows for children. The puppets were handmade by a magic carpenter many years ago. The puppeteer had bought them in a sale and had no idea that the puppets were alive.

The puppeteer had made some musical instruments for his puppets.

A tube, made of cardboard, became a trumpet. With a little glue and some scissors, a small box became a violin. He made a piano out of a little box and painted it black and white. He made a tiny piano accordion out of folded paper.

What the puppeteer didn't know was that every night

these paper toys became real musical instruments.

One evening, the puppets arranged a party. The princes put on their best silk clothes and the princesses wore their beautiful silk dresses. The band played their instruments and the puppets all danced and sang songs together. The clowns made everyone laugh at their turns, tumbles, and funny steps.

After the party was over, all the puppets returned to their places in the trunk. When the puppeteer opened the trunk, all the instruments were back in their boxes and the puppets were lying still, as if nothing had happened.

The snowball fight

enjamin and his two little brothers, Lucas and Damien were having a snowball fight. Lucas pushed Damien over into the snow.

'Ow, that hurt!' cried Damien.

'Oh, you're such a wimp!' laughed Lucas.

Benjamin tried to calm the boys, but Lucas and Damien kept fighting for so long that Benjamin fetched their mother.

'Lucas started it!' said Damien.

'It wasn't me!' mumbled Lucas.

'I saw you from the window so don't pretend you didn't start the argument Lucas!' said Mother, crossly. 'You can go up to your bedroom until lunchtime!'

'But Lucas wasn't the only one! We were both fighting,' said Damien.

'Then, you can both go to your rooms!'

A little later, their mother said, 'Lunch is ready. Benjamin, please go and get Lucas and Damien from their rooms.'

'It's lunchtime,' he said.

'I'm not hungry, I don't feel well,' said Lucas.

His mother came upstairs, felt his forehead, and said, 'Oh, dear, you've got a temperature. Stay in bed. You got soaked during that snowball fight and now you're ill.'

Lucas snuggled under his duvet, glad that his mother wasn't angry with him any more.

The new arrivals

The big old oak tree was buzzing with activity. That morning Mr and Mrs Robin's babies had hatched. Four tiny pink things broke out of their shells at daybreak. The first visitor was Mrs Wise Owl who was returning home to sleep.

'Well done hatchlings!' she hooted as she passed the robins' nest. 'I hope those babies don't squawk all day!'

Trust Mrs Owl to find something to grumble about. On the other hand, Mr Brush the squirrel was delighted to see the new chicks. He hopped off to tell all their forest friends the good news.

When Mr Brush reached Addie the snake's house he could was very out of breath.

'Addie, they've been born!' he gasped.

'Good, good,' hissed the snake. 'Please congratulate the parents for me.'

Everyone was very kind. The mouse family gave them a few nuts, the ants brought some grain, and Jackie the jay said he would be on lookout for any birds of prey hovering thereabouts.

Mr and Mrs Robin said thank you to everyone, but they didn't have time to celebrate. The four little chicks were their first babies and the tiny things were starving! They didn't have any feathers yet, but they already knew how to squawk for food.

What a busy life it is for parents!

Marjory's tale

There was lots of chatter and excitement in the big oak tree this morning. Everyone woke early because Marjory the owl was going to make an important announcement about what she had seen the night before. As soon as everyone was settled, she began her tale.

Marjory was perched high up on a branch, looking out as she always did when everyone else was sleeping. All of the other animals were curled up in the tree hollows, snoring gently. It was a clear and starry night and Marjory could see for miles around.

According to Marjory, during the quietest hours of the night when all of the forest was completely silent she distinctly heard the sound of bells ringing in the distance. It seemed as if the sound was coming from the sky. But how could that be?

She looked up and was amazed to see a sleigh flying through the air. Sitting inside the sleigh was a jolly-looking man dressed in red. He had a long white beard and said 'Yo, ho, ho!'

The sleigh flew overhead so quickly that Marjory didn't have time to follow it. She really wanted to know where it was going, and where it had been!

Nobody in the oak tree really believed Marjory's story.

Sometimes she did act a little strangely, but how could they explain the fact that each of them had a little present under their pillows this morning when they woke up?

Can you guess who was the mystery visitor?

What's that noise?

The three little seals called Splish, Splash, and Splosh, had just come out of the water. Their mother had told them many times not to stay out on the ice field for too long because a big polar bear might get them. The playful seals always stayed longer than they should do. The ice field was so beautiful when the sun shone on it. The ice sparkled like precious stones. Today the seals could see for quite a long way because there was no fog. So if a polar bear did come along they knew they would have time to escape.

But what was that strange noise that sounded like icicles blowing in the wind? 'Ding, ding, ding!'

Puzzled, the three seals turned to slide back into the sea. But they could see something in the distance. It was still tiny because it was very far away.
'Ding, ding, ding!'

'Maybe we should get back into the water now,' said Splish.

'No, we've still got time. I really want to see what it is!' said Splash.

The 'thing' was getting closer. It wasn't a bird or a seal, or even a bear. What could it be? 'Ding, ding, ding!'

The sound got louder as it approached. Suddenly Splish, Splash, and Splosh dived into the water. It was time to go! Moving very fast, the strange thing passed right by the three seals. It had lots of feet and a big sledge behind it.

Our three little friends didn't know it, but they had just seen Mok the young Inuit boy in his sledge, pulled by ten husky dogs!

One step at a time

Charlie had wanted to go climbing for a long time, but until now he had been too young. At last the day had finally arrived when Charlie was allowed to join his dad on a hike. They weren't exactly climbing the Alps, but it was a big rock face about the height of a two-storey house, and that was quite enough to start with.

As soon as they were dressed, Charlie and his dad prepared their bags. They needed a safety cord, pins to attach the cord to the rock, a hammer to knock the pins in, and safety helmets. When everything had been checked and double checked they set off.

After a long walk, Charlie and his dad reached the rock they were going to climb. Charlie sucked in his breath as he looked up. It was very high! His dad explained what Charlie had to do, then he attached the cord to both of them and started climbing. As his dad climbed the rock, all Charlie could see were the soles of his dad's shoes!

When he reached the top, his dad called, 'Come on, son. It's your turn now! Look where you're putting your feet and don't take one hand off until you're sure you have a firm grip. Don't be frightened, I'm holding the rope steady for you.'

Very slowly, Charlie began climbing the rock. It was no more difficult than climbing trees and he soon reached the top without any problems.

'Well done!' said Charlie's dad. 'Before long, you will be a proper mountaineer. Next time we come out climbing, we'll try a real mountain.'

Down in the dumps

Darren went to visit his best friend Chloe one day. She was ill in bed which meant they couldn't play together.

'I've got a sore throat,' said Chloe in a tiny croaky voice.

'Don't worry, I'll read some stories to you,' said Darren.

'Sit next to me and we can read together,' whispered Chloe, looking happy and cosy under the duvet.

'Hey, you're boiling!' said Darren.

'I know, my temperature is quite high,' said Chloe. 'That's why I have to take my medicine. I also have to chew these banana throat lozenges.'

Darren really wanted to taste all Chloe's delicious sweet-smelling medicines, but he couldn't because he wasn't ill. So he picked up

his book again and read to Chloe all afternoon. By the evening, Chloe was feeling much better.

'I feel fine now,' she said. 'That medicine worked very quickly.'

But now Darren didn't feel very well! He had a sore throat and a dizzy, aching head.

'You do look pale,' said Chloe. 'I'll ask my mother if you can have a spoonful of my medicine and a banana throat lozenge.'

The syrup and the throat lozenges tasted delicious, but Darren didn't enjoy them because his head and his throat hurt so much.

'I suppose I shouldn't have wished I could try your medicine, Chloe,' whispered Darren.

New-found friends

There was once a big forest where all the animals made friends with each other. Cora the crow would have liked to have a special forest friend, but she had only just arrived and didn't know anyone.

Late one night, Cora was flying about the forest when she heard a terrible cry. Swooping down, Cora landed on a tree branch. There, just below her in the bracken was a poor little cat caught in a trap!

Cora pulled, pushed, and tapped the trap until she managed to free the injured cat.

'I'll look after you,' cawed Cora. And she did. Within a few days, Puddles the cat was fit and strong again, thanks to his new friend.

'I wish the hunters who set these awful traps would leave the forest so that we animals could wander freely,' sighed Puddles as he sat with Cora one day.

'I know! Let's hide in a cave,' said Cora.

'No, the hunters will find us and it's so cold in caves,' sighed Puddles. 'I think it would be better to move somewhere far away from here.'

'How about going to Africa? If we go there, we will have hot weather!' said Cora excitedly.

'It's a great idea, but I think you're forgetting that I'm not a bird,' said Puddles. 'I'm not able to fly all the way to Africa like you, Cora.'

'You could ride on my back!' said Cora.

The next morning, the two friends set off on their long, exciting journey to Africa.

Shepherd days

As Edward the shepherd opened the big sheep gate, his flock of sheep all began pushing and shoving, each one trying to get out of the pen first.

'Ding! Ding! Ding!' went the bells around their necks. 'Baaah! Baaah! Baah!' went the playful sheep. They were all making such a noise!

'Those animals are so stupid!' sighed Barney the sheepdog as he watched nearby.

When the sheep reached the meadow they continued to run around as if they were being chased by a pack of wolves. At last they slowed down and looked around. They were in the field and it was time to stop running and time to start eating the grass.

Edward followed his herd and when he saw that they had calmed down, he settled under a tree for a little nap. Barney sat down next to him, but kept a sharp eye on the sheep.

Suddenly, a lamb who had lost her mother in the crowd began to bleat. The rest of the sheep looked up to see what was wrong. When they saw the little lamb wandering alone, they passed her from one to the other until she saw her mother.

After eating their fill, the sheep lay down near the shepherd and chewed contentedly.

As the sun set, the sheep, the shepherd, and the sheepdog wandered home for the evening. What a wonderful life!

Special Easter eggs

Finally, the holidays had arrived! Megan was in a hurry because tomorrow was Easter Day and she needed to prepare nests for chocolate eggs. She had already made three nests out of twigs and scraps of wool. Megan took them to her grandma's so that they could be filled with chocolate eggs ready for tomorrow. It was so exciting!

'Hello, little one!' smiled grandma, opening her arms to give Megan a huge hug.

'Oh, what beautiful nests you've made! I've been so busy, I haven't bought any eggs.'

Julie fought back the tears. 'How could her grandma forget the Easter eggs?' she wondered.

'Don't look so sad, Megan,' said her grandma, 'I have something else for you, and with a bit of luck, you will enjoy tomorrow's surprise.

Knowing her grandma, the surprise was bound to be very special, so Megan went to bed feeling much better.

Early the next morning, grandma woke Megan. 'Come quickly! There are some surprises that can't wait!' she said.

Megan and her grandma tiptoed into the barn and there, under a light in a see-through bucket were ten chicken eggs.

Megan heard a tapping noise and suddenly one of the eggs moved. A little beak appeared, followed by some yellow downy feathers. One by one the ten eggs cracked open and the chicks hatched.

Megan thought seeing the chicks hatch was much better than finding chocolate eggs.

Whose prints?

It's white and it's cold. You can make balls out of it. You can also make men and big sculptures out of it. It doesn't know how to keep a secret. What is it? Have you worked it out yet?

Snow, of course! It's white, you can make snowballs or snowmen, and it shows everything that happens on it!

When there is snow around, it's impossible not to leave signs. It shows footprints, car tracks, and even animal tracks. That's why hunting is forbidden when it's snowing. It would be too easy to follow the animal tracks to the hides. All animals leave prints that are easy to recognise, almost like a signature.

Here a hare has jumped across the field toward the bushes. Behind him a fox. Did he catch the hare? No, the hare tracks disappeared under a tree and the fox turned round and went off towards the woods. Over there, a family of wild boars have crossed the snow. What a mess they made!

Look, there are Chuck the sheepdog's tracks. He went to see the sheepdog at the next farm. When a cat saw Chuck's tracks, it padded off in the opposite direction.

That night, as snow fell thick and fast, the forest animals said to each other, 'There were two creatures here today. They each had two feet, and one pair was much bigger than the other. What were they?'

The prints of a young boy out walking with his dad, of course!

The noisy tree!

Strange things had been happening in the big fir tree for some time. There were some very odd noises. *'Crrrrr....crrrr... crrrr.'*

Sly the snake was asked for advice as he usually had good ideas about what to do. He promised to help the creatures who lived in the fir tree. Just a day later, he kept his word when Doctor Peck the woodpecker arrived.

Doctor Peck asked for complete silence so that he could listen to the noise. It was quite difficult to get the ants to stop their work as they liked to work day and night. To stop the baby mice laughing, their dad had to threaten to keep them indoors for a week! Then they all had to wait for the wind to stop whistling through the leaves.

It took quite a while, but at last Doctor Peck was able to make his diagnosis.

'I believe I know what the problem is. There are worms in the tree. I am pretty sure that's what is making the noise. I will get to work right away!'

Doctor Peck started pecking *toc-toc-toc-toc* the trunk of the old fir tree and before long, the worms came wriggling out of the bark.

'Help! That's hurting our ears!' cried the wriggly worms.

Sly explained to the worms that the fir tree was a home, not a source of food. He suggested that they live in an old tree trunk nearby, which would be both a house and a food store for them.

Finally, the inhabitants of the old fir tree could sleep in peace.

Twice as nice

Bella had been asking her parents for a little brother for quite a while. Nearly all her friends had one and they were always telling her how much fun they had dressing him, feeding him, rocking him, walking him in his pram, and all those sorts of baby things.

Bella was a little jealous and she didn't understand why her parents always said, 'Soon!'

Bella was sure her parents were only saying that to stop her going on about a little brother. But the other day, she heard her mother say to her dad, 'The doctor told me that it's alright this time.'

What were they talking about? Bella was very worried that her mother was ill.

'No, I'm not ill, it's just that it can sometimes be a bit difficult to have a baby,' her mother explained. 'Your Dad and I are impatient too, but this time it's alright. The babies are here in my tummy.'

'Why did you say 'babies'?' Bella asked.

'We're having twins!' smiled her mother. Bella was thrilled! Two little brothers to take care of!

Finally, the big day arrived. Her mother was just about to come home with the newborn babies. Bella's mother was tired, so Bella helped her as much as she could. There was always something to do! Two little mouths crying at the same time for food. Two diapers to change! The twins were always in her parents' arms! But there were also four round cheeks to kiss and Bella could kiss them as much as she liked.

Full speed ahead!

This year the Wilson family spent their holiday on a barge on the canals. The family had everything arranged. One by one, they took charge of the steering wheel while the others watched the front or the back of the barge. Canals aren't very deep or wide, so you have to be careful!

The children had brought their bicycles and often they would go on long bike rides or go to buy bread in a nearby town.

There were plenty of locks on the canal. Sometimes they came across another boat and they would tell each other what they had just passed. One day, a French family invited the Wilsons to lunch on their barge.

The family stopped whenever they liked. The children often got off the barge to stretch their legs in the fields, and then rejoined their parents and the barge further along the canal.

They loved waking up in the morning on the boat in the middle of the countryside, listening to the birds singing in the trees.

Douglas even discovered fishing on the trip, and now he was mad about it. But what they all enjoyed more than anything else was going through the locks. They felt so small at the bottom of the lock and they liked it when the water rose. It took their breath away as the big, heavy gates opened onto the flowing river ahead.

The Wilsons became real sailors that week! Who knows what exciting adventure they would go on next year!

Name games

Nuel and Shunko lived in a house on the outskirts of London. They went to school nearby, spent Saturdays shopping in the mall, and Sundays playing football in the park. Every evening, they watched far too much television, like most little boys!

Sometimes they got annoyed when people pronounced their names incorrectly. For Shunko it was easy, because everyone called him Shun. At their school, there were pupils from all over the world, so there were lots of names that were difficult to pronounce correctly!

The brothers' teacher, Anne, said she loved their class because when the children said their first names one by one, it was like a pretty song that echoed all around the world.

Nuel and Shunko had a secret. They were Guarani Indians from South America. Nuel means 'tiger' in Guarani and Shunko means 'little boy'. At home, their dad spoke to them in Guarani language. Nuel and Shunko loved it when their dad closed his eyes and sang softly while he played his drum. Then he would sing louder and louder and his beautiful voice would ring sweetly round the house.

Nuel and Shunko wanted to grow up fast because Dad had promised them that when they were twelve he would take them to his country, Paraguay, for the big coming-of-age ceremony. If Nuel and Shunko passed the tests, they would be accepted into their grandfather's tribe. But in the meantime, they had to go to school, just like every other boy and girl!

The Chinese proverb

here is an old Chinese proverb that says you should never sell a bear skin before you kill the bear. It is so true, but you would be amazed how some people ignore these wise words. Fai was one such person.

Fai was a little boy who lived near Shanghai. One day, he went to explore his grandpa's attic. While he was there, he discovered a wonderful porcelain vase. Fai was sure it was a Ming vase. A vase like that would be worth a lot because it would have been made hundreds of years ago!

'This vase could earn me a lot of money,' thought Fai to himself. 'With the money I could buy a beautiful house, a lovely car, and a restaurant. The restaurant would earn me even more money that I could spend on opening other restaurants all over the world. I would meet a rich woman who would give me a son, who could take over the business when I am old.'

Excited by his ideas, Fai jumped up, tripped, and knocked over the vase. The vase smashed into a thousand pieces!

'What's going on up there?' called Fai's grandfather.

'I've broken the Ming vase!' cried Fai.

'What Ming vase?' asked his grandfather, heading up the stairs to the attic. 'Oh, you mean this vase,' he laughed. 'This is just a cheap imitation. I bought it at the market, many years ago.'

At last, Fai understood the proverb: you shouldn't sell the bearskin before you've killed the bear!

The unicorns' song

You must have heard of unicorns, those magical creatures that look like horses with a beautiful shiny horn on their heads. Nowadays no one ever sees a unicorn, but there are many legends about them.

One such legend says that Noah forgot to take unicorns onto his ark so they were all sent to another planet. But that isn't true. I will tell you the real story.

A long time ago, unicorns lived in an enchanted forest with fairies. Only fairies could look after them because they were so pure of heart. At that time, people were not wicked unless they had been transformed by a wizard. Every time a wizard made a person wicked, the unicorns would cry. It was a beautiful mournful sound.

To make the person good again, the fairies gave them magic water to drink. The water came from a spring in which an ancient unicorn had dipped its horn. As soon as the person drank the water, they would become pure and good. At that exact moment, the forest would be filled with the beautiful song of unicorns. But one terrible night, the wizards invaded the forest and killed all the fairies and unicorns! A short time later, the evil wizards were destroyed by a huge flash of lightning from the heavens. But there were still some humans who had been made wicked, and no unicorns left to make them good again.

And that is how unicorns disappeared. But if you listen carefully, every once in a while you might hear the unicorns' song. And if you keep a pure heart, then you might be able to help another person hear the unicorns' song.

Dad's indecision

t was a very cold winter's day. Alice's dad came home from work, shivering with cold.

'*Brrr*! I think my ears are going to freeze! I need a scarf!' her dad gasped, closing the front door.

Mother and Alice glanced at each other and smiled. At last they knew what to get dad for his birthday next week! They always tried to find him a present that was attractive as well as useful, and a a new scarf would be perfect!

"If you had a scarf, would you like it red or blue?' asked Alice.

"Definitely blue,' said her dad.

The next day, Alice's mother bought a big ball of blue knitting yarn. But by the time dad came home from work, he had changed his mind.

'You know, I think I prefer red,' he said, 'yes, red it is!'

So the following day, Alice's mother bought a ball of red yarn. But then her dad had lunch with his old friend Tom. That evening he said, 'Tom was wearing a very smart green suit today. I do love green.'

Alice and her mother raised their eyebrows. This was getting ridiculous! Luckily, mother had an idea.

A few days later, when Alice's dad opened his birthday present, he saw a fantastic hand knitted scarf. It had stripes in red and blue and green!

'What a beautiful scarf! It's a shame there's no purple in it, though!' said dad, 'I do love purple...and yellow...and brown.'

'Here we go again,' thought Alice and her mother!

Jimmy's guardian angel

Mrs Pratchett was a horrible, grumpy old woman who didn't like children very much. Unfortunately, she worked for an orphanage where thirty young boys and girls lived.

Every morning, Mrs Pratchett would grab a child and poke them until their cries woke the other children.

'Time to get up, little monsters!' she would call.

Every evening as he lay in bed, Jimmy prayed to his guardian angel, 'Please let us get a new kind mistress.'

One morning, Jimmy saw a strange man enter the dining room. He was small and a strange light seemed to glow around him. The man said, 'I'm sorry I'm late.'

'Who are you?' asked Jimmy, a little afraid.

'A friend,' smiled the man. Without saying another word, the man lifted up his huge coat and Jimmy saw that he had two large wings! The man flapped his wings and rose into the air. He flew over to the horrible old lady, picked her up and carried her away.

'Bye, bye, Jimmy,' he softly called as he disappeared.

Jimmy looked around, but the other orphans were just eating as if nothing had happened. They hadn't seen a thing!

'It's strange that we haven't seen Mrs Pratchett this morning,' said one boy.

So the childrens' dream came true. They never saw the grumpy lady again.

Too many toddlers!

amuel didn't have any brothers or sisters. He envied his friends when he saw them playing with their siblings.

'I think that one little Samuel in this house is quite enough,' smiled his dad, 'and one rascal who tramples on my vegetable patch and leaves muddy footprints on the carpet is more than enough too!'

His dad was talking about the little accident the other day when Samuel was pretending to be an explorer in the vegetable patch. Rascal or not, Samuel longed to have a brother or sister to play with.

The following day, Samuel went to visit his friend Beth. But when he arrived at her house, Samuel saw not one, not two, but ten babies playing on the carpet while lots of grown-ups were chatting around the table!

'It's their mothers' meeting," explained Beth. 'It's held here once a year.'

Samuel felt something near his feet. Looking down, he saw a chubby baby trying to climb up his right leg! When Samuel looked up again he saw another baby had climbed up onto a wobbly chair. Samuel stepped over and picked up the baby. Just as he was putting him down on the carpet, he saw another baby tried to pull the leaves off a pot plant. Samuel dashed over to stop him, and gave the toddler a cuddly toy to play with instead.

It carried on like that all day and Samuel left Beth's house feeling exhausted!

When he arrived home that evening, Samuel sat beside his dad and said, 'I think you're right. One child in a house is more than enough!'

Let the music begin

 he pupils were surprised to see a new teacher waiting for them in the classroom. He was quite old, with white hair and eyebrows that were so long they fell into his eyes.

'Hello!' he yelled at the top of his voice, 'I'm Mr Ludwig!'

The pupils looked at him with wide eyes.Why was the new teacher speaking, or rather shouting, so loudly?

'Do you think he needs to speak just a little louder?' Leo sniggered to his friend Xavier.

'What did you say?!' bellowed Mr Ludwig. He might have been old and a little hard of hearing, but Mr Ludwig had seen Leo whispering.

'Um, I didn't say anything,' said Leo, looking embarrassed.

'Speak up! I can't hear you!' shouted the teacher.

'I said I didn't say anything important!' shouted Leo. Xavier and Chris, who were sitting either side of Leo, nearly jumped out of their seats.

This time, the teacher heard Leo. 'Good! Perhaps we can start the lesson now!' he boomed.

The pupils in the front row soon began to regret sitting so close to the teacher's desk. It was obvious that Mr Ludwig couldn't hear a thing and had no idea his voice was so loud.

Intrigued, Catherine looked at the old man's ears. When he turned his head, she saw something glint in one of his ears. Catherine knew what had happened. She wrote a note and handed it to Mr Ludwig. He smiled, said thank you, and put his hand up to an ear to switch on his hearing aid.

At last, the class get could on with the music lesson!

Call the detectives!

The triplets had been stuck indoors all day. Outside the wind was blowing and snow was falling. Anthony, Annie, and Adrian were pretending to be detectives. They had already solved the mystery of the lost sock. Now they were trying to work out the puzzle of the disappearing cake.

'It's stopped snowing at last,' said Anthony. 'Let's play outside!'

Adrian was the first to get ready, and as he ran out of the door said, 'When you're ready, you have to try to find me!'

'I've got an idea,' said Annie. 'We can play at detectives again and follow Adrian's footprints in the snow.'

The footprints led from the house all the way down the yard, around the house, and toward the summer house. Then they stopped!

'He must have gone in here,' said Anthony. But the summer house door was locked.

Suddenly, Annie and Anthony heard a stifled laugh behind them. It was Adrian, holding a cake in his hand!

'So detectives, have you worked it out yet?' he laughed, 'I came out, I walked around the garden, I went toward the summer house, and then I retraced my steps in the same footprints that I made in the first place. Did you think I'd disappeared?'

'Well, the mystery of the footprints and the disappearing cake have been solved at last!' laughed Annie.

Just as Adrian lifted the cake to his lips, a snowball knocked it out of his hands. Now, where had that come from?

Crash, bang, wallop!

other looked horrified when she received a letter in the post one morning.

'What's wrong?'" asked Dad.

'HE is coming to spend a few days with us!" whispered Mother.

'HE? Oh, No! Don't tell me. HE is coming!' gasped Dad.

Who were they talking about? A storm? A cyclone? No, it was worse than that. They were talking about Joshua, their seven-year-old nephew!

Whenever he came to stay, it was always one disaster after another. The last time he stayed, Dad had to redo the plumbing in the bathroom, and lay new tiles in the kitchen. This time they needed to be prepared!

Dad put anything breakable up into the attic, and they even took up the carpets.

Eventually, when everything was ready, Joshua arrived. He had changed since the last visit and was much calmer. It was a miracle! His stay was fine and there weren't any disasters.

At lunchtime on the day he was due to leave, Joshua's uncle and aunt praised Joshua's good behaviour. Then Dad said that it was time to go, so everyone, including Joshua, got up. As he was a sensible child now, Joshua had tucked the tablecloth into his trousers so that he wouldn't drop any crumbs on the floor.

BANG! SMASH! There was a great clatter as plates, cups, and saucers went flying through the air and landed on the wooden floor. Mother and Dad looked at each other and sighed.

"Next time, I think we'll come and stay with you, Joshua," groaned poor Dad.

The greedy monkey

Boola loved bananas. In fact he ate them all day, every day. He jumped from branch to branch searching for a good bunch of bananas and then settled down to eat every last one. When he was full, Boola would go to see his friends and his family and tell them about his new recipe ideas for bananas.

Everyone loved Boola, but they all thought he was a little too obsessed with bananas. He had even started to put on weight and that's not very good when you are a monkey. Boola wasn't bothered by his friends teasing him because they obviously didn't understand the pleasure of eating bananas.

One evening, just as Boola had finished eating his fourth bunch of bananas, a big tiger silently crept toward him. Boola saw the tiger and he let out a cry. He tried to climb a tree but couldn't because he was too fat. Poor Boola tried as hard as possible but there was no way he could even reach the first branch. The other monkeys tried to encourage him, but it was no use! Boola was just too heavy. Thinking his final hour had come, Boola closed his eyes and waited to be eaten.

The tiger ran up and was about to pounce, when he slipped on a banana skin, went flying into a tree trunk and stunned himself. That gave the other monkeys just enough time to jump down from the trees and rescue Boola.

When he had recovered from his nasty shock, Boola looked at his friends and said, 'You know, I think I've had enough bananas for the time being!'

The courageous camel

romedaries have one hump and Bactrian camels have two. But Callum the camel was very special because he had three humps! Callum was often the laughing stock of the other camels, who teased him and said his extra hump looked silly. But Callum wasn't the only one being teased. His owner Youssef was always being laughed about by the other camel owners.

'How can you let yourself be seen with a camel like that?' they crowed. 'You are the embarrassment to the desert! We've never seen anything like that freak. Fancy a camel with three humps!'

'My camel is strong, brave, and hardworking. He's a good camel,' Youssef would argue.

Callum was pleased that he had such a good master. He served him well and he was very hard working and brave indeed.

One day, the camel drivers had to go to a village on the other side of the country to sell spices. To get there, they had to cross a hot, dry desert. They rode and walked for hundreds of miles without seeing a drop of water. After a week, their stores of water ran out, and the camels didn't have enough strength to carry their supplies. All of the camels, except Callum, had to stop.

'It's not far now,' said Youssef to his companions, 'Callum and I will go and get some water and bring it back for you.'

Callum and Youssef collected some water and took it back to the others. All thanks to Callum and his extra hump!

The sheep wolf

esley the wolf wasn't like the other wolves. Even when he was small he didn't like playing with the other young wolves because he hated their rough games. Wesley preferred looking at nature, going for walks, or studying his books. His ambition was not to be the head of the pack like his father. He would leave that to his brother, Brutus. Wesley dreamed of a more peaceful and thoughtful job.

'Are you coming to play?' called the other wolves.

'No thanks, I'd rather read,' said Wesley.

'What are you reading?' growled his father.

'Just a novel,' answered Wesley.

'What's it about?' asked his father.

'Lots of things,' stuttered Wesley.

Wesley's father wanted to know more about what his son was reading, so he searched his belongings and found the book. It was called *How to Become a Sheepdog*!

'How could you want to become a sheepdog? You're a disgrace!' scolded Wesley's father.

'But Dad, it's a good job,' said Wesley, 'You go on long walks, you protect lives, and you are well fed.'

Despite his dad's suspicions, Wesley took an exam and got his diploma.

He was quickly accepted by the shepherds, and he won their trust and the trust of the sheep. There has never been a better sheepdog than Wesley as no wolf would dare go near his herd!

Silly little sparrow

ester the little sparrow was always criticising his friends.

'You are such pathetic little sparrows,' he said to them.

'We are very happy the way we are,' answered the sparrows.

'That's because you don't have any ambition!' said Nester.

One day Nester said to his mother, 'When I grow up, I'm going to be an eagle!'

'No dear,' replied his mother. 'When you grown up, you will be a sparrow.'

'No, I'm going to be a powerful bird of prey!' said Nester. 'I will start by catching a sheep!'

The little sparrow circled over a herd of sheep grazing in a field. Swooping down, Nester dug his little claws into a lamb's fleece.

'What's tickling me?' giggled the lamb.

'It's me!' shrilled the sparrow, 'I have you in my clutches, you are mine now!'

'Who are you?' said the lamb, crossly. 'I can't even see you.'

'I'm an eagle!' said the sparrow. Just as he said that, Nester slipped and fell down between the lamb's feet. The lamb bent down to take a closer look.

'Oh, right an eagle, are you?' laughed the lamb, 'Well I'm really frightened!'

The sheep picked up the little sparrow in his teeth and took him back to his mother. Mrs Sparrow raised her eyebrows when she saw her son, but didn't say a word. That was the last time Nester tried to be an eagle!

The crocodiles' tale

In a little African village where Suli lived, the villagers had been working non-stop. To gather the harvest they had to cross the river, but recently there were some troublesome newcomers to the river. The newcomers were a family of snapping crocodiles!

Ever since they moved there, anyone who had tried to cross the river had been frightened away by the crocodiles! The villagers were worried about how they were going to eat if they couldn't go and harvest their crops.

One day, Suli had an idea. He went to fetch the village story teller. The old man's stories were so fascinating that as soon as he spoke you couldn't help but listen. The story teller was also very wise and he knew how to speak in animal languages. Suli took him to the river where the crocodiles lived, and as the old man began telling a story in crocodile language the horrible creatures gathered round.

The crocodiles hung on the storyteller's every word! But right in the middle of the story, when he was at the most exciting part, the storyteller suddenly stopped!

'Carry on, carry on! Finish your story!' shouted the crocodiles.

'I will,' said the storyteller, 'but only if you allow my brothers and sisters from this village to cross this river.'

The fierce crocodiles readily agreed. Now, every week the storyteller amuses the crocodiles while the villagers gather their harvest without fear of being gobbled up!

Little Buffalo

I bet you can't guess what Guy's best game was, can you? Give up yet? Well as you can see, he's dressed in the costume ready to play. Have worked out what it is? It's indian braves, of course.

He loved dressing up as a courageous chief with paint on his face and feathers in his hair. Lots of the other boys preferred to be cowboys, but Guy knew that indians are the best.

Whenever he goes to a fancy dress party, he doesn't need time to choose his costume. He just plucks his indian outfit out of the wardrobe and transforms himself into Little Buffalo!

Guy was really looking forward to his own birthday party this year because they were going on an outing to the riding school. Guy was going to ride a horse for the first time! He couldn't wait to ride a horse like a real indian brave.

The day for the outing arrived and Guy and his friends were taken to the riding school. Guy felt really excited, but also a bit nervous when he saw the horses. They looked so huge!

All the children were given riding hats and taught how to sit on a horse. Then, they were off!

They trotted around the paddock and Guy imagined he was galloping across the plains on his wild stallion.

Everyone had a great day out and Guy decided he would take riding lessons so he could be just like Little Buffalo!

Matt's crush

ouise was more than just a best friend to Matt. She could tell Matt secrets that she wouldn't tell anyone else. Matt talked about Louise so much that one day his mother said, 'I think you are in love!'

Matt blushed. He had never thought of it like that before, but it would be great if Louise would be his girlfriend!

Matt went to school the next day with a beating heart and sweaty hands. At break time, he saw Louise talking to one of her friends. Matt tiptoed closer and hid behind a tree. He wanted to wait until Louise had finished talking so he could tell her how he felt.

But when Matt heard what Louise was saying, he was shocked!

'Listen, I'm sure that he's in love with me, and I'm certain he thinks I'm in love

with him, but I'm not! How can I tell him?' Louise said.

Matt couldn't believe his ears and burst into tears!

At lunchtime, Louise came over to Matt and said, 'I have an audition at the theatre this evening. Could I practice in front of you so you can tell me what you think?' she asked.

Matt said she could and Louise began, 'Listen, I'm sure that he's in love with me, and I'm certain he thinks I'm in love with him, but I'm not! How can I tell him?'

Matt knew he had heard these exact words before. Louise had been acting! With his heart pounding, he interrupted Louise and asked if she would be his girlfriend.

'Of course,' she said, smiling happily.

Spot the difference

The teacher looked quite confused as she introduced the new pupils to her class one morning.

'This is Amelia and Justine,' she said.

The other pupils looked at the twins. It was impossible to tell them apart! They had the same hairstyle and they were wearing exactly the same clothes.

By the end of the morning, it was obvious that nobody could tell one girl from the other. Lunchtime was the worst part.

'Haven't I just given you apple juice?' asked Justine's teacher.

'No, that was Amelia,' replied Justine, innocently.

Five minutes later, the teacher went up to Amelia and said, 'Haven't I just given you a piece of cake?'

'No, that was Justine,' said Amelia, taking a slice of cake.

When the bell rang, the teacher kept the twins back.

'I need to be able to tell you two apart.'

'Do you mean something like this?' asked the twins, taking out two badges with their initials written on them. The teacher didn't know whether to be angry or relieved. At last, she would be able to tell who was who!

Once the teacher had left Felix, who had been listening, asked the twins, 'Do you wear those badges every day?'

'Yes,' answered the twins. 'But what really is fun is when we swap labels!

I'm in charge!

obert was surprised to see his mother knitting some little pink bootees one day. They were much bigger than the one's she had made for his cousin Ellie's doll.

A little later, Robert heard his mother say to his dad, 'The scan has confirmed it, David. Isn't it wonderful!'

The scan! Robert wasn't stupid, he knew that his mother had ordered a little sister for him. What a disaster! Robert didn't want a sister, he wanted a little brother who would play pirates and football. What could he do with a little sister? Girls' games are so silly!

'Well, darling, you're going to have a little sister soon,' said his mother.

Robert didn't answer. He just looked at his dad. He would be

annoyed about it too! Mother must have made her order without even asking his opinion.

At school, the next morning, Robert talked to his friend Joe who had learned lots of things from his older brother.

'Robert, your mother didn't choose what baby she wanted,' said Joe.

'What do you mean?' asked Robert, puzzled.

'Mothers don't choose what baby they get, it just happens. Imagine if our mothers had chosen girls instead of us. We would have been really annoyed. Anyway, a sister, at least, won't want to borrow your toys.'

In the end, Robert was quite happy whether his mother had a little brother or sister for him. At least he would still be the big brother either way!

The rainbow's end

Mr Bootle the librarian, was always telling amazing stories. Billy and Jasmine loved to go and listen to them after school. One afternoon, Mr Bootle told them a story about a fairy who found gold at the end of a rainbow. Billy was listening very closely because it was raining outside. When they left the library, the rain had stopped.

'Hurry! We have to find the end of the rainbow before it disappears!' said Billy, pulling his sister along.

There was a beautiful rainbow stretching across the sky, but it was already beginning to fade. It seemed to end in a nearby garden. Billy grabbed a bucket and ran across the garden and jumped over the fence into a bed of tulips!

A few minutes later, a man ran toward Billy, shouting, 'Billy! What do you think you're doing? Get out of my flowerbed!'

At that moment, something glinted on the soil that Billy had kicked up.

'That's unbelievable!' gasped said the man. 'That's the wedding ring I lost last year!'

The man was so pleased to have his ring back, he couldn't stay angry with Billy any longer and invited the children inside for a snack. Outside, the rain had started to fall again.

When they arrived home a little later, Billy and Jasmine saw another beautiful rainbow in the sky. But this time the end of the rainbow was in their garden!

'Let's get digging!' cried Billy.

Can we help?

rs Church was very tired today. She looked at the pile of washing up in the kitchen sink and sighed, 'What a bore!'

'Can we help you?' asked Gwen and Mark.

'Do you know how to wash up properly?' asked their mother.

'Of course!' they answered.

While the children set to work, their mother went to sit down in an armchair. But she had barely closed her eyes when the trouble started! Gwen turned on the tap really hard and a huge jet of water sprayed all over the sink, the walls, the cupboard, and Gwen and Mark themselves! Then, Mark squeezed washing up liquid all over the dirty plates. As the water ran, huge bubbles of foam appeared. Of course, Gwen and Mark couldn't resist having a bubble fight and soon entire kitchen was covered in foam. But what about the washing up in the sink? Why is all that water on the floor? Oh no, the tap! Gwen, switched it off but it was too late, the floor was soaked! The two little demons were sliding around the kitchen floor. Oh dear, it looked like their mother was waking up! It was time to seriously start work on the washing up.

By the time the plates were clean, Mark and Gwen were soaked. As Mark carried a pile of plates, he slipped on the wet floor, *CRASH*! The plates fell and smashed on the floor!

What would their mother say now? She ran in and when she saw the mess she cried, 'I don't know why, but I seem to feel even more tired now than I did before my nap!'

The monster in the cupboard

Some days the teacher had trouble keeping the class under control. One day, she asked the pupils to read in silence while she went to fetch a book from her office. But she had only just stepped out of the classroom when the pupils started messing around and being noisy.

Popping her head back into the room, the teacher said, 'While I'm out of the room, I suggest you keep an eye on the cupboard to make sure they don't escape. If you make a noise, you'll surely wake them up!'

What was she talking about? The pupils were silent when their teacher left the room.

'Perhaps there's a monster in the cupboard that eats naughty children?' whispered Gail.

'Shhh!' whispered Charlie. 'It's definitely a monster. They love dark places.' The children were terrified! Why hadn't the teacher come back yet?

'I'll just go open and close the door really quickly, then at least we can see what it looks like,' said Sebastian, bravely as he tiptoed to the cupboard and slowly opened the door. There was nothing there! Phew!

Sebastian explored the cupboard, but he bumped into a bucket and broom. The bucket fell and there was a loud *BANG!*

'Close the door!' shouted the others, 'There's a big, hairy monster in there!'

When the teacher returned, the pupils were reading quietly. 'The 'monster in the cupboard' game always works,' thought the teacher.

Midnight noises

One night when everyone else was sleeping, Jacob woke up with a start. He had heard a noise and thought it might be burglars. He crept out of bed and tiptoed down the corridor. Suddenly, Jacob heard his door close behind him with a loud CLICK!

Tina came out of her room. 'I thought I heard a noise, like CLICK!' she said.

'It was me,' answered Jacob. 'Shush, don't make a sound!'

Tina knocked an apple out of the fruit bowl and it bounced across the floor, BOING! Then, Nicholas came out of his bedroom. 'I thought I heard a noise, like BOING!'

'It was me,' said Tina. 'Shush, don't make a sound.'

But then, Nicholas bumped into the bookshelf and a book fell out onto the floor, THUD!

John came out of his bedroom. 'I thought I heard a noise, like THUD!' he said.

'It was me,' said Nicholas. 'Shush, don't make a sound!'

But John hadn't seen his father's shoes in the doorway as he came out and he knocked them over with a loud CLACK!

Their mother came out. 'I just heard a loud sound, like CLACK!' she said.

'It was me,' said John. 'Shush, don't make a sound!'

Suddenly, they heard a sound. They crept to the kitchen to find dad, munching a sandwich.

'I was peckish,' he grinned.

'Shush!' said Jacob, Tina, Nicholas, and Mother. 'Some people are trying to sleep!'

A lesson learned

 olin was a spoilt child who was never satisfied with what he had. One day, his grandpa decided to teach him a lesson. He went to see his friend, Mr Archer and told him of his plan.

When Colin came home from school, he announced, 'I want a bike!'

'Well, you should go next door then,' said his grandpa, 'the magic bird that lives there will grant your wish.'

Colin rushed next door.

'Let me introduce you to my magic bird, Aral,' said Mr Archer. 'Ask him anything you like and he will give it to you.'

'I want a bike,' said Colin as Mr Archer left the room.

'If you give me some money, I'll give you what you want,' said the bird in his funny voice.

So, Colin picked some blackberries and then sold them at the market. He went back to see the bird with the money he had made.

'I need more money than that,' cackled the bird.

With his money, Colin bought some clay. He sold the models he made at the market.

When the bird demanded still more money, Colin did jobs for his parents. Eventually, he had earned enough money.

'Great,' said the bird, 'now you can buy yourself a bike!'

Grandpa appeared from behind the wall where he had been hiding and pretending to be the bird's voice! Colin understood and he promised not to behave like a spoilt child ever again!

Hidden treasure

ixies are always hiding treasure. All you need to do to become really rich is catch a pixie. But pixies are also very cunning and love playing tricks.

Adam was walking across a field one day when he heard something in the bushes. He tiptoed up and saw a funny little man not much taller than a child. It was a pixie! Without making a sound, Adam crept closer and grabbed his arm.

'Where is your treasure hidden?' he asked the pixie.

'If you let me go I'll take you to it,' replied the pixie.

'No funny business. I've got my eye on you!' Adam warned.

Adam and the pixie crossed one field, then another, then another and after a while they reached a huge field of sunflowers. The pixie went up to a sunflower and said, 'The treasure is under this one.'
Pixies never lie so Adam believed the little fellow.

'Alright,' said the boy, 'I'll put my cap here to mark it. Don't touch it!'

'Promise,' said the pixie.

When Adam went back to the field, he saw an astonishing sight. The pixie had put a cap just like Adam's on every sunflower so that it would be impossible to find the treasure!

The pixie hadn't told a lie because he had kept his promise not to touch Adam's cap. What a clever little creature he was.

Henry's secret cave

Henry was a little worried because he was going to go exploring with his dad. He thought it might be dangerous. What if there were monsters in the caves.

'Dad, are you sure we should climb to the top?' asked Henry.

'Yes, of course!' said his dad.

'Um, well...' began Henry. As his dad started climbing, Henry became more anxious.

'Are you coming?' called Henry's dad. Henry gathered up his courage and made himself catch up with his dad, who had found the entrance to the cave. It was quite difficult to see because it had been concealed behind bushes and trees.

Nervously, Henry followed his dad inside. A long corridor led into a big open room and there they had a surprise! They saw some wonderful ancient pictures of bison, horses, and bears painted on the walls.

'Mother, we found a prehistoric cave!' Henry blurted out, as soon as they got home.

'We will have to contact the tourist board,' said his mother.

'No, we can't tell them! Imagine what they'll do!' gasped Henry. 'They'll make it into a noisy tourist attraction or they'll stop the public entering so that the paintings don't get damaged and we'll never be able to go in there to see them again!'

Maybe they were right, maybe they were wrong but Henry and his family decided to keep the cave a family secret.

The brave little prince

Once upon a time, the king's son sat on his horse at the bottom of the belfry. Striding towards him was the brave knight Godfrey, arriving for the big tournament.

'Your highness, are you ready to take me on in the tournament this year?' asked Godfrey.

The little prince looked at the knight. 'Oh, if only I could,' he said, 'but there are too many brave knights taking part.'

'That is a great *atchoooo* pity!' said Godfrey.

'You have a nasty cold,' said the little prince. 'Perhaps you should rest in the belfry!'

'Yes *atchoo* thank you, I think I will,' said Godfrey.

Poor Godfrey was beginning to feel quite ill. His legs were weak and his head really ached, but Godfrey was a brave knight and knew that he would be expected to take part in the tournament.

Just as Godfrey was about to go for a nap in the belfry, the king arrived with his three ministers.

'Oh, father!' said the young prince, 'Godfrey is quite ill. I think he needs to rest.'

'Knight Godfrey, seeing as you stand at the foot of the belfry on such a cold day,' said the king, 'it's not surprising that you catch colds. Because I am king, I insist you rest and withdraw from the tournament.'

'But who will *atchoo* take my place?' asked Godfrey.

The king's son smiled when his father said, 'Little prince, it is your chance to take part in the tournament!'

Think before you speak!

Perhaps you don't believe the fact that babies are born in cabbages? But it's true! Some babies are born in lettuces and others in roses, and some are even born in the treetops! Of course, these are not human babies, at all.

In big, green cabbages there are creepy-crawly caterpillars that grow into beautiful butterflies. In lettuces, there are little slugs, and in roses there are millions of greenflies! In the treetops, there are birds' nests with little chicks in them. The tiny things need their parents, just like you! So it's worth thinking about questions before you answer them!

Of course, it's not really true that your nose grows if you tell a lie, but you do know the story of Pinocchio. When he lied, his nose grew very, very long indeed! Have you ever stood in front of a mirror to check your own nose?

If you looked yourself straight in the eyes and said, 'I promise I will never eat any sweets again.' Be careful! It might just happen that your nose grows so long it touches the mirror!

So, you see, it's worth thinking about things before you speak!

Most people believe that boys are stronger than girls, even girls think that, don't they? But if that were true, then surely newborn baby boys should be able to beat a girl at high school in a game of football, then? You don't really think that's possible, do you?!!

So, it's worth thinking about things before you speak!

The forgetful squirrel

Scratchy the squirrel had spent weeks running around gathering his supplies for winter. His house was stuffed full of nuts, but he was still worried he didn't have enough. He hid them everywhere and often couldn't find them again. Everyone knew about this and so when this morning he started shouting, 'Burglar! Burglar!' nobody took any notice.

'Someone has stolen my nuts!' wailed the squirrel, 'I'm sure that it's those little rascals nibbling nuts below! Those mice have been taught how to steal.'

'Oh no, they are far too cute to be thieves,' said Mrs Blackbird. 'They may be cheeky, but they're not thieves, and anyway, you take things as well Scratchy and nobody ever calls you a thief! Have you looked everywhere? You can be a little forgetful.'

Scratchy haughtily cried, 'What do you mean, forgetful? I haven't forgotten anything! It was those mice, I'm sure of it!'

'Don't get angry, Scratchy,' said the blackbird. 'It's just that the other day I found a few nuts hidden in the corner of a branch and I thought that perhaps they were yours.'

'Well it's possible,' muttered the squirrel.

'Those young mice did not steal the nuts. I saw you give those nuts to their mother myself!' said Mrs Blackbird.

'Hrmph! Yes I remember now,' said Scratchy, looking slightly embarrassed. 'I gave her some nuts in exchange for a little of her spare straw for my nest.'

What's cooking?

Lucinda's parents had gone shopping and left Lucinda to look after her little sister. Lucinda loved cooking so she decided to make something. She put salt, pepper, chilli, tomato ketchup, and sugar into a bowl, and then mixed the ingredients together. When it looked ready, the two sisters sat down to eat.

'Yuck! It tastes disgusting!' said Lucinda's sister, pulling a face.

Lucinda tasted the mixture and although it was horrible, she tried to pretend it was nice.

'Mmmm, yummy! It's disg...delicious!' said Lucinda.

'Well, let's make Mother and Dad taste it and see what they say!' said Rachel.

'No way!' said Lucinda.

'Why not?' asked Rachel, 'if it's good, then they'll like it too!'

'Well no, because it's a special anti-adult potion! They really can't touch it,' said Lucinda, rather quickly.

To make sure her parents wouldn't tease her, Lucinda threw the horrible mixture into the bin. When her parents came home, her mother said, 'There's a very funny smell in the kitchen. Did you make something while we were out, girls?'

'I tried to make something for us to eat,' said Lucinda, knowing she had to tell the truth, 'but it was horrible so..'

'Yes, she did, and she told me it was an anti-adult potion and then...' began Rachel.

'How about if we ask Mother to teach all three of us how to make pancakes instead?' Dad said. Everyone thought that was a great idea!

No more chocolate!

esterday, the mailman delivered a parcel.

'It's from my godmother!' shouted Kay, excitedly. 'She's sent us a New Year's present. Let's open it!'

'This parcel isn't for you. Look at the label, it's for your mother,' said Kay's dad.

'But Dad, my godmother sent it, so I should be allowed to open it. I'm sure that it's chocolate! She always sends me chocolate at New Year, said Kay.

'You'll have to wait until Mother gets home!' said Dad.

As soon as her mother came home and opened the parcel, Kay dived into the chocolate box and ate one after the other.

'That's enough, you'll make yourself sick,' warned her dad.

'Just one more please, just one,' begged Kay.

Dad hadn't noticed that naughty Kay had already sneaked some chocolates into her pockets. At dinnertime, Kay wasn't hungry at all, but she managed to force down a little soup, so that she was allowed one more chocolate before brushing her teeth.

But during the night, Kay woke up feeling very hot, very sick, very yuk!

'Mother, I've got a tummy ache!' she called.

Of course, Kay's mother knew exactly what was wrong. The box of chocolates! Kay spent the whole night running to the bathroom. The next morning, she was still feeling poorly.

'Kay, how about a chocolate for breakfast?' joked her dad.

'No! Don't ever talk to me about chocolates again,' Kay groaned.

Making friends

ulia found that time was passing very slowly. Her best friend Mary-Jane, hadn't been to school for a week because she was ill. Usually, they were always together.

Julia and Mary-Jane weren't very kind to their classmates. In fact, they loved teasing the other children. They would walk past a group of girls and whisper loudly to each other. The other girls would know the terrible two would be saying something awful about them. Were they whispering about their clothes, their hair? What was wrong with them? When Julia and Mary-Jane were together, nobody would dare approach them.

Now Julia was all alone. She wondered how she could tell the others that she and Mary-Jane were just joking. They didn't mean to be nasty. Julia was finding it difficult to talk to anyone in her class.

There was always Marc, who looked kind and friendly.

Oh, no! Julia couldn't bring herself to speak to him, she had laughed at him with Mary-Jane just the other day. But now she had been looking at him for too long and he had turned round and seen her. Julia looked so lonely that Marc went up to her and said, 'Hey Julia, what's wrong?'

'I-I want to make friends with the other children in class, but I don't know how to,' said Julia.

'I know it will be difficult at first. After all, some of them are cross with you and Mary-Jane, but just try to be nice and I'm sure they will grow to like you,' said Marc, kindly.

Marc took Julia's hand and led her to the others, and before long, she had made lots of friends.

Julia learned an important lesson today about true friendship.

What a dear little girl

Every time Katie and her mother went shopping, grown-ups would stop and say the same thing, 'What a dear little girl! What's your name? Don't be shy, tell me.'

Then they would ask her age, if she worked hard at school, if *blah, blah, blah*. Katie had heard it so many times that she pretended to be shy and hid her face behind her hair. When the grown-ups didn't get a reply from her, they would give up and leave her in peace.

But the grown-ups always had a question for Katie's mother too. 'When is she going to get a little brother?' they would ask, over and over again!

That was the final straw! Katie didn't want a little brother, she wanted a little sister. She was fed up with boys. They pulled her hair, stole her bag, and were always annoying her. But a little sister would be soft and sweet. She could do her hair, dress her up, sing songs to her, and take her to play in the park. They could sleep in the same bedroom and when everyone else was asleep, she could tell her baby sister stories about princesses and magic castles, fairies and elves.

Katie wanted her sister to be pretty with curly hair, big eyes, and little hands and feet. Of course, Katie's little sister would never ever cry.

But thinking about it, Katie decided that she could do the same things with a little brother. A brother would be fine, as long as he didn't touch her things!

Shazam does it!

awny the owl announced the news in the early morning. The night before she had been perching on the highest branch of her tree, as she did every evening. Everything was calm until suddenly she saw something moving. 'Excellent, there's my supper!' she hooted, happily.

But it wasn't her supper, because it was much too big. Tawny stayed still and didn't make a sound. The creature finally came out of the bushes and Tawny saw it by the light of the moon. 'It was long and red with a tail.'

'That tail is more beautiful than yours, Bushy,' said Tawny.

Bushy the squirrel was confused. Nobody had a tail more beautiful than his. Nobody, except, of course... but that would be impossible!

Tawny then explained that the creature had a pointed nose and small beady eyes.

'Like a bird?' asked Robbie the robin.

'Worse,' replied Tawny, 'much worse!'

'My friends, I think I know what it was,' said Bushy. 'The only animal in the world that has a tail nearly as beautiful as mine is the fox. We must be careful.'

'A fox!' gasped the creatures. 'What will happen to us?'

'There have always been foxes in the forest and we are still here. Don't worry, I'll go and speak to him,' said the Shazam the snake.

Nobody knew exactly what the snake said to the mysterious fox, but he disappeared that night and was never seen again.

Thank you, Shazam!

Busy dancing bees

Zandra the bee had just come back to the hive with her bags full of delicious nectar that would make wonderful honey. She quickly went to put them down, then she rubbed her little feet together so the two big piles of pollen that she had collected would fall off. It had been a heavy load and Zandra was tired. But bees never rest and she needed to tell her family the good news. Zandra had found a big lavender bush in flower!

Zandra stood on the edge of some honeycomb and started to dance. Yes, dance! That's how bees talk to each other.

Sometimes, Zandra would dance slowly and then quickly. First just one bee followed her dance, but soon all the others joined in until eventually all the bees were dancing round as if they could hear music playing! Then, one after the other, the bees stopped dancing and flew in the direction that Zandra had told them to go. The clever little bees didn't make a single mistake and quickly found the lovely lavender bush.

When Zandra's sister Zara flew home, she did a dance to tell the bees she had found a place where thistles were growing.

'Thistles!' cried the bees, excitedly. 'Great! Thistle honey is so tasty! Quick, Zara, do your dance to tell us where it is!'

Zara started to dance, and little by little the bees learned the location of the thistle field. The thistles were in flower, so the bees quickly set to work.

The golden ball

Faith and her friend Clive were always causing mischief when they were playing together. One afternoon, instead of playing quietly near their homes, they ran into the woods.

'Look, there's a golden ball! I saw a golden ball!' called Clive, excitedly.

Faith ran to where Clive was pointing, but there was nothing there.

'I promise you, it was just there on the ground behind that bush,' said Clive.

Faith was very disappointed. She searched everywhere, but the golden ball was nowhere to be seen. Suddenly, they saw a glint of light from behind a tree trunk. Faith glimpsed something shiny just as it disappeared. The golden ball! The children started running through the woods.

'It was here! I saw it!' said Faith. 'I saw it over there,' said Clive.

'No, it was over there!' called Faith.

The children spent the whole afternoon chasing after the magic ball. As night fell, Clive and Faith decided to go home. They were exhausted, but still convinced that the beautiful golden ball existed.

The next day, the children began searching again but still they didn't find the golden ball. When Clive and Faith told their parents where they had been, the grown-ups were angry. The children could have easily got lost in the woods.

Clive and Faith weren't allowed to look for the golden ball again. So, they never knew for sure whether the ball existed or not. Have you seen it?

Meet the Rainbow family

The Rainbow family were reunited at Grandma White's house. Auntie Beige and Uncle Black were there, too.

Auntie Beige was very small and gentle, but she was always very boring. Her smile was dull and so her eyes never sparkled. Uncle Black was a sombre fellow. He was very strict and serious all of the time, but every now and then the Rainbows saw him do something magical.

Red, Blue, and Yellow had just arrived with all their cousins. Blue the eldest, was very happy because he was in love. He loved the sea, the sky, bluebells, and his girlfriend's eyes. They were the most beautiful shade of cornflower blue he had ever seen.

Red was a very fiery character! How she shouted, and raged. She made lots of noise and you just couldn't help noticing Red.

Yellow was as warm as a summer's day. She smiled all the time like a sunflower. She was gentle and kind, and loved the sunshine more than anything else. She spent hours sunbathing, but she was always careful because she didn't want to get too tanned like her cousin Brown or too red like her elder sister Red.

Where was Violet? She had gone for a walk in the garden with the twin sisters, Orange and Pink. They liked nothing better than a stroll amongst the wildflowers.

The jay's special call

Among the inhabitants of Goodwill forest there lived a little bird called Jools the jay. He was so secretive it was easy to miss him if it weren't for his unbelievable voice. It sounded like a creaky door! *Sqwaaaaaaawk, craaaaaaaak*! What a horrible, horrible sound!

Everyone in the forest laughed at Jools, so one day he asked Mr Thrush to teach him how to whistle properly.

'It's impossible,' said the thrush. 'You were not made to whistle, Jools.'

'But I can try, can't I? You can squawk like me, so why can't I try to copy you?' asked Jools. 'I'm different, I'm an artist,' said Mr Thrush, pompously.

Rubin the snake said, 'Jools my friend, don't listen to Mr Thrush's horrible words. It's because your voice is so unusual that you can warn everyone in the forest if there is any danger. You are our alarmbell, and I don't think an alarmbell that sounded like a singing nightingale would be very effective! I think you have a beautiful voice.'

Rubin had exaggerated his claims just a little. You see, snakes cannot hear very well so he hadn't really heard the jay's voice. But he was right. When you go into Goodwill forest, everyone who lives in it will know you are there thanks to Jools the jay, who will have announced your arrival.

Sqwaaaaaaaaawk, craaaaaaaaak! There's some people coming to see us, but you don't have to hide, they aren't a threat.'

Clara's cousin

One day the cows in the fields weren't grazing because they were too busy talking about Honshu, Clara's cousin. That morning, Clara had received a letter from her cousin Honshu, who lived in a busy city, far away in Japan.

Honshu was quite something! She had once lived in a field like Clara and friends, but she had recently moved and was living in an eight-storey building! Tower blocks for cows weren't all that unusual in Japan, you see! On each floor there were six apartments, each inhabited by eight cows. They rarely went out and food and hay were brought up to them in a lift.

Honshu was very proud of living in such a modern style and enjoyed her good view of the city. The only thing she didn't like was being stuck in the apartment.

'It's obvious why they are kept indoors so much,' said Celestine, a very wise cow. 'They're frightened that the cows would try to escape that horrible home! Clara, I really don't think you should visit her. You may never come back!'

Clara felt very sad about her cousin, but she thought Celestine was probably right. It was better to stay where she was able to roam freely in the lush, green fields.

'It's a pity, though,' sighed Clara. 'I think I would have liked to visit Japan and have a ride in a cow lift!'

The woodland wedding

The day of Miss Robin's wedding was a day of grand celebration in the forest. All the animals had gathered together to welcome wish the happy couple well.

Miss Robin met her future husband at the beginning of spring. She had been rehearsing her singing all winter, perched on the highest branch of a tree. She sang from dawn until dusk.

A young robin was passing one day and when he heard Miss Robin's singing, his heart filled with love! He perched on a nearby branch and began to sing too. His song was so beautiful that Miss Robin stopped to listen.

'Who is singing?' she chirped.

The sound of the male robin's voice had set her heart a-flutter and when she saw the handsome young bird she fell deeply in love. Now, they were to be married!

They had received permission from the forest warden to build their nest in Miss Robin's special tree. In a few weeks time, Mrs Robin could lay her eggs in it.

There were hundreds of guests at the wedding. There was a banquet of dried fruits, seeds and nuts, and when it came to music they were spoiled for choice! Tap the woodpecker set the rhythm and the songbirds from all around the forest sang happy songs.

Everyone danced until sunset. Then, it was time for the woodland inhabitants to wander contentedly home.

The violinist

One cold night, a man who was dressed very scruffily stopped in front of Madison's block of apartments. The man looked so poor and sad. He didn't have a home, any friends or children, or even a dog. He had nothing except the violin that he played in the road to earn a little money.

The man was still standing by the door when Madison came back from her music lesson.

'Are you a musician?' he asked, when he saw the violin case that Madison was carrying.

'I play the violin,' said Madison. 'So do I, but it's too cold to play this evening. My fingers are too stiff,' said the man.

Madison didn't hesitate. 'Can you wait here for a moment?' she said. 'I'll be back in just one minute.'

Madison rushed upstairs and told her parents about the poor man. Madison's dad came downstairs with her and they invited the busker to dinner. After the meal, the man took out his violin and began playing music from his home country. It was very beautiful.

When the busker was readying to leave, Madison's dad said, 'Do you give violin lessons?'

'It is funny that you should ask. I used to be a teacher but now…'

'Well, would you agree to give lessons to Madison?' asked her dad. 'She could learn a lot from you, Mr Vilovik.'

Madison has made great progress, and Mr Vilovik has become a close friend of all her family.

The short-toes

ean was staying with his aunt and uncle for the school vacation. The other evening, Uncle Ted came in from the fields and said, 'The short-toes have come back.'

'Who are the short-toes?' asked Sean. 'Are they staying at the next farm?'

'You could say that,' laughed Uncle Ted. 'They only live here in the summer.'

'Are they tourists, then? Where do they live?' asked Sean.

Uncle Ted looked at Sean mysteriously and said, 'I'll take you to see them tomorrow, but you'll have to be good, they don't like to be disturbed. If you leave them alone they can be useful!'

Sean asked his aunt lots of questions about the so-called short-toes, but Aunt Maggie wouldn't give anything away. 'If I explained them to you it

wouldn't be a surprise,' she smiled. 'It's better if you see for yourself.'

The next morning, Sean was excited about going to meet these short-toes! He wondered if they lived on a farm because ten minutes outside the village, Uncle Ted was striding heading for the woods!

'Don't move, just look up,' Uncle Ted whispered.

Sean looked up and there was a huge powerful-looking bird, carrying a wriggling snake in its beak!

'It's an eagle, a short-toed eagle,' said Uncle Ted. 'They nest here every year and live on snakes. We're quite happy to have them around.'

Jackie the jay

ackie was a jay bird and he lived in a big park in city, in the branches of an oak tree. Jackie was the only jay who lived in the park, but he didn't mind, he was happy sitting on his special branch and watching people come and go. Sometimes he would even call out to some of the people to see if they noticed him, but they never did.

Autumn came and less people came to the park. This didn't worry Jackie though because autumn was his busiest time of year. This was the time that the oak tree dropped its acorns on the ground for Jackie to collect and bury in the ground for the winter. Jackie was very good at this job. He could collect as many as six acorns at once and hold them in his mouth until he had dug a hole big enough to put them in.

When all his work was done, Jackie was very satisfied and he sat on his branch studying the patch of earth where he had buried his food, so that he wouldn't forget where it was.

Suddenly, Jackie noticed something that he had been too busy to notice before: all the people were gone! This was strange because even in colder weather people still came to walk their dogs. Then, Jackie noticed something else! There was a big fence around the park, and men were coming with big trucks. Jackie could only watch as he saw the big machines churn up the oak tree and the earth where he had buried his food. He thought he saw the acorns, but it would be too dangerous to save them now.

Jackie was sad, but he decided to leave the park and look for a new home and new food; there was still time before winter. Maybe he would find some other jay birds! So, he stretched out his wings and said goodbye to his special oak tree.

Bear dreams

Let me tell you a funny story. Here's the recipe for this story:

One little brown bear with two blue eyes, three wooden buttons, and four paws— one, two, three, four.

His five naughty cousins arrived at five after five with six pumpkins, six sausages, seven lollies in their socks, and eight big raindrops to throw in puddles.

It's nine minutes after nine! And there's an egg missing in the chicken coop!

'Egg number ten,' called the rooster.

Eleven ducks were swimming in the pond as twelve clucking hens sat on thirteen nests facing fourteen fat dogs. Has anyone spotted the fifteen little kittens?

And what's that? Let's see, it must be a plane. No, a boat? A black cat? A grizzly bear! No, not a grizzly bear. What is it then? A polar bear? No, it's...

A little brown bear with two blue eyes, three wooden buttons and, four paws— one, two, three, four. His five naughty cousins arrived at five after five with their six pumpkins, six sausages, seven lollies in their socks, and found him asleep in bed.

The little brown bear was probably dreaming about chickens and ducks. When the fourteen fat dogs appeared, waiting for the fifteen kittens, he would have to start again, otherwise the little brown bear would wake up and know it was time to get out of bed! One, two, three, NOW!

The right hand?

ally was very happy at school. She loved to paint pictures and play with the other children. Then one day Sally's class at school started to learn to write letters and words. This was the best thing Sally had ever done! Soon she could even write her own name, Sally. She wrote it again and again, all over the piece of paper, because the next day the children were going to meet their new handwriting teacher, and Sally wanted her writing to be perfect.

Sally wondered what the handwriting teacher would look like. However, the teacher that came into the classroom was not like Sally had expected. She was stern and sullen.

The handwriting teacher told Sally that she was left-handed and that she should try to write with her right hand instead. Sally tried and tried with her right hand, but no matter how hard she tried, her writing was not as neat as it was with her left hand.

Sally decided to ask her mother what to do. 'The teacher said I should write with my right hand, but my writing is much neater with my left hand!'

'Well,' said Sally's mother. 'All the people in our family have always been left-handed. Your father paints beautiful pictures with his left hand and your grandmother used to write books with her left hand. Do what comes naturally to you, dear.'

Feeling much better, Sally decided to explain this to the handwriting teacher.

This happened many years ago, and Sally is now all grown up. She teaches children English, and especially handwriting. All the children love her lessons because she is kind, but mostly because she has the most beautiful writing ever!

The barking house

liver loved mysteries and today there were definitely some strange things going on at the house next door. Mr and Mrs Vidal and their dog Sparky had just gone on vacation.
They had given their house key to Oliver's parents so that they could water the plants. Oliver watched them leave and he was sure that Sparky went in the car with them.

But then last night Oliver heard barks coming from their house. At nine o'clock precisely, a light went on in the living room. Then at ten o'clock, the light went out and a different one came on in the bedroom. Oliver thought that the family must have come home. But then the next day they called from Spain to say they had arrived safely. How strange!

With his heart in his mouth, Oliver crept into the Vidal's yard and the barking stopped! It was odd because the dog's bark was much deeper than Sparky's. He would have to talk to his parents about it.

When Oliver explained what he had heard, his parents burst out laughing, 'Well done, you little detective! We must have forgotten to tell you that Mr Vidal set up a system in his house to scare off burglars. As soon as anyone goes near the house there is a sensor that makes a tape play barking noises and every night the lights are set to go on and off automatically. Clever, isn't it?'

Some grown-ups are very odd, thought Oliver.

Whose move?

 hess is a great game that uses wonderful characters. They are heroes from medieval times. On each side there's a king and a queen, and their castle towers. There are also knights, bishops, and an army of soldiers.

The king is the most important person. He is so fat and his crown is so heavy, he can only take one step at a time. Luckily, the others are there to protect him so that he is not taken prisoner.

Next to the king is the queen. She loves to run and despite her crown and her long robe, she can go wherever she likes. If anyone is in her path, they should beware! She'll soon knock them out of the way!

On each side of the royal family are the two bishops. No one knows quite why, but they insist on going everywhere sideways like crabs.

The knights live at the foot of the castle. They are very useful as these men and

their horses can jump over the heads of everyone else.

At the outside edges of the chessboard are towers that protect the castle and its inhabitants. They can move too, but only in straight lines. In the front is a row of soldiers who can only move when they're told to, one at a time.

'One step forward,' orders the king from the back row.

'One step only,' replies the soldier.

A fun game, isn't it?

The little gardeners

Gregory the gardener lived alone in his little house at the bottom of his garden. Gregory often invited the children of his village to help him in his garden.

The children loved learning how to grow vegetables, and Gregory was a fantastic teacher. In spring, the children planted potatoes, all sorts of lettuce, carrots, radishes, and flowers for their mothers. Every Wednesday, they would weed the garden.

The children loved picking the vegetables. It was amazing what happened underground! They planted a potato and for days and days they watched the shoots grow. They watered their plants and after a while, four or five little potatoes grew around the one they had planted. The children had no idea how many potatoes would grow around each plant or how big they would eventually be.

The time came to dig up the potatoes. All of the children put on their boots, rolled up their sleeves, and set to work. What a crop! By the end of the day, hundreds of potatoes had been dug up from the soil.

Gregory was very pleased with his little gardeners. The potatoes were huge! He shared them between the children and they took them home for dinner.

How to be a hedgehog

Paula and Tom the two little scatterbrained hedgehogs, never listened to their mother's advice. Mrs Hedgehog was always worried when her children went off alone. She was afraid they would come across a hungry fox.

Paula and Tom had only just entered the forest when they heard footsteps in the bushes. Without thinking, the two little hedgehogs lay on the ground and covered their eyes. They were sure they were to be attacked by a fox.

'Look, Dad,' said a girl's voice. 'What are these little creatures?'

'They're hedgehogs,' replied a man's voice, 'but I have no idea why they're doing that. Come on, let's leave them in peace.'

Paula and Tom ran home to tell their mother what had occurred.

'There were two-legged foxes, but they didn't try to attack us,' said Paula.

'What did you do?' asked Mrs Hedgehog.

'Nothing,' said Tom, 'we were too frightened! What should we have done?'

For once, the two hedgehogs listened to their mother's advice.

'When you see a fox, even if he hasn't seen you, roll up into a ball and bury your nose in your prickles, and don't move!' said Mrs Hedgehog. 'The fox won't be able to get hold of you and he will leave you alone. When he goes, get back onto your feet and run away! If you do all of that you'll be safe.'

'We'll remember that,' smiled the young hedgehogs.

Hair of the rabbit

When she was helping at the farm, Michelle was never bored. Yesterday, they went to collect honey from the beehives, and today they were going to comb the angora rabbits. Michelle was surprised.

'Do we comb the rabbits to make them more beautiful?' she asked the farmer.

The rabbits were very pretty and had long white fluffy fur, like fresh snow.

'No, it's not to make them beautiful, it's to make them healthy. If I don't take off some of their fur, they will get too hot,' said the farmer. 'Several times a year, they shed fur and they grow a new coat.'

'So you have to take off their coat? But won't they be bare afterwards?' said Michelle. 'It must really hurt them a lot!'

'Not at all,' smiled the farmer. 'I wouldn't do it if it hurt them. Don't worry, the rabbits' fur grows back really quickly.'

The farmer took the first rabbit out of its cage and put it on his lap. Then he gently pulled tufts of fur from the animal. Little by little, he put fur into a basket. Michelle put her hand into the basket and felt the fur. It was so soft!

'Do you throw all this fur away?' she asked.

'No, it's very precious. It can be made into a lovely sweater,' explained the farmer.

When he had finished, the rabbit looked very strange.

'It doesn't matter to the rabbit,' smiled the farmer. 'In a week, he'll be beautiful again. Let's get to work on the next rabbit.'

Mushroom picking

Finally the rain started! Scott had been waiting for this moment since he arrived at their new home near the forest. Scott knew that if the weather had been just right, there would be lots of mushrooms to pick.

At the end of a hot, dry week, his mother announced that it was time to look for mushrooms. She got out her mushroom book, her basket, and two plastic bags.

Why do we need all these things?' asked Scott.

'Well, you must never confuse mushrooms that you can eat with ones you are not sure about,' explained his mother. 'A tiny bit of the wrong kind of mushroom could poison a whole family!'

'The book will tell us which ones are safe, won't it?' asked Scott.

'Yes, but I also need to know that you will remember what should you put in the basket?' asked Scott's mother.

'Only the mushrooms that we know are safe, those that are good to eat,' said Scott.

'What do you put in this plastic bag?' asked his mother.

'The mushrooms that you are not sure about, so that you can check later if they're safe to eat,' said Scott.

'And in the other plastic bag?'

'The mushrooms that are not at all familiar,' said Scott.

Scott and his mother soon found some delicious mushrooms hidden under a tree. They were bright yellow things in the moss and there were also some orange ones. What a feast they were going to have!

Big boy's bike

Luke got a new bike for his birthday. It was a red, shiny bike with a chrome frame, just like he had always dreamed of. There was just one problem! The bike didn't have training wheels, and Luke wasn't sure he was ready for it.

'Come on, Luke,' said his dad. 'You've been riding for months on your old bike. I am sure you are ready for this new bike.'

'But I'm afraid of falling off!' said Luke.

'There's no need to be afraid! I'll hold you,' smiled Dad.

Luke wasn't very sure of himself on the new bike. 'Ooooh!' he cried, wobbling all over the place. 'Don't let go of me, Dad!'

'Don't worry, you're doing it! Go a bit faster now, that will stop you wobbling!' laughed Dad. 'Go, Luke, go!'

Luke tried as hard as he could. He felt much calmer now and he rode along easily!

'Dad, are you still holding me? Am I doing alright?' asked Luke. He could hear his dad puffing and panting.

'You're doing really well, Luke, but I haven't been holding you for ages! See, you don't need training wheels at all. But can you stop now, I'm exhausted!'

Luke looked round to see his dad way behind him. Could it be true that he was cycling all by himself?

'Yippee! I'm a big boy, riding a big boy's bike!' cheered Luke.

A tall story

One afternoon, Holly's grandmother told her how boats were invented. This is how her story went...

Long, long ago, people could only travel on foot or by horse. There were no boats, and men could not travel on the sea. They would fish at the water's edge, casting their lines into the shallow water. Then one day, a boy threw a piece of wood into the sea.

'Look! The wood didn't sink!' said the child.

As the waves carried the wood away, a man watching nearby had an idea. He chopped down a tree and set to work, hacking out a hollow in the trunk of the tree. When he had finished, the man pushed the trunk into the water, climbed into the hollow and floated away.

That is how boats were invented.

At first it was difficult to work out how to make boats move in the right direction. One day, a fisherman fell into the water. To dry his shirt, he stuck a pole upright in his boat and hung on the shirt on it. The wind blew into the shirt and the boat was gently carried along by the wind. So the other sailors put their shirts up and the boat moved even faster. Soon, a clever fisherman took the sheet off his bed and attached the corners of the sheet to a mast. The boat sailed through the water so quickly that it had crossed the bay in just a few minutes. When the boat reached the reef, the sailor took down the sail and the boat slowed down. And that is how sailing boats were invented.

Holly wasn't sure she believed her grandmother's story, but it was fun to listen to!

Fruit fight

here was a big discussion going on in the fruit bowl.

The mandarin said, 'I'm soft and sweet, and my skin comes off easily, which is why children can eat me without making a mess. I'm everyone's fave fruit!'

The lemon said, 'It's exactly the opposite with me. I don't like being peeled, I don't taste sweet, and I don't like being eaten!'

'Oh dear,' said the mandarin. 'You have such a nasty, sour personality!'

'I'm meant to be bitter. However, I am full of good vitamins,' said the lemon.

'Sorry to disagree with you,' said the kiwifruit, 'but I think you'll find that I provide the most and best vitamins.'

The lemon started to get angry! 'Who is used for salad dressing, you or me? Who goes well with fish? Who, with just a few drops, gives a lovely taste to a big glass of water?' it said, bitterly.

'There's no point arguing about it,' said the banana. 'Children prefer me because they can put me in their bags and take me to school. We exotic fruits are always the most popular aren't we, pineapple?'

'That's true,' said the pineapple.

Just then, the door opened and James came over to the sideboard.

'Oh, no! We've run out of apples again!' he sighed. 'Oh well, I'll have a glass of milk, instead!'

Too much noise!

The fir tree was a good place to live. The shade was cool and the wind blew gently through the branches, rocking the babies in their nests. Everyone was safe from foxes, which was why it was such a popular lodging.

On the ground floor, the mouse family and their many children were scurrying around as they always did. On the first floor, Hooter the grumpy old owl slept all day. She often got annoyed with the little mice disturbing her rest.

On the second floor lived Reddy the squirrel. He was worried all the time about losing his store of nuts. He was rather forgetful and often couldn't remember where he had put them.

Hooter decided to talk to Velma the cuckoo. Velma was deaf, so Hooter had to shout at her to explain her problem.

'THE MICE MAKE TOO MUCH NOISE! I CAN'T SLEEP!' she hooted loudly.

'Really,' answered the cuckoo. 'Are you quite sure? They never disturb me. I'll see what I can do for you. Come back tomorrow.'

The next day, Hooter knocked on Velma's door, but she didn't hear at first. Eventually after much banging, Velma appeared at the door, smiling. 'I was just about to go out and eat some snails,' she said. 'I saw the mice yesterday and they said they would play elsewhere during the day, if you would twit-twoo further away during the night because everyone has been saying that you make too much noise and wake them up.'

Hooter was speechless!

Time for a nap

It was a summer's day and the heat was stifling. Sidney the snake didn't mind, it just made him sleepy and so he would settle down anywhere he could find for a nap. But the other day he settled down in rather a silly place.

After a good lunch, Sidney felt very sleepy. His eyes had become heavy and he found himself in a strange place where the ground was black and very hot. It was the perfect time for a nap and soon he was fast asleep.

Suddenly, Sidney had a strange sensation inside his skin. Snakes are completely deaf, but they can feel any slight movement around them through their thin, sensitive skin. He opened one eye as a shadow passed by. It must have been a fox or a deer. Sidney went back to sleep unworried by some silly old fox!

Vroom! There was another strange vibration and then a shadow that quickly disappeared. This time, Sidney was completely woken up and put in a very bad mood.

Vroom! This time the thing passed right in front of his nose! Actually, I should say the 'things' because there were two, one behind the other. Sidney didn't have time to see them properly, but it looked like they were black and round. He didn't know their smell, but whatever they were, they weren't very clean.

Sidney quietly slithered off the black surface toward the grass and disappeared. It was lucky that he did move because just at that moment two fast cars drove right over the part of the road where he had been taking a little nap! Sidney must learn to be more selective about where he decides to take a nap!

Tania's deal

ania and Tamara, the two little mice didn't dare leave their house at times. There was a rather large and unpleasant dog who lived a few doors down from them, and who frightened them to bits. When the dog was ill, they could go out without worrying about anything, except bumping into an alley cat. But the two mice needed to think of something because they couldn't stay at home forever.

'Why don't we just go and see the dog? We could try and make a deal with him,' said Tania.

'And do you think we would convince him? That dog is a greedy scavenger,' said Tamara. 'What could we offer him, apart from ourselves?

'You'll see, trust me,' smiled Tania.

Off they went toward his dog house. When Growler the dog smelled them coming, he licked his lips greedily. But then Tania, who was sat on a wall addressed him very politely. 'Mr Dog,

we have a suggestion,' she said. 'We've noticed that your masters don't give you much food or snacks. If you let us pass safely, we will bring you lots of extra food from the market.'

'Like what?' barked Growler.

'Like cheese, meat, and biscuits,' said Tania.

'Biscuits? Yum!' said Growler, suddenly becoming interested. 'Okay, it's a deal.'

Delighted by the idea of a good meal, Growler was happy to stay in his dog house when they passed. The two little mice can now skip down the road without a care in the world.

The giant's sore eye

Once upon a time, there was a giant so big that he couldn't find any shoes to fit him. Who could make him some shoes as long and wide as a valley? The giant decided to ask his grandma, the old giantess. She lived very far away, and the giant had to stop several times to rest his sore feet.

The giant was sitting on a mountain with the clouds drifting past his nose, when a strange noise made him look up. The giant couldn't see anything, but felt something land in his eye. He lifted up his hand to rub his eye and meanwhile accidentally kicked out with his left foot. By mistake he kicked up an entire forest! The poor forest animals went flying in all directions.

A little monkey found himself clinging to the giant's pocket! He didn't dare look down because he was so high up.

Eventually, the monkey climbed up to the giant's hand.

When the giant saw the creature he said, 'Who are you?'

'I am Monkey. I'm very sorry, I didn't mean to land on you,' said the little fellow.

'I need some help,' said the giant in a gentle voice so as not to frighten the animal. 'I've got something in my eye, could you check it for me?'

'Certainly,' replied the little monkey, as the giant lifted him up to his face.

'Well,' he said, 'can you see anything?'

'How can you not see it?' replied the shocked monkey. 'There's an airplane in your eye! Hold up your finger again, I think there are some passengers wanting to get out!'

The perfect student

Dan and his friend Giles had to try to choose which one of them would go and ask the teacher to give them back their ball which she had confiscated. They tossed a coin and Dan cried 'heads!' When the coin landed, it was tails! So poor Dan had to ask Miss Jones for their ball. It was not going to be easy because Miss Jones was the strictest teacher in school.

Dan decided he needed to pick the right moment. First of all, he mustn't do anything silly, like talking in class or chewing gum because Miss Jones hated that sort of thing. She also hated people sucking their thumbs or giggling in class. He would also pay attention to what she was saying, instead of daydreaming like he usually did.

It was break time, and Dan had been trying so hard to be good that he was exhausted! But now he had to try to retrieve the stupid ball. As everyone left the classroom, Dan went up to the teacher.

'Excuse me, Miss,' he said, feeling a little nervous. 'I wondered whether you might be able to give me our ball back? I promise we won't throw it in the pond again.'

'Oh, so that's what you were up to,' said the teacher. 'I wondered why you were being so well-behaved in class. Continue behaving like that for another week and I'll think about returning the ball.'

Poor Dan, how ever was he going to be able to stay good for a whole week!

Pilot and the whale

he blue whale was eating his usual lunch of plankton when he heard a noise. Pilot the lonely little fish was flopping exhausted on a rock near to the blue whale's eye.

'What's that noise?' asked the blue whale. 'It's beginning to really annoy me!'

'It's me,' said Pilot.

'What are you doing?' grumbled the big blue whale.

'Well, I was passing by and not paying attention, when you sucked me in and blew me out. It's a good job I landed here to tell you to be more careful next time!' said Pilot.

'Oh, I am sorry,' said the whale. 'You're not hurt, are you?

'No, just a bit shaken up that's all,' said Pilot. 'You're very kind. I'd like to be your friend. Because I'm so small, I'm always alone.

Could I stay with you? I could get rid of any parasites that come near you and you could protect me from fierce sharks.'

'Okay,' smiled the whale.

The huge whale and the little fish became friends. But the whale was sad. 'I would love to find my brother White Whale, but I don't know where he is.'

Pilot decided to help and swam off to look for White Whale. He asked all the sea creatures if they had seen White Whale and one fine day he returned to his big buddy with White Whale following him.

The two whales were so happy. Now Pilot didn't have just one friend, he had two!

Mending hearts

Naomi was sitting at the table with the grown-ups, listening to her cousin Andy talking about his future. At the end of the year he would be a qualified speech therapist, helping children who had problems speaking. Naomi thought that was a good job, but she had other career plans.

'When I grow up, I'm going to mend hearts,' she said, loudly.

'You want to be a surgeon like Uncle Arthur?' said Aunt Geraldine.

'No, I don't want to make hearts better with medicine, I want to mend them when they are broken,' said Naomi. 'Ever since Grandpa died, I have heard Grandma saying that her heart is broken. It's true, because you don't see her laughing much any more. The other day, Vanessa came round and she cried. Mummy said it was because Vanessa had heartache. They talked for a while and Vanessa was better. So I want to learn how to use words to make people better and how to comfort people. Then, each time someone says 'I don't have the heart', I will help them. I will listen to them, comfort them, and they will leave feeling better with a happy heart. They will see pretty flowers, hear birds singing, and feel the wind blowing through their hair again. That way, there will be happiness everywhere.'

'Well, my darling, you have chosen an excellent profession,' said her dad, hugging Naomi tightly. 'I'm sure that you will be very good at mending hearts!'

The lucky monkey

A baby monkey was crying at the foot of a tree one day when a huge tiger walked by. He had just eaten a big meal and was in a very good mood. He was surprised when he saw the little monkey, who didn't even try to run away.

Puzzled, the tiger said, 'Why are you all alone?'

'I'm waiting for my mother,' cried the little monkey. 'I don't know where she is. She went to the other side of the forest and she still hasn't come back for me.'

The tiger felt sorry for the monkey. 'Oh, I see,' he said, stroking his whiskers. 'Maybe she was, well, maybe she's running late. Don't stay here alone. If a tiger passes by he may get some ideas. Climb up into the trees as fast as you can!'

'But I'm not strong enough,' said the little monkey, as big fat tears rolled down his cheeks. 'Just eat me now and forget about me.'

'Well, I would,' said the tiger, 'but I've just had lunch and I really couldn't eat another thing. Now, climb on my back and I'll carry you to the big rock over there and then you can jump up onto a branch.'

The monkey was so surprised, but didn't need to be told twice. With a big jump, the tiger leapt onto the rock and the little monkey scampered up a tree.

From the top branch the monkey called out, 'Thank you, sir! I hope I can repay you for your kindness one day.'

'I shouldn't think you will,' said the tiger. 'If I see you again, I'll probably be eating you!'

Around the world

ee was excited because his Uncle Paul was coming back today. He had been away for over a year. Lee had lots of questions for his uncle who had been everywhere: Canada, the Rocky Mountains, the Pacific coast, South America, and the Amazon rainforest.

'Lee, calm down,' said his dad. 'Don't fire questions at your uncle the moment he walks in!'

But Uncle Paul had barely settled into an armchair when Lee was sitting on his lap and asking him all kinds of questions.

'Did you go skiing? said Lee.

'Well, I went walking on frozen lakes,' smiled Paul.

'And did you see bears in the mountains?' asked Lee.

'How do you know so much about the places I have been to? Did you learn about them at school?' asked Paul.

Proudly, Lee told his uncle that he had kept all his postcards and that he had looked up all the places he had visited in library books.

'Where else did you go?' asked Lee, bouncing up and down.

'Well, I went to Mexico, Bolivia...' began Paul.

'Did you see any lions?' asked Luke.

'No, there aren't any lions in those countries, but I did see alligators, monkeys, and all sorts of birds,' laughed Paul.

Paul had to leave, even though Lee had lots more to ask him because he was planning his own trip! Lee wanted to know if there were big cats in America. If there weren't, then he didn't want to go there!

Gone to the stars

I am very sad because my friend Mrs Pendle, the old lady who lived in a hut outside the city has gone. She lived there with her cat Branston and I often went to see them. She taught me lots of things about plants, animals, and the stars. She didn't have a television or a refrigerator in her house because there was no electricity! She managed very well even though she was poor. One day, when she was showing me a box of books she said, 'I'm not poor when I have these. You see, wealth is not money or cars, wealth is here in these books.'

Mrs Pendle would often read me stories. She would ask me questions about school, and sometimes she would lecture me. 'Spelling, my dear girl, is the most important thing of all,' she would say. 'That's what you need to learn now, because at your age you'll learn words easily and never forget them.'

After school one evening I went to see Mrs Pendle to tell her that I had passed my spelling test with no mistakes. But Mrs Pendle wasn't at home. Instead, there was a grumpy, old man who said, 'She's not here any more. She's gone.'

I knew what that meant because Branston and the box of books were still there. Mrs Pendle would never have left either behind. I opened the box and there was a little note inside for me.

'Goodbye, dear girl. I've gone to the stars. These books are for you.'

Every night, after I have finished my reading I say a quick 'hello' to Mrs Pendle in the stars.

Above the clouds

 ate was lying down in the grass with Sausages, her pet dog. She was cloud watching. Where she came from there were no fields and very little grass. Here, out in the country, the sky was big and the grassy hills stretched for miles. It was great that Kate could spend her vacations here!

Suddenly, Kate heard a strange quiet noise. What could it be? Sausages didn't seem concerned at all, he was snoring away.

Feeling a little unsure, Kate went to the kitchen to see her mother.

'Mother I just heard a strange noise, but I don't know what it was,' said Kate.

'Was it a plane?' asked her mother.

'No, I don't think so,' said Kate.

'Let's go and have a look,' smiled Aunt Lucy.

They left the house and Kate's mother looked up. 'It's a glider, look how beautiful it is!'

'But why can't I hear a motor?' said Kate, looking puzzled.

'That's because it doesn't have a motor, it just glides on the wind like a bird,' explained her mother. 'A little plane tows it into the sky. When the wind picks it up, the pilot releases the towing rope.'

'Is there someone inside it?' asked Kate.

'Yes, there is some lucky person inside! I'd love to go gliding one day!' sighed Kate's mother.

How amazing it would be to see Mother in a glider!

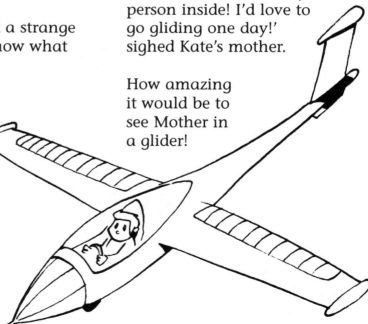

Baby blues

One day in the jungle, a very sad noise was coming from behind a banana tree. it sounded a little bit like mewing and a lot like crying.

'*Boo hoo! Waaa, meow,*' went the noise.

Mick the monkey decided to investigate the strange noise. He poked around under the tree and found a tiny fluffball, curled up and sobbing away underneath a banana leaf.

'Hello little one,' Mick softly said. 'Why are you crying?'

The little fluffball looked up at Mick with tearful eyes and spluttered, 'My mama! My mama, they took her away!'

Mick knew what had happened, and became very angry. This poor little fluffball, a baby leopard, had been orphaned by evil poachers. The jungle animals hated the cruel ways of the poachers and often devised plans to outwit them.

'There, there little leopard. I'll make sure you are OK,' he whispered soothingly. 'I am sure Mrs Jaguar will be more than happy to look after you. She is very kind and will treat you as if you were one of her own.'

'Thank you Mister Monkey,' said the little leopard, drying its eyes.

And so Spotty the leopard cub was brought up by Mrs Jaguar, thanks to the help of Mick, the clever monkey.

Flying is fun!

Uncle Richie had gone back to America, and Michael was sad because he loved going fishing with him. But a letter arrived from Uncle Richie yesterday, inviting Michael to spend the summer vacation with him in New York. Michael was thrilled, but also a little worried, because it meant he would have to travel by plane to America. It would be the first time he had flown. He would also be on his own for the journey. Uncle Richie would be waiting for him at the other end.

Finally, it was the big day! Michael had a bad night's sleep the night before, dreaming about being trapped in a plane that was falling into the sea. It fell, fell, fell, and then Michael woke up in his bed!

Michael's parents took him to the airport. After lots of hugs and kisses, his mother and dad handed him over to a steward who would look after Michael during the flight. He sat next to a window and could see the engines turning.

The stewardess helped Michael fasten his seatbelt. Then Michael felt the plane speeding up until it was going very fast. Before he knew what was happening, they were in the air!

The houses became really tiny and Michael could see nothing but clouds. It was as if they were floating on them. Michael started to float too as he drifted off to sleep.

'Wake up, sleepyhead! We've arrived,' said the steward.

'Huh! Flying is a piece of cake!' grinned Michael, stretching his arms and yawning.

Impishness

Legend has it that if a human sees an imp, it will vanish immediately. But what the story doesn't say is that imps will disappear completely if people stop believing in them.

There was once a village where the children had never seen an imp, so they had stopped believing that they existed. It was a matter of great concern among the local imps.

'What will become of us?' said the imps. 'We must do something quickly, otherwise we won't live to see next spring!'

Sylvian, the smallest of the imps had an idea. As night fell, he crept into the village school, and put little pieces of paper on each desk, which had the following message, 'You must believe in imps. They really exist!'

The next morning, when the teacher went into his classroom he saw the children holding up little pieces of paper. When one of the children read out the note, he said, 'It's a joke. Imps don't exist!'

'Yes they do!' said the children.

At that moment, the tree in the schoolyard became covered in blossom even though it was the middle of winter. Sylvian, hidden in a corner of the classroom, had cast a spell that had created the flowers.

Without meaning to, the teacher had proved that imps did exist! Sylvian ran to tell his friends.

'That's wonderful news!' they cheered. 'If the children believe in us, then we will never disappear!'

Sylvian the hero!

I don't believe it!

Once upon a time, there lived a wealthy king who wanted his daughter to get married. But she couldn't marry just anyone. The king thought he knew everything and nothing could shock him. So he decided that the first suitor who surprised him could have his daughter's hand in marriage.

Now the king's daughter was secretly in love with a shepherd, and the shepherd was in love with her, but the king would not allow such a union.

'He is far too poor, my dear!' said the king.

The king announced that if someone could tell him something extraordinary, then he could marry his daughter.

Attracted by the famous beauty and intelligence of the princess, gentlemen came from all corners of the kingdom to try their luck.

They told the most wonderful stories about dragons, exploring the world, and even about meeting the devil himself! But after each tale the king said, 'Well, that's not so surprising.'

One day, the young shepherd arrived. 'Don't tell me you are here to ask for my daughter's hand in marriage!' shouted the king.

'Certainly not,' said the shepherd. 'I think your daughter, the Princess, is ugly and stupid!'

'What!' roared the king. 'I don't believe it!'

'Well, if you don't believe it, then I should be allowed to marry her!' said the shepherd, with a mischievous smile.

The king kept his word, and the happy couple were married.

Del's prickly encounter

el, Nell, and Del the three little hedgehogs went out to find some apples for dessert one day.

'You must wait until the apples fall, but don't wait around too long because the badger may get you,' said their mother. 'He's so greedy, he never leaves any apples for others to eat and gets angry when he sees others taking a share of them. If he is lurking there, then turn round and come straight home! He might confuse you with one of his precious apples, the greedy old thing!'

Feeling a little nervous, Mel, Nell, and Del decided to walk slowly through the forest. At first, everything was fine. It was quite windy, but that doesn't bother hedgehogs. Soon they were happily running through the forest when suddenly, the two sisters stopped. 'Where's Del?' said Mel.

Del was far behind because something spiky had just fallen on his nose. It was very prickly, and looked like a hedgehog rolled into a ball.

'Can you look where you're going before you jump out of trees!' yelled Del, thinking he was talking to another hedgehog. The prickly thing didn't reply or move at all. 'It's no use pretending you can't hear me,' said Del. 'Look at my sore little nose!'

Del went up closer and pushed at the prickly thing with his paw. It was just a chestnut in its spiky case!

By the time his sisters appeared, Del was finishing off his tasty snack. Forget the apples, try the chestnuts!

Prince from the stars

anute the camel was crossing the desert with his family and a caravan of nomads. They walked through the night because it was far too hot when the sun was out. During the day, the men would lie in their tents to keep out of the sun and Canute could wander freely around the camp.

One day, Canute was walking along, dreaming of a refreshing oasis shaded by big palm trees. Suddenly, a snake slithered over his foot.

'You frightened me,' said Canute. 'I didn't see.'

'No one ever sees,' answered the snake.

'Why are you out in the sun when you could hide in the cool sand?' asked Canute.

'I have an appointment,' replied the snake, secretively.

'There's no one here, apart from us!' said Canute.

'That's why the meeting is here,' said the snake.

'Well, can you tell me who your meeting is with?' asked Canute, growing curious.

'A prince from the stars. I said I would help him get back home,' said the snake.

Canute started to ask whether the snake had been out in the sun too long. A prince from the stars! Suddenly, Canute remembered a story that a sand fox had told him. An unbelievable story about a prince who had become his friend and who had talked about going back to the stars. Canute thought it was all a little strange.

Canute returned to the camp, and for ever after wondered about the mysterious prince from the stars.

Newsflash

Leo the lion wanted to be a newsreader on television. He knew a lot about the job because he could see his keeper's television from his enclosure. His most liked program was the news with the well-dressed man who wore a different tie each day. Leo didn't always understand what the man was saying, but he really thought that he would be able to be a good presenter if someone would lend him the clothes.

One night, Leo escaped from the zoo and ran into the town to find the television studio. By morning, he had found a tall building that said 'TV1' on the front. 'Excellent!' thought Leo. Now, I can be on television!

When Leo entered the building, everyone panicked. The security guards ran out and the receptionists climbed onto their desks. Leo needed to find out what floor the news desk was on. During his search, he terrified technicians, journalists, producers, directors, and even a silly, fluffy poodle that belonged to the fashion reporter.

Eventually, Leo found the news desk. As usual, the newsreader was talking about disasters, wars, and new discoveries. At the end of the broadcast he noticed the lion.

'I know you. You're the lion from the zoo,' said the newsreader.

Leo was flattered that the man recognised him. Leo explained what he wanted and made the newsreader laugh. Funny things can happen on television, and if you watch at the right time you might see Leo presenting the wildlife program.

Ready to set sail!

elly and her dad had finished cleaning the fishing boat at last. They had spent all morning scrubbing the port, tidying the nets, and polishing the brass fittings. Kelly and her dad were tired, but they were pleased with their work.

'Kelly, I'm too tired to sail now. Fishing is hard work and I'm too old to pull in the nets after cleaning the boat all day,' said her dad. 'I think it may be time to sell the boat.'

'But you can't sell your boat!' said Kelly. 'You've always had it and you love it. You can't get rid of it!'

'I must,' said her dad. 'I need the money. If I sell the boat, I can retire and pay for your studies at college.'

'I don't care about my studies. I want to be captain of this boat!' cried Kelly.

Despite her dad's protests, Kelly stopped her college studies and prepared to pass the boat captain's exam. The old seamen laughed at her, and said she was too young and weak. The big, strong sailors said it was no job for a young girl.

But Kelly was brave and determined! With her dad's help, she learned the rules of fishing, and in the evenings she studied navigation books. When the day of the exam arrived, the whole village came to the port to watch. Kelly's dad looked very proud when she climbed aboard the boat and prepared to set sail.

There were shouts of joy when the boat arrived back into the port and Kelly received her diploma. The whole village celebrated her victory.

Kelly threw her arms round her dad's neck and said, 'Dad, your boat's not for sale any more.'

Polly saves the day!

Polly the Octopus was bored. She was bored because she didn't know what to do. She had finished her work and tidied her cave. She thought a visit to her friends would cheer her up. But when Polly reached them, she found Walter the whale was asleep, Sam the shark was out hunting, and Harry the hermit crab was busy looking for a new home. Everyone had things to do except Polly and so she went home.

'What can I do? What can I do?' sighed Polly as she munched a prawn in her cave. She was about to catch another prawn when she felt a ripple of water. It was Walter, Sam, and Harry!

'Polly, there's just been an oil spillage. Look at us! We're covered in oil and we're not the only ones. We need to get clean quickly, otherwise we will die,' cried the friends. 'Oh, what can we do?'

'I know what to do!' said Polly. 'Go and find all the sponges that grow at the bottom of the sea, then ask all the other oil covered sea creatures to come here as soon as they can. Hurry now! There's no time to lose!'

Walter, Sam, and Harry returned with lots of sea creatures, and more sponges.

Polly took a sponge in each of her eight long arms and began scrubbing the oil off her friends. When they were clean, it was everyone else's turn. As she scrubbed and cleaned, Polly chatted away to her many friends, pleased to find something so important to do.

Taro and the tiger

very morning, Taro cut down wood in the big bamboo forest. He always sang as he worked and each morning he made up a new song. Taro's voice was powerful and his melodies carried through the bamboo right up to the village.

'Ah, Taro must be cutting down bamboo,' said the villagers when they heard him.

One day, the wind carried Taro's voice further than usual, deep into the forest where a tiger lived. The following day, as Taro was working and singing, a huge tiger appeared in the clearing. Taro was terrified because he had never seen such a big tiger before. His legs shook so much that he had to lean against a tree.

The tiger looked at Taro with burning eyes and said, 'Is it you that sings every morning?'

'Yes, I am very sorry if it annoys you. I can sing more quietly if you like,' Taro said carefully.

'Oh no,' said the tiger, 'I would like you to sing for me.'

'Tiger, I am happy to hear that you like my music, but aren't you going to eat me?' asked Taro, nervously.

The tiger didn't eat Taro. Each day, he came to listen to his beautiful voice. At the end of the day, Taro would go home to his little hut and the tiger would go back to his den.

Deep in the forest, long and soft purrs are sometimes heard. Some people say it is the singing tiger who was taught to sing by a man. What do you think?

Cooking lesson!

heung was in trouble again!

'Eat your rice!' ordered his mother.

'No, I don't like it,' said Cheung.

Every night it was the same scene as Cheung refused to eat his dinner. His mother would threaten to get the dragon to come and punish him.

'For the last time, eat your rice or I'll call the dragon,' said his mother.

'I would rather you did that than make me eat this rice,' said Cheung.

So raising her arms to the sky, Cheung's mother prayed to the dragon. When she finished, a furious and terrifying dragon appeared in a cloud of smoke.

'I have came all the way down from the skies to make you eat rice? I'm so angry!' snorted and grumbled the dragon.

'Me too,' said Cheung, completely unfazed. 'I'm furious that I have to eat it. Taste this!'

After one mouthful, the dragon spat it out amidst flames. 'It's disgusting!' he shouted, turning to Cheung's mother. 'How can you make rice so badly?'

Cheung's mother burst into tears. Sobbing, she explained to the dragon that she had never learned how to cook and that's why her rice tasted so awful.

The dragon whispered a delicious recipe for rice in her ear. Ever since, life in that house has been much better.

Cheung eats up all his rice, and every Sunday the dragon comes round for a delicious dinner. Ever had a dragon to dinner?

Can you do bat stroke?

renda the bat wanted to learn how to swim.

'We bats are meant to fly not swim!' said her mother.

'But I want to learn how to swim,' insisted Brenda.

'Brenda, you have decided to learn skating, photography, and even singing, and they've all ended in tears,' said her mother.

Brenda went out feeling very annoyed. As she flew around she told herself that her mother might not be wrong about the other things, but she knew that she wanted to swim more than anything else in the world.

Brenda headed for the sea, where she met some flying fish.

'How can I learn to swim, little fishes?' asked Brenda.

'Well, you need a teacher,' said one of the flying fish. 'There's always Mr Shark, but he's often too busy hunting, or there's Wally the whale, but then again he's so big he probably won't even see you.'

'What about Manta the ray?' said another fish. 'She would be a perfect teacher for this bat.'

Brenda got on wonderfully with Manta. They spent a fantastic day together and Brenda made great progress.

When Brenda went home that evening, her mother said, 'Have you forgotten about that silly swimming idea?'

Taking out a few shrimps from under her wing, Brenda smiled and said, 'Mother, have you ever eaten shrimps?'

'They are tasty,' said Brenda's mother after tasting one. 'Where did you get them?'

'From the sea,' said Brenda. 'I've learned how to swim!'

Who stole the cake?

Rosie the chicken was in tears because someone had stolen her cake. It was a beautiful cake that she had taken ages to make. She had just taken it out of the oven and put it by the window to cool. Then, Rosie had gone out to do some shopping and came back to find, that the cake had disappeared!

The tearful hen explained what had happened to Barry the cockerel. Barry assured her that he would find the thief. He went to look by the window where the cake had been cooling and found a duck's feather!

'That's strange,' he said to himself. 'Ducks have no business being near the hen house.'

Barry looked for footprints. He found a trail and followed it. Further away, he found some dog hairs.

'How peculiar,' said the cockerel. 'These are not dog footprints.'

The trail stopped just in front of a little bush.

Barry could hear noises coming like *mmmmm* and *slurp*.

The cockerel knew who the thieves were. It was Quack the duck and Yappy the dog.

'Got you, you rascals!' said Barry. 'You will be judged by the farmyard council for stealing Rosie's cake!'

The two young thieves were given the punishment of making a cake for Rosie, once a week for a month. They did a good job and turned out to be the best bakers on the farm. Soon, visitors from miles around came to taste their delicious cakes.

The magic spell!

oor Fargo the magician
seemed to have lost his
magic touch. Until now, all the
imps and elves had depended on
his powers, potions and magic
spells. But now the situation had
changed. Whenever Fargo
opened his spell book and read
a spell, it hardly ever worked!

'Abracadabra, by magic you
will became as transparent as
the air!' said Fargo.

'It hasn't worked. You can still
see me,' said his talking newt.

So, the old magician tried again,
but it was no use.

'I can't do it any more, my
dear Newton. I must be
too old,' sighed Fargo.
'I'll have to give up
because a magician
with no magical power
is completely useless!'

'Don't give up,' said Newton.
'Perhaps you are just tired?'

'Perhaps you're right. Pass me
my spell book, would you?'
asked Fargo. 'I'm going to
make myself a special potion.
Let's hope this one works!'

Fargo opened his spell book and
read, 'Three kilos of straw, some
old letters, some…

'What are you saying?' said
Newton, looking over the
magician's shoulder. 'That's
not what the spell says!'

Perched on the magician's
shoulder, Newton read out loud
'three kilos of strawberries, some
fresh lettuce…'

'I know what's wrong!' laughed
Newton. 'All you need is a pair
of reading glasses!'

The wizards' feud

 ong ago, there were two wizards called Biggle and Boggle. These two wizards had great powers and they hated each other. For many years they had been at war, trying to chase each other out of the country. One day, they decided to end the dispute once and for all. The wizards faced each other in a forest clearing, then Biggle turned into a huge furry poisonous spider and went for Boggle.

'You don't frighten me, Biggle! Prepare to die!' roared Boggle, turning himself into a huge spider-eating frog.

Boggle was about to gobble up Biggle, when Biggle turned into a fox with sharp teeth. But then a big hungry bear appeared. It was Boggle, of course.

'Are you shaking, you wimp? Say your prayers!' said Boggle.

Boggle had barely finished his sentence when a flame zoomed down in front of him. He looked up and saw a fire-breathing dragon. It was Biggle!

'What were you saying?' roared Biggle.

'With my powers, I will destroy you!' cried Boggle, turning back into a wizard.

'I have the same powers as you, you fool,' shouted Biggle, and he also turned back into wizard form.

The two wizards were face to face again.

'Isn't this a bit ridiculous?' said Biggle.

'A little bit,' agreed Boggle.'If we made peace, there would surely be enough room for two wizards in this country.'

So off they went and decided never to be at war again.

The nosy badger

All the animals in the forest met up today to discuss a problem. The animals suspected that Toffee the badger had been reading all their mail before delivering it.

'That's impossible,' said Marco the bear. 'Toffee's my friend and I don't believe he's dishonest.'

'He might not be dishonest,' said Ralph the hare. 'He might just be nosy.'

'Whatever he is, we need to know!' said Picpoc the porcupine. 'I have a plan.'

The next day, Toffee was doing his usual delivery when he saw an envelope that looked more interesting than the others. It had *'For Jojo the mole, highly confidential. Do not open'* written on it. Toffee looked left and right, and when he was sure he was alone, he opened the letter. This is what it said:

Mr dear Jojo, Here is the treasure map I told you about. Don't tell anyone about it.

Thanks for all your help. Yours in friendship, Picpoc.

Toffee read and re-read the letter. He couldn't help being nosy, and now he would simply have to go and look for this treasure!

The young badger followed the map, and after winding and wiggling through the forest, he entered a huge clearing where all the animals of the forest were waiting for him! He knew he had done wrong, and he knew it was bad, but he was nosy, what could he do?

In the end, the other animals forgave Toffee when he promised never to read their post again.

I can fly!

No, it was impossible! He was never going to be able to do it. He would never have the courage to throw himself off the edge of the nest! He was too high up and too frightened.

The little bird's feathers trembled just thinking about it. How did everyone else manage it? His brothers had already learned to fly and now there was only him left.

'Everyone is going to think I'm such a coward,' sighed the bird.

'Come on, jump! You can do it!' called his mother.

But despite her encouragement, the little chick was pinned to the edge of the nest with fear.

'I want to stay in this soft nest,' stuttered the chick. 'I don't want to leave. I'm happy here.'

But when the chick saw his brothers flying around, he did envy them a little.

'They do look happy,' he thought, 'and they're free. If only I wasn't so scared!'

Just then, a noise stirred the chick from his daydream. It was wind tearing through the tree.

Suddenly, the tree began to shake and the branch where the little bird's nest rested kept moving from side to side until the nest fell out! The little bird felt himself falling and without even meaning to, he felt his wings start to flap. He was flying! What a wonderful feeling it was!

Later, when the little bird grew up, he never forgot his first flight and how exciting it felt.

The bravest knight

here was once a kingdom where two knights were fighting for the love of a young princess. The princess knew which knight she preferred, but her father the king, had to choose which man she would eventually marry.

'You will marry the bravest of the two!' said the king. 'I'm going to ask these two knights about their most dangerous adventure and then I will decide which of them is the bravest.'

'As you wish,' sighed the lovelorn princess.

The princess was sad. She knew that the other knight was very boastful. 'He will win my father's challenge,' she sighed. 'He will make me miserable.'

The next day, the two knights came before the king.

'Sir, I want to hear about your adventures,' said the king to the knight that the princess loved.

'Well... ' began the knight.

'Let me speak!' interrupted the other knight. 'I'm not frightened of anything. I killed two dragons just before I came here and I was already tired because I had spent the night defeating an army of two thousand men who were trying to invade your kingdom. I was armed with only a sword and I...'

'Excuse me, sir,' said the first knight, 'I think you should know that you have a mouse stuck in your armour!'

'A mouse! Oh, Mother, help!' shrieked the knight as he fled from the castle.

The king then understood which knight was the bravest, and to the joy of his daughter, chose the first knight as her husband.

The precious gift

Camilla's mother had a pretty box that she kept in her bedroom. The box was always locked and Camilla was curious to know what was inside it. One day she asked her mother, who replied, 'I will tell you, my dear little one. The story goes back to the time when I was a little girl.'

'When I was a child, I used to love looking out into the garden where there were beautiful trees and hundreds of birds nesting in them.

One day, when I was looking out, I saw a bird at the foot of a tree and it looked as if it was in trouble. The poor little thing was shaking and it couldn't fly. I went outside and saw that the bird had a broken wing. I picked it up and could feel that its little heart was beating very fast, so I took it into the house and asked my dad, your grandpa, for something that would help to make the bird better.

With a lot of love and care, the bird got better and after a while it could fly again! But I was so attached to it by then that I didn't want to let it go. I knew it wouldn't be fair to keep the bird inside, so one day I opened the window and let it fly away. I watched it fly higher and higher until it disappeared in the clouds.

I felt very sad to see the bird go, but when I looked down, I saw that it had left behind a little feather. I put that feather into the box that I keep in my bedroom. It is like a precious jewel to me. I will give that box to you one day and you must take care of it and it will remind you to be kind to others.'

The magic feather!

Mother gave Camilla the box just as she promised, and inside was the beautiful feather from the little bird that her mother had rescued when she was child. Camilla loved the present and it became her most precious thing.

Every evening, before she went to bed, Camilla would take the key, open the little box and look at the black, glossy feather. She tried to imagine her mother when she was her age, and it seemed strange. Did Mother do silly things? Was she told off by her mother? It was funny imagining her mother as a little girl.

For Camilla, the black feather was a magical object. One day, when Camilla was opening the box, she heard a tap-tap-tap tapping noise on the window. Camilla was a little afraid, but she still went to take a closer look. When she drew the curtain, Camilla saw a black bird, pecking at the window with its little beak. Camilla was very surprised. She opened the window and to her amazement the bird spoke.

'I'm not like other birds. I'm the little bird that your mother saved a long time ago,' said the bird. 'I left as soon as she made me better and I never thanked her. Don't tell her you saw me, because adults don't understand that sort of thing. I just wanted to tell you that the feather I left behind for her is magic. As long as you keep it with you, only happy things will ever happen to you. I must go now, goodbye!'

With that, the bird flew away, leaving Camilla alone with her little feather that she kept safe and close by her whole life like a wonderful precious jewel.

Safe and snug

lover was a young hermit crab. A hermit crab is a little sea creature that lives in a shell that has been discarded by another shellfish. Clover the hermit crab, like all members of its species, was looking for a new home. But for some reason it was difficult to find any homes at the moment. That morning, a group of hermit crabs had met up.

'Have you found anything?' asked Claws, peering out from a dilapidated shell.

'Well, as you can see, no,' said Clover, who was tucked into a little cave for the moment. 'I'm busy searching, just like you.'

It was a very serious situation, because hermit crabs without shells make easy prey.

One day, Clover had enough. 'I can't bear this any more,' he sighed. 'Life is too dangerous without a shell and it's very cold in the water! So while I'm searching for a permanent home, I'll find somewhere else to stay temporarily.' Clover gathered up all the bits of moss and algae that he could find and made himself a big green coat.

That evening, he went to find the other hermit crabs to show off his new home. The other hermit crabs burst out laughing. 'Look at that piece of walking moss! Does he think this is carnival time?'

'Alright, I know I look a bit strange, but it's just until I find a proper home,' said Clover.

Suddenly, all the other hermit crabs stopped laughing. A huge catfish was coming their way! In an instant, it gobbled them all up, all except Clover! The catfish had thought he was a piece of moss!

The final battle

oto the chief of the lice lived on the right hand side of Emily's head.

'What are you doing there?' asked Toto, rather crossly, when he saw Cracka at the parting.

'You have no business here!' replied Cracka, the chief of the lice living on the left hand side of Emily's head.

'We will have you removed!' said Toto. 'This is our territory!'

Neither chief or his army moved. The stand-off went on for ages. The problem was that today Emily's mother had parted Emily's hair in a side parting.

When the lice arrived on Emily's head, two clans were quickly formed. There were terrible battles, where many lice on both sides met their end. But as the lice became wiser, they shared out Emily's head into two vast areas, with Toto on the right and Cracka on the left.

But today, things had gone wrong because Toto and Cracka thought they were in each other's territories and neither would back down. The tension mounted between the two armies as they waved their antennae and clicked their pincers together.

'For the last time, retreat Toto!' cried Cracka.

'You retreat, Cracka!' replied Toto.

The lice war promised to be terrible. Each side was preparing for battle when there was a call of alarm. Suddenly, a deadly cloud appeared from above!

'There, that should do it,' said Emily's mother. 'This new lice shampoo should kill all of those nasty creatures.'

It was true! Not one lice survived!

The last lie

arla was delighted that her cousin Hugh was coming to stay. She hadn't seen him for ages! When he appeared with his parents in the front garden, Carla ran outside to meet him.

'Hugh, it's really good to see you again!' she called.

'Really?' said Hugh, sarcastically.

'Of course!' smiled Carla.

'You're too honest, Carla,' said Hugh, putting down his bag. 'You should always lie, it's much more fun. I'll teach you how to lie and you'll see how much fun it is. Now take my bag please, it's making my arms sore.'

Carla picked up Hugh's bag and carried it into the house to the spare room. When Hugh walked into the room, he burst out laughing. 'That was your first lesson,' he said. 'I never get sore arms, I just lied so that you would carry my bag. If you lie, you can get anything you want. When I came here, I told my parents I was really sad about leaving my cat and so they gave me a new video game to cheer me up.'

Hugh spent all day trying to convince Carla that lying was lots of fun.

Hugh has really changed,' thought Carla.

The following day, Carla had a word with her cousin.

'I really don't like you any more, she said, 'so don't speak to me.'

'What?' said Hugh. 'That's impossible.'

Hugh cried and looked very sad, so Carla gave him a hug and said, 'Hugh, I just lied to show you how much hurt lies can cause. I will be your friend if you promise not to lie any more.'

Hugh readily agreed to Carla's deal, and ever since they have been the best of friends.

The Queen of Hearts

The Queen of Hearts was angry with the Queen of Spades because she had stolen her servant, the Jack of Hearts from her. Looking very cross, the Queen of Hearts went to see her cousin the King of Clubs, who was playing a game of patience on his own.

'Hey, King! Are you asleep? Wake up!' called the Queen of Hearts. 'I need you!'

'What for?' mumbled the King of Clubs, who was still half asleep. 'It wasn't me, I'm innocent! Leave me alone!'

'You idiot!' said the Queen of Hearts. 'It's me, your cousin! The Queen of Spades has stolen my servant and if I don't get him back there's going to be a war!'

'Oh, I'll sort it out!' sighed the King of Clubs.

The Queen of Hearts and her cousin went straight to the King of Diamonds' palace and found the king playing chess.

'Well, I don't know how you can get her servant back,' said the King of Diamonds. 'The only thing I can suggest is that you search the King of Spades' house as he's married to the Queen of Spades, who is a friend of my wife, the Queen of Diamonds. Don't count on your sister the Queen of Clubs. She won't like being disturbed.'

'I've got an idea,' said the Queen of Hearts.

A few days later, the Queen of Hearts was being followed by a handsome new servant. When people congratulated her on her choice she replied, 'He's ace!'

Joko to the rescue!

One day in the very north of Canada it was colder than ever. As the snow fell, a sled pulled by dogs moved across the huge white landscape of ice. The sled driver was a famous explorer who had decided to study the local wildlife during the coldest months of the year. He was pulled by six dogs, each as strong as a bear. There was a seventh, younger dog called Joko, who was a brave little puppy. But because he didn't have much experience, he was put in charge of pulling a little sled carrying supplies.

One evening, the explorer said, 'We will leave tomorrow morning on an important mission, Joko. You stay here to guard the camp and your sled. Don't worry, we will be back tomorrow evening.'

Joko wanted to protest, but the oldest dog in the team told him he was too young and weak for this mission.

Joko waited patiently until the

evening. But when the team didn't return, he started to worry. 'Something must have happened to them,' he said to himself. 'I'm going to follow their tracks with my sled.'

Most creatures would have turned back in the intense cold, but Joko wouldn't give up and at last he found the others. Their sled had turned over and the dogs were stuck in a deep snowdrift. During the accident, the explorer had broken his leg and couldn't rescue the dogs or even drive the sled.

Of course, Joko was given a hero's welcome and the other dogs barked with joy. That day, they arrived home safe and sound, thanks to brave Joko.

The maxi taxi

Max was a taxi driver who loved his job and the town he worked in. He liked finding all the little hidden roads and secret alleyways. When his customers had the time to spare, he would take them on a scenic route over the old bridge or to the town square where there was a beautiful fountain decorated with dolphins. Max's customers were delighted because they got the chance to see such pretty places and sights.

Max was happy if his customers were happy. But not everyone in the town was as happy as Max's customers. In fact, the other taxi drivers were jealous of Max's popularity. They weren't very friendly and would just drive from one side of town to the other without talking.

One evening, as they sat in Sal's cafe, the drivers talked about Max. 'I won't stand for it any more,' said a grumpy old driver. 'We will have to teach Max a lesson to stop him taking all the customers. Everyone must meet tomorrow in the town square.'

Three taxi drivers challenged Max to a race. They said they wanted to see who could cross the town in the shortest time. Max happily accepted the challenge, and the race began with a hoot from a taxi horn.

Who do you think won the race? Max, of course!

He won because he was the only driver who knew all the back streets. The other drivers used the main roads and were constantly stuck in traffic jams!

Max drove slowly, admiring the beautiful scenery! The other taxi drivers had to concede that Max really was the best taxi driver in the town!

The poetic pig

Spencer the pig was having a spot of trouble! 'Oink, groink, gronk,' he went. 'Oink, groink, gronk!'

That morning, all the farmyard animals were gathered round Spencer. He was wearing a big hat and a scarf round his neck. With his body upright, two of his trotters planted on the ground, and his head pointing to the sky, Spencer was reciting poems.

Spencer had decided to be a poet, you see. He knew that he had many important and beautiful things to tell the world. The problem was that no one else understood the beauty of his poems. They were all about ham, gherkins, and bran. The farm animals looked at him wide-eyed. Had Spencer gone completely mad?

'You are all ignorant,' said Spencer. 'I am going to the farm next door. They will understand.'

But at the farm next door, the pig had the same reaction. What was Spencer trying to say with a poem about boiled eggs and chopped liver?

Furious, Spencer went off to a third farm. On the way, he came across a wolf, who was delighted to have come across such a fat, juicy pig.

Spencer began reciting a new poem about buns, pies, and pastries. Now, the wolf hated poetry and the fact that a pig was reciting poetry to him seemed really weird! It was clear to the wolf that the pig had gone mad. All wolves knew that the meat from a mad pig tastes awful so the wolf left the pig alone.

Taking off his hat, Spencer made up a new poem, devoted to the peculiar wolf who did not gobble him up!

Some things don't change

By the garden pond there was a tadpole and a caterpillar who were the best of friends. They loved meeting up each evening for a chat.

'Dear tadpole, don't you think life is beautiful?' sighed the little caterpillar.

'It's wonderful, but I can't wait to be a frog,' replied the tadpole.

'And I can't wait to be a butterfly!' said the caterpillar. 'You've already changed a lot, you know. Look, your back feet have grown.'

'In a few weeks you will have beautiful wings on your back,' said the tadpole.

'That's true,' said the caterpillar. 'When you are a frog, do you think you will mind spending all your time in the cold water and mud?'

'Oh, no!' replied the tadpole.

One evening, the caterpillar said, 'It's time for me to make my cocoon. In a few days, we will both be transformed. You will be a frog and I will be a butterfly. Promise me that we will always be friends.'

The days passed and the tadpole changed little by little into a strong magnificent frog.

'Hoorah!' cheered the young butterfly as he came out of his cocoon. 'Now, I must go and find my friend the frog.'

The butterfly flew to the pond, but where was his friend?

'I'm over here,' croaked the frog. And so the butterfly fluttered over the pond chatting to his amphibian friend every day from that day on.

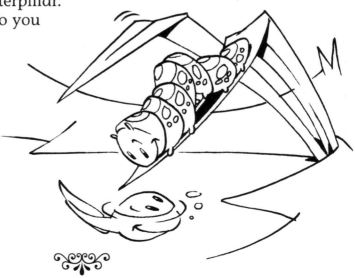

The littlest dinosaur

Dino was a very small dinosaur. When his friends started to grow big and strong, he remained little and frail. Sometimes, the other dinosaurs laughed at him. 'You are so weedy!' they called.

Dino didn't understand what was wrong with him being small. He thought he looked fine as he was and his mother reassured him.

'Don't listen to those other dinosaurs, Dino. Small or big, I love you just the same,' she smiled.

The dinosaurs lived at the foot of a big volcano that was thought to be extinct. But in fact, the volcano was still active and one morning, the dinosaurs heard a terrible rumbling noise. The volcano was erupting! First big puffs of black smoke came out of the top of the volcano, then boiling lava poured down the sides. The dinosaurs were terrified! Even the older ones who had mocked Dino, were trembling with fear.

'It's going to erupt!' they cried. 'We're all going to die!'

'What's the point in being big and strong if you don't use your strengths?' said Dino. 'If you are so strong, why don't you take those big rocks over there and build a wall to protect our land from the lava?'

The dinosaurs set to work. They had to be quick because the lava was moving fast. But with Dino's urging them on and encouragement, they worked as hard as they could to build the wall that saved them. Dino was never laughed at again.

Green with envy

Rascal the rat had always wanted to know the secret of the magic potion that gave imps the power to become invisible, but he had never been able to find out the closely guarded formula.

'One day, I will know the imps' secret. Then, when I become invisible, I will be able to steal anything I want and I will be rich as rich as a sultan!' laughed the evil rat.

Rascal had an idea. He called together a motley crew of his fellow rats and told them his plan. But he didn't know that an imp called Piccolo had been listening in. The imp ran to warn Balthazar the magician, who had invented the potion.

'Don't worry,' said Balthazar. 'Those horrible rats don't scare me. Let us play a trick on them.'

When night fell, the rats crept into the magician's cave and hid in the darkest corners.

'Shhhhh! Don't make a sound,' whispered Rascal. 'Look over there! The old magician is preparing the magic potion. Make a note of what the idiot is saying and then at last, we will know the recipe.'

Balthazar put one ingredient after another into his big cauldron and called out the recipe in a loud voice. When he had finished, the rats quickly scampered out and ran off to prepare their own potion.

Rascal wanted to be the first to taste the potion. But he had barely swallowed the first mouthful when he began to look decidedly queasy. Then, little by little his fur started to turn a violent shade of green. Balthazar had given them a recipe for a potion that would turn their fur green for a whole month!

Bubbles' adventure

Bubbles the goldfish was bored of being stuck in his bowl. 'I've had enough of swimming round and round and always seeing the same room!' he sighed. 'I want to have adventures and live an exciting life. I want to go out into the ocean, meet other fish and make friends from around the world.'

A stream ran next to the house where Bubbles lived and his bowl was near to the windowsill. One day, when the window was open, Bubbles took a deep breath and hup! He dived into the stream. The little stream ran into a river that led to the sea!

Finally, Bubbles reached the sea. What freedom! The water stretched out forever and it was full of millions of mysterious creatures like crabs, squid, mussels and shrimps. Bubbles felt a little nervous when he saw big fish looking at him with huge round eyes.

A little sardine swam past Bubbles and said, 'You'd better leave before you get eaten!'

'Eaten?' gasped Bubbles.

'Don't you know what happens here?' asked the sardine. 'The big fish eat the little ones. That's the way things work. You have to be on your guard every day, because there are thousands of enemies. Even if you escape the big fish, you might be caught in the fishermen's nets.'

'But that's awful!' cried Bubbles.

Bubbles used all his strength to swim back along the stream. His owner spotted him and put him back into his little bowl.

'Phew!' gasped Bubbles. 'Perhaps it's not so bad here, after all!'

The genie's rose

On the day he came to power, Sultan Kalim received gifts from all the regional governors of his land. At the end of the day, the last visitor was announced. Sultan Kalim was astonished.

'I thought I had seen everyone in the world,' he said to himself.

'Sultan, I have come here on behalf of the good genies. There is a custom that we should also give you a present, so please accept this,' said the visitor.

The genie held out a golden rose. 'This rose has great powers,' he said. 'Each petal is worth a fortune, but you must never separate them because it could cost you your life.'

At that moment, the genie disappeared and the reign of Sultan Kalim began. Now, the sultan liked to gamble and often

lost! In fact, he gambled so much that his fortune got smaller and smaller each day. Sitting in his palace, the sultan had an idea. 'Each petal on the genie's golden rose is worth a fortune,' he smiled. 'Surely if I separate just one and sell it, nothing bad will happen. When I have more money, I can buy the petal back.'

After selling the petal, the sultan soon lost all his money again. So he peeled off a second petal and lost the money again! This went on and on until there was just one golden petal left.

'Right, this is my very last chance,' the sultan said to himself. 'It's a good job I don't believe in prophecies.'

When the sultan took off the last petal it turned into a wilted daisy petal and his palace vanished. The sultan truly had lost his life.

Pumpkin soup anyone?

I t was Halloween and Lucas was very excited. His friends were coming to a party at his house. They were going to wear fancy dress costumes and play spooky games.

Before the party began, one of the most important jobs was to prepare the pumpkins. Lucas put them on the kitchen table, sat down and began to carve faces into them. The pumpkins needed to look as scary as possible. Lucas did a good job. They were very scary pumpkins, and with candles inside they glowed brilliantly.

Suddenly, something strange happened. Lucas saw one of the pumpkins' eyes move.

'That's impossible!' gasped Lucas. 'It must have been the candle flames that made the pumpkins' eyes appear to move.'

But, no! It happened again! Two pumpkins turned their cruel eyes towards Lucas and their mouths broke into evil smiles.

Lucas shook with fright. He wanted to scream, but no sound came out of his mouth. The two pumpkins started to fly and dance around him.

'Ha, little boy! You thought you were the master of the pumpkins, did you? Well, you were wrong. You will see who is in charge now!' cried the pumpkins.

Lucas closed his eyes, finally found his voice and shouted as loudly as he could! Then he heard someone softly say, 'Lucas, Lucas, wake up darling. Your friends are here.'

Lucas recognised his mother's voice. He had been dreaming!

'I don't like Halloween! Let's make soup with the pumpkins.'

Dreams do come true

Mr Rollo was the owner of a beautifully painted and decorated merry-go-round. In every village in the land, Mr Rollo set up his merry-go-round for a few weeks. Its pretty music could be heard for miles around and the children rushed to have a ride on it. They could choose to ride on pigs, horses, lions, or even unicorns. But what the children didn't notice was that one of the animals was very sad. He was beautiful, loved by everyone and adored by the children. It seemed that he had nothing very much to complain about, but despite all this the little horse was very unhappy.

You see, what he wanted was to be a real horse. His life seemed so boring, always turning in the same direction. When winter came, the toy horse was shut away in a barn and had to wait for the fine weather to return. The only thing that made him happy were the children.

One day, someone special climbed onto the horse's back and said, 'My beautiful horse, I am a little fairy and today I am going to make your wish come true,' she whispered. 'I have read your mind and I know what you want most of all. So, in return for all the joy you have brought to children over the years, your wish will be granted. I am going to turn you into a real horse.' With a wave of her magic wand, the fairy cast a spell and the horse's dream came true!

The little wooden horse is now a beautiful pony who trots around the fields, taking children for rides and is as happy as can be.

Joseph and the beaver

oseph lived in a log cabin near a river. The young man lived on fruit and vegetables and loved nature more than anything else in the world. He wasn't rich, but he was happy.

One day, when Joseph went home, he noticed something strange. The posts that held up his house were a little shorter as if someone had sawn them off.

'They must have been worn down by age,' Joseph said to himself. 'I will check all the posts tomorrow.'

The next morning, when Joseph looked at the posts, they had become even shorter!

'Who could have done that?' wondered Joseph. He needed to find out who was trying to damage his house before it was too late, so he hid in the bushes and kept a look out. After a few moments, he was surprised to see a beaver run up to the posts and start nibbling them. Joseph came out of his hiding place and caught the beaver.

'Why are you doing this?' he asked, crossly. 'I've never done anything to you.'

'Yes you have. 'Humans are always hurting animals,' said the beaver.

'But I've never hurt an animal in my life. I love all of nature, I promise you!' said Joseph.

Joseph managed to convince the beaver that he intended no harm. Within a short while, the man and the beaver became friends. Together, they used their talents to make log cabins, which became popular all around the world.

The flying boat

autilus was a little boat that still had a lot to learn, and the first thing to learn when you're a boat is how to sail. If you don't know how to do that you won't get anywhere!

'Mother, I can't do it! I'm going to sink!' cried Nautilus, as he floated in the water.

'Just try a bit harder, son. What will you do with your life if you don't learn how to sail?' asked his mother.

'Oh, I don't want to do this anymore. I've had enough!' said Nautilus, crossly.

The worst thing about having to learn how to sail was the fact that he didn't even like water!

Nautilus's parents were very worried about his future. They often spoke about it. Then one day, Nautilus's uncle came to visit. His name was Volo and he was a handsome airplane.

Nautilus loved his uncle and admired him greatly.

When Nautilus's parents told Volo about their worries he said, 'Let me speak to Nautilus.' Together, Nautilus and Volo went for a walk and when they returned, Volo was smiling. 'I don't think your son was made to be a boat. I think he would make a far better plane!'

So the little boat's parents entrusted Nautilus to his uncle Volo, who bought his nephew a wonderful pair of wings and taught him how to fly. Nautilus was much happier as a seaplane!

Nina's glasses

ina wasn't happy at all. 'What about these, do you like them?' asked her mother.

'No, they make me look ugly!' said Nina.

Mother had spent over two hours with Nina trying on pair after pair of glasses at the opticians.

'Right, that's enough!' said her mother. 'You need to get a pair of glasses now, so choose the ones you like best and let's get out of here.'

Finally, Nina chose a red pair and looked at herself in the mirror. Oh, dear! What would her friends think? Most of all, what would Ben think? The optician made the adjustments and said that the glasses were ready.

Nina spent the whole evening worrying about going to school and everyone seeing her wearing glasses. She could already hear the children calling her 'four eyes' and 'speccy'.

Next morning, Nina ate her breakfast in silence. Then, she picked up her bag, put on her glasses and set off for school. As she stood at the school gates, Nina said to herself, 'Come on, there's no point in hiding them, be brave!'

As Nina walked across the playground, some children looked surprised, but she didn't hear anyone calling 'four eyes'.

As she headed for her group of friends, Nina felt a hand on her shoulder. It was Ben and he was wearing a brand new pair of blue glasses!

'Hi Nina,' he said. 'Your new glasses look great.'

Suddenly, Nina felt happy that she was wearing her red glasses.

Pip the penguin

Far away in the north pole lived a penguin called Pip, who had always promised himself that one day he would make a journey to unknown lands. Today, Pip set off across his little ice field. He headed south to the sea, where he found a large iceberg and climbed aboard.

Pip spent a lovely night lying down watching the stars and the beautiful northern lights. He caught a couple of little fish for his lunch and was setting his course when he saw a huge boat coming toward him.

'Hey, little penguin, do you need some help?' called the captain.

'No thanks, Captain,' said Pip. 'Have a good trip.'

Pip continued south and saw more boats and animals who offered to help him. Nemo the whale asked Pip if he wanted a lift on his back, and Happy the dolphin offered to pull Pip's iceberg to make it go faster. But Pip politely refused all these offers. The days went by and Pip's iceberg carried on toward the south. As he went further south, the iceberg began to melt.

One morning, there was only just enough room for Pip's feet and by the evening, the penguin had to balance on one foot so that he didn't fall into the water.

'I think I might need a bit of help now,' said Pip.

'Of course, young penguin,' said Nemo the whale. 'I've been following you all the way in case this happened. Climb onto my back, and if you need any advice on your journey, just ask me.'

Tom gets tricked

Tom the cat was a very good hunter. It was worth seeing how Tom approached his prey, without so much as a quiver of a whisker giving him away. Just when a mouse felt safe, Tom would pounce, play with him for a few moments, and then let him go. Then, proud of his conquest, Tom would lie in the sun.

Unfortunately, Tom lived with Dodo the dog.

'Yahoo! Tom, I've just been hunting. It was great! I dived into the pond to catch a duck! I got covered in mud! Look, it's still all over me!' called Dodo, rubbing his face on Tom's nose.

'You're disgusting!' groaned Tom. 'Go and have a wash.'

A little later, Tom saw a mouse coming toward him. Tom was just about to pounce when...

'There we are. I'm all clean again now!' barked Dodo.

'You idiot! You've just scared off the mouse I was hunting!' said Tom, crossly.

Tom was about to pounce on another mouse when...

'Come on, Tom. I thought we'd made up,' said Dodo. 'Look, I stole a sausage for you and....'

'I don't want anything from you. Do you see this claw? Well, it's for you if you don't clear off!' snarled Tom.

It was like this all day, as Tom tried to catch mice and Dodo lumbered about. That night, the not so foolish dog was in deep conversation with some mice. 'Now listen, mice, we'll stick to the same plan, but you need to give me two bones for my help.'

Spring is in the air

Although it was the first of May, it was still very cold. The winter weather didn't seem to want to end. There was snow everywhere and all the lakes and ponds were frozen. The fields were covered in frost and there was nothing for the wild animals to eat. The smaller creatures tried to keep warm in the nearby barns, while the birds fed on breadcrumbs thrown out by the farmer's wife. Nick felt really sorry for them, but what could he do? Why wouldn't the spring start?

Nick thought it was cold because the sun hadn't come up properly yet. During the winter, the sun appeared for a short while, but the night was longer than the day. Nick ran into the garden with his dog, turned to the pale sun, and called, 'Wake up, sun! We all need your heat. Come out and shine!'

From the frosty branches above, a weak *tweet-tweet* could be heard.

'Sun, everyone is waiting for you. Please wake up!' Nick shouted.

Nick's dog barked three times, then they heard a cockerel crow in the distance and then some cows mooed. The animal voices grew louder and louder, and the joyful sound encouraged the sun to wake up. Even the trees tried to stretch their branches towards the sun.

Soon, the weak light of the sun began to grow stronger and stronger. At last, the sun had come up! The snow and the ice began to melt and wild flowers and grass appeared. The flowers brought a warm glow to the spring landscape.

Spring was finally here, thanks to Nick and the animals!

The friendly fruits

In a beautiful orchard, an apple tree and a pear tree grew next to each other. One of the apple tree's branches was touching one of the pear tree's branches. On each branch there was one apple and one pear. Ever since their first bud and their first flower, they had been together. The days passed peacefully for them as the rainy days were followed by sunshine.

Soon it was summer and the apple and pear could feel themselves getting bigger, fatter and riper.

'Apple,' said Pear, 'I don't want to get ripe because I don't want to be picked.'

'Pear,' said Apple, 'I don't want you made into jam.'

'Stop!' cried the pear. 'Don't talk about such things. Let's just enjoy our last days together.'

'But then,' Apple said, 'we will be separated and eaten.'

'Apple, if you want us to remain friends then we're going to have to think of something quickly. Perhaps we should jump out of the tree?' suggested Pear.

'If we were to jump, what would we do once we were in the grass? Call a taxi?' joked Apple.

'This is terrible,' sighed Pear.

Suddenly, a big hand plucked Apple and Pear from their trees.

'These fruits looks delicious!' said a giant. He ate Apple and Pear in one mouthful.

'Hey, Pear! Here we are in a giant's tummy, but at least we're together,' said Apple.

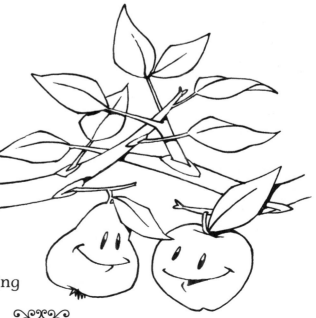

Aunt Jo

Rob and Fred weren't very happy when they found out that one of their elderly aunts was coming to spend a few days with them. They had never met the old woman before and didn't know anything about her. Their mother had said, 'Aunt Josephine isn't young any more, so she'll need a bit of peace and quiet.'

The boys understood exactly what that meant. They would have to whisper and tip-toe around for days. Their aunt would probably be wrapped in a shawl, and spend the whole time sitting in an armchair with a rug over her knees. How boring!

When Aunt Josephine arrived, the boys had a surprise. 'Please don't call me Aunt Josephine,' she said. 'Call me Jo.'

Jo was quite unusual for an aunt. She wore a long string of pearls that she twirled in her fingers. She spoke loudly and told the boys' dad off for not washing his hands before his meal. Rob and Fred thought she was fantastic. Despite all this, the brothers still did as their mother had asked and made as little noise as possible.

This went on for three days, until Fred said, 'I can't keep quiet any more!'

'Let's go and play football in the garden,' said Rob.

The boys had been playing football for a few minutes when they saw Jo stride out from behind a tree.

'At last!' she shouted. 'I was starting to get a little bored.'

With that, Jo turned and booted the football between two trees.

'Goal!' she shouted. 'Beat that!'

Make a wish

One day, Boris the little hedgehog heard that if you see a rainbow and make a wish then it will come true. The trees above Boris blocked out the sky completely, so he had to venture out of the forest. It was raining that morning, a fine rain that landed on Boris' prickles and eyelashes. When he finally got to the edge of the forest, he waited for the rain to stop before continuing.

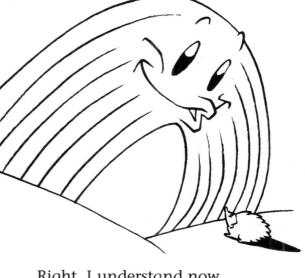

When he was out in the open, he looked up at the sky. High above his head a huge arch crossed the sky. It was beautiful!

'That must be the rainbow, so I must make a wish,' said Boris to himself. 'But what should I wish for? Now let me think...'

The little hedgehog really wanted to make a wish, but his mind had gone blank.

'Your wish can be anything you hope for,' said the rainbow.

Right, I understand now. I hope... ' said Boris.

'But WHAT do you hope for?' asked the rainbow, becoming impatient.'

'Nothing... or everything!' said the hedgehog.

'Ha!' laughed the rainbow. 'See you later, Mr All or Nothing!'

With that, the beautiful rainbow disappeared!

'Maybe all was too much and nothing wasn't enough,' thought the little hedgehog. 'Next time, I'll ask for a little something!'

Flower power

hloe loved flowers. While other children liked to look in the toy shop windows, she would think of ways to get her mother to stand by the florist's window.

'Mother, what's that flower called? Mother, please buy some flowers! Mother, why are those flowers in the same vase even though they're different?'

Chloe's questions just went on, and on, and on!

'Chloe, you're going to make us late! We have to meet Dad,' sighed her mother. 'If you're good, then tonight I'll tell you a secret about flowers.'

When she was tucked up in bed, Chloe learned the secret about flowers.

Can you guess which is the prettiest flower? Is it the dusky rose or the lily of the valley? The sensible pansy or the secret violet? What about the delicate hortensia or prickly holly? Perhaps the crocus or the hibiscus? How about the forget-me-not, the iris, the lily, the daffodil, or the daisy? Is it the dahlia or the carnation?The cornflower or the bluebell? The alpine daisy or the fragile water lily? Perhaps it's the daisy. Could it be the gladioli with its long leaves, or the first snowdrop of spring?

Don't be impatient, I'll tell you the truth. The prettiest flower is the one that you choose! If you give someone flowers, then do it with your heart!

Chloe dreamed of a garden full of flowers, blowing gently in the breeze. Ah, flowers must be the most beautiful things in the world!

The vegetable patch man

There was once a strange man who looked just like a vegetable patch. He was very sad and lonely because everyone laughed at his appearance.

'Look, he has a nose like a ripe tomato and his hair looks like wilted lettuce!' people would say. 'His eyes are like shrivelled plums, and he has string bean eyebrows, and cabbage leaf ears! His chin looks like an old, gnarled turnip!'

The vegetable man was so sad that he would often cry. He was terribly lonely, but he preferred being on his own than with other people as their teasing hurt him. He thought life was very cruel. The man hadn't chosen to look like this and the worst part was that he had no one to share the love in his delicate artichoke heart with.

One day, the strange-looking man saw a beautiful girl.

'How lovely she is,' he said. 'Her hair is blonde like wheat and she has rosy cheeks and pretty ears like two shells. Her eyes are brown like nuts and her mouth is like raspberries. Everyone must love her.'

The girl overheard what the man had said and replied softly, 'You know, it all depends on how things are said. The same words can be kind or cruel, compliments, or insults! Tomato, green bean, shells, nuts, raspberries! I think you are handsome just as you are. Let's be friends!'

Ever since that day, the vegetable man has never felt sad. If people laugh at him he doesn't care because he has a very special friend.

Bernard Bunny

G emma had received a birthday present from her uncle.

'Wow! I wonder what it is?' she squealed, excitedly. It was a lovely toy rabbit with a letter in its hand. 'Mother, will you read it? It'll be quicker if you do.'

'Are you sure?' asked her mother. 'It might say something secret.'

'If there's a secret in it, then you'll just have to forget it after you've read it!' laughed Gemma.

So, Gemma's mother opened the letter and read it out loud, 'Hello, Gemma. I am a rabbit. When you grow up I will be very sad, so please hug me often. I don't have a name, so you can give me one. If you hug me and carry me with you all the time, then I will be your friend forever. Take good care of me.'

At the bottom of the note there was a curly signature, which Gemma thought said 'Bernard'.

'Bernard! What a funny name for a toy rabbit! Oh well, Bernard it is!' said Gemma.

'No, Bernard is your godfather. He wrote the note,' said Mother.

'No, the letter says it is from the rabbit,' insisted Gemma, making her mother laugh loudly.

'What's so funny?' said Dad.

'Mother's just read this letter that came with Bernard,' said Gemma.

'Did Uncle Bernard write you a note?' asked Dad.

'No, not Uncle Bernard. Bernard Rabbit!' said Gemma.

'If you say so,' smiled Dad.

Funny names

ne day, a strange insect landed on a soft leaf.

'Pleased to meet you,' said the leaf. 'What's your name?'

'I'm a praying mantis. What about you?' asked the insect.

'I'm wild mint,' said the leaf. 'Are you very religious?'

'Not really,' replied the insect, 'it's just my name. Are you wild?'

'Not really, it's just my name too,' said the leaf.

'Goodbye,' said the mantis to the mint as he flew away.

One day, a beautiful reindeer came to lie down in a meadow. A flower whispered in her ear, 'Pleased to meet you. What's your name?'

'I'm called Big North, and you?' asked the reindeer.

'I'm Queen of the Meadow. Why are you called Big North?' asked the flower.

'Because I'm the queen of the north. Why are you Queen of the Meadow?' asked the reindeer.

'Because I grow here,' said the flower.

One day, a farmer put a harvest sheaf in his kitchen. The calendar said, 'Hello, what's your name?'

'I'm an ear of corn. What about you?' asked the ear of corn.

'I'm a calendar year.'

'Goodbye, I hope it's a good year,' said the ear of corn.

'Goodbye, I hope you're a good ear,' said the calendar.

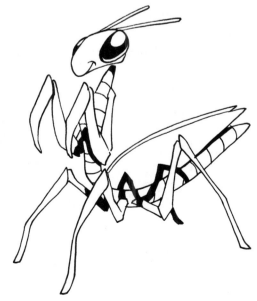

Mother's joke

 haron wanted her mother to play games with her.

'I can't right now, dear. I'm working on a joke for later this evening,' said Mother.

'Can I help?' asked Sharon.

'No, because the joke is for you and Dad,' said her mother.

'Wow!' said Sharon. 'When is the joke for?'

'For supper,' replied Mother.

Sharon was quite excited thinking about how much fun they would have tonight when Mother made her joke. Poor Dad didn't know anything about the joke.

The joke seemed to be taking a long time to arrange. Mother had been shut in the kitchen for hours! Perhaps she was using ingredients from the kitchen cupboard. Mother was singing, which was always a good sign.

Eventually, Dad arrived home from work and they all sat down for supper. Sharon pulled faces at her mother to try to get her to start the joke, but Mother just ignored her.

Then, Mother brought in the casserole dish which had a lid over the top of it. Removing the lid, Mother said, 'Ta-raaaa!'

Inside the dish was a plate of stuffed tomatoes, each with a little face and hair made from other vegetables. Mother and Dad burst out laughing, but Sharon sulked. She hated tomatoes.

'Why do parents laugh at things that really aren't funny at all?'

Strange sayings

veryone in the house had felt a little nervous for two or three days because Sarah's dad was having an interview and it seemed to be important. Last year, the car had to have an 'interview', but that only made dad nervous afterwards, rather than before. He came home in a really awful mood, holding a piece of paper.

'It's bad news!' he said, wagging the paper at Mother.

'Oh, dear! So the car failed, did it?' sighed Mother.

Sarah couldn't understand how a car could fail an 'interview'. What did it do? A car wasn't able to speak, was it? Anyway, after all the fuss Dad had made, the car's 'interview' went OK in the end, and the car came back looking like it was brand new.

As Dad paced around the room, Mother said it would be alright. She tried to reassure Dad, but said he shouldn't count his chickens before they hatched. Sarah wondered what they were on about. Dad didn't own any chickens.

'Grown-ups seem to do and say some very strange things!' Sarah thought.

Dad had bought a new suit last year and Mother said he looked like a million dollars. Sarah had a closer look in the suit's pockets when no one was around, but she couldn't find any money.

Sarah thought her parents were acting very strangely at the moment!

Hopefully, Dad's interview would be a piece of cake, and then they could all eat it for tea!

Archie's secret power

Archie was a little boy who liked being naughty sometimes, just like any other. But he was different to other boys in a special way. His eyes were of different hues. The left eye was blue and the right eye was brown. He looked both strange and beautiful, and the other children sometimes teased him about it.

'Where did you find your eyes - in a button box?' called one boy. 'You could have chosen matching ones, at least! Ha, ha!'

Archie didn't take any notice. His eyes were as they were and there was nothing he could do to change them.

Archie would stare at the other children with his charming brown eye and his piercing blue eye, and when he did that they would soon stop teasing him. But they wouldn't tease him at all if they knew his secret! You see, Archie had a great power. With just one look he could tell what people were thinking! Yes, he knew exactly what was in their minds and hearts!

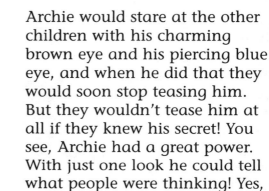

Archie's blue eye saw evil and nastiness in people and his brown eye saw sweetness. So ever since Archie was young, he was sure of one thing: nothing in life is just black or white, brown or blue.

Archie could see sadness in joyful people and tenderness in rough people. But most of all, Archie knew that everyone had a secret.

So remember, be careful what you say or think because someone close by might just be able to read your mind!

The white zebra

ephyr was a little zebra who lived in a circus. He was neither sad nor happy, and tried to accept his destiny and not to think about his beloved homeland in Africa. As they moved from town to town and from place to place, the circus brought joy to all who came to see it. But as he ran round the ring with the other animals, the audience paid little attention to the zebra plodding along behind, unable to keep time with the music.

The highlight of the show was when the graceful white horse danced and waltzed under the bright lights of the big top. Zephyr often wished the audience would applaud him as much as they applauded the white horse.

One day, Zephyr decided to have a moment of glory. After the procession, he broke away from the camel and the lama, and went to the back of the big top where

there was a big box of chalk. He rolled around in it until he was covered from head to toe, then he jumped back into the ring. The ringmaster couldn't believe his eyes as Zephyr began his performance.

Zephyr danced so elegantly and gracefully that everyone thought they were watching the white horse. The lights glowed on his back and he was truly magnificent! The crowd cheered and applauded loudly.

Ever since that day, from town to town, and from place to place, people come especially to see the zebra and the white horse perform. And Zephyr is just a little bit happier, it's true!

Grandad's book

elix had found a big, old book belonging to his grandpa. 'What's in this book, Grandad?' he asked.

'Ah, that's the book of my life!' replied Grandad.

'Can I read it?' asked Felix.

'No way!' said his grandpa. 'Everyone has their secrets and I don't want anyone reading mine!'

Felix was very disappointed, and went off thinking that adults were not much fun.

One afternoon, Felix waited for his grandpa to go out, then he took out the big old book. Sitting on the floor, Felix turned to the back of the book as he always liked to read endings first. On the last page Felix read, 'One afternoon, Felix made the most of Grandpa going out, he opened me and read me from start to finish, despite Grandad telling him not to!'

Felix quickly closed the book! But curiosity got the better of him and he opened the book again and read, 'That day, Felix did three naughty things. He had been disobedient, he had been disrespectful and he read the book from start to finish. His punishment would follow soon.'

Felix left the book and ran out, terrified. He thought he had avoided suspicion, but he had read either too much or too little as in the book there was a final paragraph he missed. It read, 'His disobedience that day came back to haunt him. He regretted it his whole life. He was never disobedient again and he never started reading a book by looking at the back page first!'

Spot count

 arianne the spotted beetle had lost her memory.

'I must have stayed out in the sun far too long! I can't remember how old I am any more!' she said.

'You must be able to remember your date of birth,' said a snail.

'I can't remember anything!' wept Marianne.

'What flower were you born on?' asked the snail. 'Go and see it and it will remind you.'

'I don't know which flower it was!' groaned the forgetful Marianne.

'Do you have to make so much noise when everyone's trying to have their afternoon nap?' moaned an old owl.

'Sorry,' said the snail, 'but Marianne doesn't know how old she is and she's very upset.'

'So much noise for such a little thing. Work it out by counting the spots on your back!' hooted the owl. 'Don't you know that it's one spot for one year!'

'Turn round, Marianne,' said the snail. 'I'll count the spots for you! One, two, three, four! You're four years old!'

'Great, but now I want to know how many brothers and sisters I have,' said Marianne.

'You are never satisfied, are you little beetle? You are always looking for complications in life. At least I can count on you for that,' said the little snail with a chuckle.

'You can't count on me for anything,' said Marianne.

Marianne was so annoyed with the snail's cheek that she forgot how old she was all over again.

Bertram the bear

This is the story of Bertram the bear. Unlike other bears, Bertram reacted in some very strange ways when he saw certain things! In fact, often he would blush a rainbow!

When it was a day, he went gray. When a wind blew, he went blue. When it snowed, he glowed.

If he saw a bed, he went red. If it was light, he went white. When he winked, he turned pink. A cello turned him yellow. A bean turned him green. In a rage, he turned beige.

And if he saw something black? Well, he'd just lay down on a sack and roll onto his back!

To make Bertram's peculiar life even more complicated, he couldn't stop doing some very silly things.

When he sucked a sweet, he would want more to eat. When he cracked a nut, he would slam a door shut. If he tasted honey, he would feel quite funny. He would chew a twig and do a strange jig. After a piece of cheese, he would always sneeze. Two leaves of a daisy made him feel very lazy.

For hot milk in a bowl, he would do a funny roll. For a tiny pea, he would laugh with glee. After an apple core, he would always want more. If he saw a frog, he would hop onto a log.

Poor, Bertram. What do you do if you can't go to sleep?

'If I couldn't sleep I would certainly weep. Wait a minute! I could count sheep and watch them leap!'

Storm in a bath

Mr Periwinkle was teaching his class. 'Brooks become streams, streams become rivers, and rivers flow into the sea,' he said. 'Typhoons and storms are the main cause of shipwrecks.'

Everything was a little confused in Camilla's head, but she had remembered one thing: all water ended up in the sea! Water must be very intelligent to know how to do that. If Camilla wanted to walk to the sea, she would probably get lost, but water always seemed to know the way.

Camilla decided to check to see if this information was true. So at bath time she used a sponge to make a little boat.

'If I let it go down the plug hole, it will go into a stream, then a river, and then the sea!' Camilla said to herself. 'If I write my name and telephone number in waterproof ink on the label, a sailor might even find it and call me.'

Camilla got out of the bath and without her mother seeing, she put her little 'boat' under the bubbles to be sucked down the drain.

When she came home from school the next day, Camilla heard her parents talking.

'Have you finished doing the plumbing yet?' Camilla's mother asked her dad.

'Yes, but it was difficult because the bath was blocked!' said Dad. 'There was a funny little boat stuck in the pipe. Luckily, we've got it out! It was almost a naval battle, though.'

'My boat was in a naval battle!' said Camilla. 'I'll have to find out if the pipes are as dangerous as typhoons.'

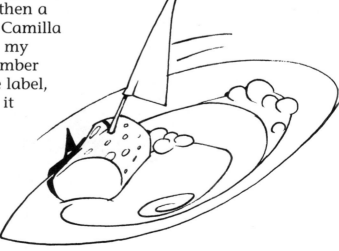

What am I?

 ne day, Peter was walking in the mountains. When he sat down beside the path for a little rest, he heard a voice whisper, 'Hello little one!'

'Who is talking to me?' asked Peter, looking around.

'Ha, try to guess! I have a body, but no arms,' said the voice.

'Are you a penguin?' asked Peter.

'No, I'm not a penguin! Guess again!' said the voice. 'I'll give you another clue. I don't lose my leaves!'

'That's easy! You must be a book because they don't lose their leaves,' smiled Peter.

'What would a book be doing out here?' said the voice. 'Here's another clue: I move, but I stay in the same place!'

'Well that's not possible, unless you are a magician!' said Peter.

Peter was becoming a little exasperated by the voice. He wanted to know what it was, and he was getting bored with its silly clues. But the voice wasn't going to give up.

'A magician! Oh, you are too kind,' laughed the voice. 'Think again. My head is in the clouds!'

'A bird! You must be a bird!' said Peter, excitedly.

'No, try again,' whispered the voice. 'When I am old, I will have lots of knots!'

'Are you a piece of string?'

'No, but you are sitting on my root!' said the voice. 'Would mind moving a little?'

'Oh, I'm sorry!' said Peter to the fir tree.

Lots of love

R uth told her mother that she thought David was unlucky to be having a brother.

'His parents will love him less if they have a new baby boy,' said Ruth.

'No they won't,' smiled Ruth's mother. 'Love is a rare thing that is unlimited. For example, I love you, and I also love your dad, your grandparents, and my brother, and my friends. I also love Coco the cat. So you see, you can love all those people at once! And the more you love people, the more they will love you back!'

'So what's the point if they just give you the love back?' asked Ruth, looking confused.

'No, I don't mean that,' said Mother. 'I mean that the more love you give, the more love you receive. It's not like sweets, where if you gave them to everyone you would have none left!'

The next morning, Ruth went to school, bursting to tell David the good news. Ruth walked into the playground, eating a delicious, home-made muffin.

'Hi, Ruth! Can I have one of your muffins?' asked David.

'David! I have to tell you something,' said Ruth. 'Cakes are like sweets. If you give them to lots of people, you will have none left! But love is different, and the more you give the more there is!'

David hung his head and slowly walked away.

'How strange,' said Ruth to herself. 'I tell David some good news and he gets in a funny mood. Oh, I don't think I'll ever understand boys!'

A quiet nap

It was time for Amanda's afternoon nap so she climbed into bed. Grandma was resting in the armchair in the corner. It was summer and the curtains were pulled to keep out the hot sun. Outside, there was a deafening noise. Whiskers was miaowing behind the door, but grandma said it was too hot to have the cat on the bed.

'Grandma, why do we have to go to sleep in the afternoon?' asked Amanda.

'Because we both need it,' smiled Grandma.

'Then why don't Mother and Dad have naps?' asked Amanda.

'Because they are always busy, and don't have time,' said Grandma. 'It's a special treat to have an afternoon nap!'

Amanda wondered if her grandma would like to swap her treat for something else.

'No, there's nothing better than a nap,' yawned Grandma.

'Do afternoon naps have to be long? If you say you've had one, but really you haven't, is that very bad?' asked Amanda.

'Well, it's bad because it's a lie and you shouldn't tells lies or disrespect a treat,' said Grandma. 'Do you know what the best kind of treat is? It's when you can sleep without anyone trying to talk to you!'

Amanda thought about what her grandma had said.

'Do you often have that treat?' Amanda asked.

'Yes, but only during term time!' laughed Grandma.